Take and Read—Endorsements

"To learn about the book that most influenced another human being is to learn not only about their mind, but also about their heart and soul. This volume gives us an astonishingly intimate window into the perspectives and passions of the most significant figures in contemporary American Catholicism."

Cathleen Kaveny
Libby Professor of Law and Theology
Boston College

"This collection is a tour de force of accessible religious reflection and a treasury of intensely personal testimony to the inspiration of great writers. In more than forty brief essays a wide range of significant Catholic thinkers reflect on the great books that have influenced them deeply. The range of authors is impressive, all of them distinguished theologians writing for a general audience. But the variety of texts they have selected is frankly extraordinary, ranging from religious classics like Augustine, Schleiermacher and Rabindranath Tagore, to novels from the pens of Georges Bernanos, George Eliot and Muriel Spark, to histories, biographies and memoirs. Karl Rahner at one extreme, Karl Marx at the other. This is a veritable feast, enriching our understanding both of the classic texts and of the present generation of thinkers who have benefited from them."

Paul Lakeland
Aloysius P. Kelley S.J. Professor of Catholic Studies
Fairfield University

"If the community of faith may be likened to a great river fed by a thousand unseen tributaries, *Take and Read* gives us a resplendent map of the tributaries. And how many of them I recognize! Dianne Bergant and Michael Daley have assembled a powerful collection of voices, each witnessing in distinctive ways to the patient if often painstaking work of faith, hope, and love seeking understanding. In one essay after another, the authors gathered here celebrate the unforgettable impact and sometimes costly grace of engaging with books that turn our complacent assumptions upside down, not least our assumptions about the mystery we name God—source of all tributaries. In this era of impatience if not outright contempt for the life of the mind, this is a beautiful and provocative book, like a boat bearing the reader up and downstream the communal river of faith."

Christopher Pramuk
Chair of Ignatian Thought
Regis University

Take & Read

Christian Writers Reflect on Life's Most Influential Books

Edited by

Michael DALEY and Dianne BERGANT

Foreword by Martin E. MARTY

Apocryphile Press
1700 Shattuck Ave #81
Berkeley, CA 94709
www.apocryphilepress.com

Copyright © 2017 by the authors as represented.
Each author retains control of their own work, with permission granted to the Apocryphile Press to sell and distribute this volume.

ISBN 978-1-944769-90-1

All rights reserved. No part of this book may be reproduced, stored in a retrieval system, or transmitted in any form or by any means—electronic, mechanical, photocopy, recording, or otherwise—without written permission of the author and publisher, except for brief quotations in printed reviews. Printed in the United States of America

Please join our mailing list at
www.apocryphilepress.com/free
and we'll keep you up-to-date on all our new releases
—and we'll also send you a FREE BOOK.
Visit us today!

Contents

Foreword by Martin E. Marty 11

Introduction: The Power of Books 13
   Michael Daley

*The Abolition of Man: How Education Develops
Man's Sense of Morality* (Macmillan, 1947) by C. S. Lewis 19
   Tobias Winright

An Asian Theology of Liberation (Orbis, 1988)
by Aloysius Pieris, S.J. 25
   Peter C. Phan

*Analogical Imagination: Christian Theology and
the Culture of Pluralism* (Crossroad, 1998) by David Tracy 31
   Edward Foley, Capuchin

The Autobiography of Malcolm X (Random House, 1965)
by Malcolm X with Alex Haley 37
   M. Shawn Copeland

Being as Communion: Personhood and the Church (St. Vladimir's
Press, 1985) by Jean Zizioula 43
   James F. Keenan, S.J.

Beyond the Text: A Holistic Approach to Liturgy (Indiana University
Press, 1987) by Lawrence A. Hoffman 47
   Julia Upton, R.S.M.

The Christian Faith by Friedrich Schleiermacher (Harper & Row,
1963) 53
   Roger Haight, S.J.

The Confessions **by St. Augustine** 59
    Gregory Baum

The Confessions **by St. Augustine** 65
    Wendy M. Wright

The Communist Manifesto
**(with an Introduction by A.J.P. Taylor, Harmondsworth, Penguin,
1967) by Karl Marx and Friedrich Engels,** 71
    Gerard Mannion

Cry of the Earth, Cry of the Poor **(Orbis, 1997)
by Leonardo Boff** 77
    Dawn Nothwehr, O.S.F.

The Diary of a Country Priest **(The Thomas More Press, 1983)
by Georges Bernanos** 83
    Elizabeth A. Dreyer

Faith in History and Society:
Toward a Fundamental Practical Theology
(The Seabury Press, 1980) by Johann Baptist Metz 89
    Bruce T. Morrill, S.J.

Gitanjali **(Chiswick Press, 1912) by Rabindranath Tagore** 95
    Francis Xavier Clooney, S.J.

God for Us: The Trinity and Christian Life
(HarperSanFrancisco, 1991) by Catherine Mowry LaCugna 101
    Richard Gaillardetz

God's Presence in History: Jewish Affirmations and
Philosophical Reflections **(New York University Press, 1970)
by Emil Fackenheim** 105
    Mary Jo Leddy

Gyn/Ecology: The Metaethics of Radical
Feminism (Beacon Press, 1978) by Mary Daly.................................111
  Susan A. Ross

Hearers of the Word (Herder & Herder, 1969) by Karl Rahner 117
  William Madges

The History of Black Catholics in the United States
(Crossroad, 1990) by Cyprian Davis, O.S.B. 123
  Sandra Yocum

History of the Council of Trent (translated by Ernest Graf,
2 vols., London: Thomas Nelson, 1957-1961) by Hubert Jedin.......129
  Massimo Faggioli

A History of Theology (Garden City,
NY: Doubleday, 1968) by Yves Congar... 135
  Catherine E. Clifford

The Imperative of Responsibility
(University of Chicago Press, 1984) by Hans Jonas 141
  John T. Pawlikowski O.S.M.

Infections and Inequalities: The Modern Plagues (Berkeley:
University of California Press, 1999) by Dr. Paul Farmer...............147
  Emily Reimer-Barry

The Interior Castle (tran. by Kieran Kavanaugh and Otilio
Rodriguez, Mahwah, NJ: Paulist Press, 1979) by Teresa of Avila 155
  Gillian T. W. Ahlgren

Interpretation Theory: Discourse and the Surplus of Meaning
(Texas Christian Press, 1976) by Paul Ricœur 163
  Sandra M. Schneiders

Jesus: An Experiment in Christology (New York: Seabury
Press, 1979) by Edward Schillebeeckx 169
Ormond Rush

Just Jesus, 3 Volumes (Crossroad, 2000) edited by
Jose Ignacio, Jose Ignacio Lopez Vigil, Maria Lopez Vigil 175
William Reiser, S.J.

"Justice in the World" by 1971 Synod of Bishops, Second
General Assembly (in *The Gospel of Peace and Justice:
Catholic Social Teaching Since Pope John*,
edited by Joseph Gremillion, Maryknoll: Orbis, 1976) 181
Michael Crosby

The Law of Christ: Moral Theology for Priests and Laity
(The Mercier Press, 1963) by Bernard Häring 187
Charles E. Curran

The Long Loneliness (Harper & Row, 1952) by Dorothy Day 191
Julie Hanlon Rubio

Memento Mori (Macmillan, 1959) by Muriel Spark 197
Valerie Sayers

Method in Theology (Seabury, 1972) by Bernard Lonergan 201
Dennis M. Doyle

Middlemarch: A Study of Provincial Life (Harmondsworth,
Penguin, 1965) by George Eliot 205
Anne E. Patrick, S.N.J.M.

Mujerista Theology: A Theology for the Twenty-First Century
(Orbis Books, 1996) by Ada Maria Isasi Diaz 211
Michelle Gonzalez Maldonado

New Seeds of Contemplation (New York: New Directions, 1961)
by Thomas Merton 217
   Ilia Delio, O.S.F.

Night (Hill and Wang, 1960) by Elie Wiesel 221
   Dianne Bergant, C.S.A.

Pedagogy of the Oppressed (Herder & Herder, 1970)
by Paolo Freire 227
   Thomas Groome

Personal Writings (translated and edited by Joseph A. Munitiz
and Philip Endean, New York: Penguin Classics, 1996)
by Saint Ignatius of Loyola.. 233
   Lisa Fullam

The Seven Storey Mountain (Harcourt, Brace and
Company, 1948) by Thomas Merton 239
   Donald Cozzens

Tattoos on the Heart: The Power of Boundless Compassion
(Free Press, 2011) by Greg Boyle.. 245
   Thomas P. Rausch, S.J.

A Theology of Liberation: History, Politics, Salvation
(Orbis, 1973) by Gustavo Gutiérrez.. 249
   James B. Nickoloff

*The Varieties of Religious Experience:
A Study in Human Nature* (Longmans,
Green & Co., 1902) by William James 255
   Sidney Callahan

What Happened at Vatican II (The Belknap Press of Harvard
University Press, 2008) by John W. O'Malley................................... 261
   Katarina Schuth O.S.F.

Foreword

"Boring!" is the first word in the first line of the first chapter in *Take and Read*. Most other words in the book demonstrate why this damning critique need not reappear. Tell us readers that this is a book in which scholars nominate the greatest, or at least most influential, book each has read, and we might be expected to suffer boredom. Eyes may glaze over when we are confronted by lists, or when as readers we confront virtual advertisements for Great Books by scholars we may not recognize or who are specialists in fields other than our own. But here: boring? Never! Let's anticipate why this collection will turn out to be exciting, memorable, and capable of inspiring reflection.

First and perhaps most notably, each chapter turns out to be not an argument but a story, a narrative witness. Certainly, theoretical discussions of books have rightful and sometimes urgent reasons to bid for scholarly attention. But they also have their limits. I have written a Foreword to a collection of essays devoted to the theme of *mentorship*. Many of the contributors have written or are capable of writing sophisticated abstract discourses on this or that element of pedagogy that merits attention as they helped shape the outlooks of readers on mentoring. Yet every writer, with no prompting from the editor, sooner or later told the story of what particular mentors—teachers, coaches, parents--exemplified, embodied, and achieved, as they became stories that shaped the mentees.

So it is here in *Take and Read*: along the way we learn that, whether the contributing authors are male or female, American or Other, proponents of fiction or "non-", they are most true to themselves, to the book that they say has shaped them, and to the reader's interests, when we read their stories. We learn which teacher commended a certain book to some as students, how often they were surprised by the hold the book came to have on them, and why they commend the books to others who ask them.

As an oft-time interviewer, I learned to ask questions that permit the subjects to probe and reveal themselves. I often ask, "Tell me three things about yourself that I won't forget!" Recently an African-American high schooler with whom I was chatting responded to such: "You don't need three things; only one." And? "That I was never stung by a bee." So? Should boredom set in? No, she explained: "When I was a little girl a bee stung my mother. She had an allergy, and died ..." I'll long remember that girl, while I will have forgotten whether some contemporary of hers got straight A's, played soccer or traveled much.

The wonder in the essays that follow is how revelatory the shaping impact of the singled-out books has been. Let me repeat a line which changed St. Augustine's life: "Take and read!" and, express hope that you will be surprised, delighted, and influenced.

Martin E. Marty
Emeritus, The University of Chicago

INTRODUCTION: The Power of Books

Jesus before Christianity (Orbis, 1978) by Albert Nolan, O.P.

Michael DALEY

"Boring." It's the death knell we fear hearing upon suggesting a book be read or assigning one to students.

Yet, our lives are testaments to the power of a book—a good book. We know firsthand how they can inspire, affirm, challenge, change, even disturb, persons. This is what we seek to convey and celebrate in *Take and Read: Christian Writers Reflect on Life's Most Influential Books*. In the selections that follow well-known and well-respected figures in the church and theological community offer captivating theological and personal reflections about the important role that books play in our lives.

In the end, we want the readers to experience, through the contributors' own words, the life and vitality, the energy and enthusiasm, that books, specifically theological and spiritual ones, can have not just for ourselves but for them as well. Far from being paperweights, these books will be seen as must-reads.

Of course, this book won't tell the whole story. How could it? Surely, you'll recognize there is another book that should have been included and that warranted consideration. We agree and, in this sense, emphasize the book as a starting point to further reading across theological and spiritual perspectives.

For me it was 1988. The winter of my freshman year at Xavier University. I'd only heard of the place and applied there because my girlfriend at the time had considered it. Suffice to say some years later, as luck would have it, she went elsewhere. As a result, my first few days on campus were a little lonely. Truth be told, I was ready and needed to get to the rhythm and routine of class. Save for a bout of kidney stones and the challenges of maintaining a long distance relationship, my first semester was uneventful. Little did I know what was to come in the winter/spring semester.

Unlike many of my classmates, I was public school bred. For whatever reason, though the opportunities were limited but still available in Lexington, Kentucky, my parents chose not to send me to Catholic schools. No twelve years of Catholic education, especially religion class, to joke or complain about. The best I could muster were CCD classes and regular Mass attendance. Admittedly, as valuable as those experiences were, my theological education was decidedly lacking and a little naïve.

I didn't know what to expect then when Dr. Paul Knitter, one of the most catholic Catholics I know, passed out the course syllabus for *Introduction to Theology*. As many a teacher and student both know, going over the course objectives, class procedures and expectations, and grading scale, can quickly incapacitate one's senses. I, however, found myself staring at one of the class's required texts—*Jesus before Christianity*. Though it makes perfect sense to me now, I had never before really put Jesus *before* Christianity. Never rooted him in his first century Palestine, Roman-dominated, Jewish context. Jesus was who he always was, or so I thought, Jesus Christ. Over the course of several months, though, through the substance of that book, much would change about who I thought I was, who I thought Jesus was, and what I thought I wanted to do with my life.

As untutored as I was at the time, the first thing that interested me about *Jesus before Christianity* (1st edition 1976), beyond the title, was the book's preface (1987 edition). In it, the author, Dominican Father Albert Nolan, expressed surprise at how popular the book had become some ten years after its first publication. What struck me, however, were two additional things. The first was an apology. For *sexist language*. I kind of knew what it was but didn't want to admit its influence on me. Didn't everyone know anyway that *mankind* meant *humanity*? Just because "*He*" was God's pronoun, we knew that God wasn't actually male. Right? In this case, *Jesus before Christianity* began a sensitizing process for me of the sin of sexism, especially the power of language to challenge or to confirm sexism and the structures that support it, and the conscious-raising privilege and burden of being born a white, male, American, heterosexual Christian.

The second thing that touched me was the book's and Nolan's stress on historical context and how it influences theological reflection. As a child of the Cold War, *The Day After* movie (1983), the "Star Wars" missile shield, and school civil defense ("duck and cover") drills, I knew of the nuclear threat. Yes, it was MAD—Mutually Assured Destruction. At the same time, in a way, I had become numb, insulated to it. The starting point of *Jesus before Christianity* though, unavoidably, was catastrophe. Not just nuclear, but environmental, even spiritual.

I was also intrigued by the author's South African heritage. In ways I and the world hadn't been made fully aware of before, the issue of Apartheid—the systematic denial of human rights to black South Africans—was becoming front page news at the time. Boycotts and protests seemed to be a weekly occurrence. Here was someone writing out of that charged social, political and religious situation. Though it was supposed to be kept a secret, in 1983 Nolan turned down the chance to become Master General of the Dominican Order to remain in South Africa. He believed that his presence there was more important, so that the theological reasons people offered for Apartheid could be challenged and, eventually, overturned. Long before the movie *The Matrix*, *Jesus before Christianity* introduced me to the reality of the "machine" and the violent means through which it exercises its control. Sadly, rather than confront and resist it, religion has often supported this system. Combined with a book on Gustavo Gutierrez by Robert McAfee Brown later on in the course, the key ideas of liberation theology—a preferential option for the poor and history as the scene of God's revelation—were unveiling themselves before my very eyes.

Only after this stage-setting did Nolan introduce Jesus "as he was before he became the object of Christian faith." A person who, in his own time and place, faced similar circumstances of oppression and poverty, not just in body but also in spirit. *Jesus before Christianity* was beginning to make Jesus relevant to me in a way he had never been before, connected to events not from long ago, but current ones like poverty, violence, war and peace.

How often we limit our experience of Jesus and church to an organization, a bureaucracy, a building, even a definition, rather than to a person and a people. For me *Jesus before Christianity* represented a time when there weren't any settled doctrines and dogmas, just the enlivening experience of Jesus trying to bring forth the kingdom of God. It was an attempt at Christianity and Christology in the making, before Nicaea's "of one substance" and Chalcedon's "two natures, one person." Tradition was still in formation. Nolan understood then (and still now) how traditional understandings of God for people, especially the young, were bankrupt, unmoving, even dead. For this reason, he said, "To choose him [Jesus] as our God is to make him the source of our information about divinity and to refuse to superimpose upon him our own ideas of divinity."

Most importantly for me, what really emerged from *Jesus before Christianity* was Jesus' humanity. Though I would eventually read more substantive books on Christology by John Meier (*A Marginal Jew: Rethinking the Historical Jesus*) and Dominic Crossan (*The Historical Jesus: The Life of a Mediterranean Jewish Peasant*), Nolan introduced me to a Jesus who was, well, like me ("in all things but sin," Hebrews 4:15). Echoing Karl Rahner's Christological critique of "crypto-monophysitism" which emphasized Jesus' divinity at the expense of his humanity, *Jesus before Christianity* began to correct this imbalance. Here I encountered a Jesus who was moved with compassion for the poor and oppressed (Mt 14:14); who was tempted to misuse his power (Mt 4:1-11; Lk 4:1-13); who wept (Jn 11:35); who expressed anger (Mk 8:32-33); and who was betrayed by his friends (Mt 26:33-35). Jesus, in the fullness of his lived humanity, discloses God to us. Therein we discover the fullness of Jesus' divinity. As Nolan makes clear: "Jesus' divinity is not something totally different from his humanity, something we have to add to his humanity; Jesus' divinity is the transcendent depths of his humanity." It made sense.

Admittedly, some decades removed from my first reading of the book, I honestly and unfortunately find myself becoming more cynical, daresay fatalistic. The state of the world doesn't exactly inspire confidence. Whether the matter involves work, politics, or church, it's easier to keep one's head down. Move along. Get along. Let's be honest: Jesus was crucified for raising his voice, going to the margins, and envisioning a new way of life. What a warning for all those who risk action on behalf of the Kingdom of God. Does it really matter what we do and say in the fight for justice?

Like Pilate and his minions, won't the compromised and corrupt then and now, whether they be persons or corporations, win out in the end?

Thankfully, every time I reacquaint myself with *Jesus before Christianity* there is a restoration of faith in Jesus. The idealism and hope of the once undergrad me returns. As it must. The Kingdom that Jesus proclaimed isn't some utopian fairy tale but something that can be brought forth and, in some ways, is already present (Luke 10:9, 11; 17:21). Discipleship in Jesus isn't only possible but attractive, inviting, and real. As Nolan says, "Faith was as attitude that people caught from Jesus through their contact with him, almost as if it were a kind of infection. It could not be taught, it could only be caught." I am able to believe again that goodness, truth, and the Kingdom will prevail.

When all was said and done, after reading this book and finishing that class, I went from business undecided to declaring theology as my major. Truth be told, accounting was a major stumbling block too. I think it was for Jesus as well. My mother has worried ever since about how I am going to support myself.

Speaking of support, it goes without saying that we are grateful to our respective academic communities that continue to be such fertile grounds. We also would like to thank John Mabry of Apocryphile Press and Mick Forgey and Dennis Coday of *National Catholic Reporter*. Finally, the contributors themselves deserve special recognition. Though the project may have been conceived by Dianne and myself, it became a reality due to their generosity of time and the substance of their reflections. Thank you to all.

The Abolition of Man: How Education Develops Man's Sense of Morality (Macmillan, 1947) by C. S. Lewis

Way beyond "the Way," but It Paved the Way

Tobias WINRIGHT, *St. Louis University*

It may surprise readers that C. S. Lewis's brief book, with its archaic title using non-inclusive language, played a significant role in my life and faith story. The reference to morality makes sense, since I am a moral theologian. So too does its focus on education, because I am a university professor. Still, Lewis (1899-1963) was a medieval literature professor at both Oxford and Cambridge, most remembered today for his children's novel, *The Lion, the Witch and the Wardrobe*, in the Chronicles of Narnia series, and for his works in Christian apologetics, such as *Mere Christianity*—each of which evangelical Protestants have found especially important.

So, how did I, a cradle Roman Catholic, happen across this book and in what ways has it been significant to me, a Catholic theological ethicist? When I was an undergraduate student, majoring in political science at the University of South Florida's Saint Petersburg campus, *The Abolition of Man* was included on the "recommended reading" list appended to a course syllabus. It grabbed my attention, because I was beginning to find myself interested in political theory and various perspectives on the human condition. My professor, the late Regis A. Factor, had done his Ph.D. in political science at the University of Notre Dame, and he often incorporated more philosophical readings into his assigned texts, as well as in his syllabi appendices. Not only did he introduce me to writings by Morgenthau,

Keynes, and Kissinger, he had me read Vatican II's *Gaudium et spes*, John Paul II's *Laborem Exercens*, selections from Augustine's *The City of God*, and Ralph McInerny's *Ethica Thomistica*. In actuality, Factor was a closet Thomist, associated somewhat with the "new natural law theory" of John Finnis and others, and at the time I was drawn to it.

You see, I was a first-generation university student in my family. Two of my younger brothers dropped out of high school, and the third has a high school diploma but no college education. Growing up, I always hoped to go to college, considering a possible career in law, politics, education, or as a priest in the church. However, my parents' divorce when I was ten years old had a very negative impact on us all, especially my brothers. During middle school, I continued to be an excellent student, but I came to hate going to Mass and became rather hostile toward religion. During high school, though, I lived with my father. He remarried and became active in the Pentecostal denomination, the Assemblies of God, where I, too, regularly attended youth group, initially due to an invitation by a girl I liked. It turned out that I became very involved in this community during these formative years—though it was a very conservative, more fundamentalist type of Christianity. Indeed, I started a morning prayer group at my public high school, included many other mostly Protestant kids, and wrote essays that were in sync with what came to be known as the Religious Right in the 1980s. I was even a regular "preacher" at a monthly religious service in the local juvenile detention center.

When I graduated from high school in 1983, I considered going to a Bible college with a view toward becoming a pastor. However, I wasn't fully on board with that, and I still thought it might be better for me to pursue becoming a lawyer. I ended up going to the local community college for my first two years. I had a tuition scholarship, but because I was living on my own (during my senior year I was thrown out of the house by my father after an argument), I needed a source of income to work my way through school. So I worked in a video arcade and then in a factory, but these made attending and doing well in classes difficult. Given my interest in law, my mother, who had become a cop after the divorce, suggested that I apply to area police departments for a job. I ended up getting hired by her department, and worked full time, mostly during the midnight shift, in the maximum security jail, while attending classes full-time during the day.

Professor Factor's courses brought many things together for me personally: politics, law, and religion—all of which eventually and circuitously led me back to Catholicism. In my work, I wrestled with questions having to do with violence, injustice, dehumanization, and oppression. In contrast to many of my fellow students, I preferred being in the classroom, where I could read, discuss, and write about such matters. Who are we? Why are we here? How ought we to live? What is true, good, just, and right? These questions, I couldn't get enough of them and devoured everything I could read whenever I could find time.

I first read Lewis's *The Abolition of Man* in that context. It met my longing at the time for something objective and virtuous, over against relativism, subjectivism, emotivism, and even propaganda. I wouldn't put it this way now, but Lewis's discussion of "the Tao" or "the Way"— probably oversimplifying a universal natural law he discerned in Platonic, Aristotelian, Stoic, Christian, and eastern religious sources—as "the doctrine of objective value, the belief that certain attitudes are really true, and others really false, to the kind of thing the universe is and the kind of things we are" (p. 29), really spoke to me.

His critique of our "conquest of nature," making it only an instrument to be controlled and manipulated to serve human interests, has stood out to me over the years, along with his warning that these same attitudes will be applied to human persons, too. "Having mastered our environment, let us now master ourselves and choose our own identity" (p. 63). Reductionism threatens to lead us to view humans—as well as the rest of the natural world—as "raw material," "mere nature," and thereby disenchanted. Of course, Lewis was writing in the immediate aftermath of World War II, and he had in mind especially eugenics, and he was concerned about its power exercised by some over others. "For the power of Man [sic] to make himself what he pleases means…the power of some men to make other men [sic] what *they* please" (p. 72). In this matrix, values are even simply human "artifacts" so that there is no objective basis for conscience, and thus, the ability to say "no" and identify limits. Out of a desire to achieve freedom from nature, Lewis argued, we actually end up losing freedom to the worst of human "nature," namely those who abuse power over others and all things.

Although I could not have seen it at the time, this major point by Lewis helped to prepare the way for me to embrace the following, more recent line: "It follows that our indifference or cruelty towards fellow creatures of this world sooner or later affects the treatment we mete out to other human beings." The latter quote is from Pope Francis, in his encyclical, *Laudato Si'* (# 91), where he is critical of the "dominant technocratic paradigm" (# 101) that gained traction 250 years ago, wherein humans have a "Promethean vision of mastery over the world" (# 116) and seek to control and dominate nature. As Francis writes, "[N]uclear energy, biotechnology, information technology, knowledge of our DNA, and so many other abilities which we have acquired, have given us tremendous power. More precisely, they have given those with the knowledge, and especially the economic resources to use them, an impressive dominance over the whole of humanity and the entire world. Never has humanity had such power over itself, yet nothing ensures that it will be used wisely…" (# 104). As he observes, drawing on the work of Roman Guardini, our technological developments (not all are necessarily advances) have not been accompanied by growth and maturity when it comes to "human responsibility, values, and conscience" (# 105). We should instead "see each human being as a subject who can never be reduced to the status of an object" (# 81), and "[y]et it would also be mistaken to view other living beings as mere objects subjected to arbitrary human domination" (# 82).

Instead of going to law school after graduation in 1987, I went to divinity school and then to graduate school to study theological ethics. I realized I wanted to teach, write, and inspire like Professor Factor had before his untimely death later in 1999 from ALS (Lou Gehrig's disease), a year after I first became a college professor myself. As a theological ethicist, I write and teach about a variety of topics: police use of force, just war, nonviolence, capital punishment, environmental degradation, climate change, and more, including bioethics. In retrospect, the nascent insights Lewis shared in *The Abolition of Man*, even though not explicitly mentioned, have remained behind much of my work.

Curiously, I suppose, I haven't assigned the book to my students, although I have mentioned it once in a while, especially to those interested in a basic, natural law type of book by a name familiar to them. Recently, however, I used it in my Ph.D. seminar on religion and bioethics, and I was surprised that none of them had read it before, let alone heard of it. Lewis was definitely prescient about much of what's happening today, as bioethics has become mostly secular.

Interestingly, I could have picked another book from that time, this one not recommended by Professor Factor: Timothy E. O'Connell's *Principles for a Catholic Morality*, with a Foreword by Charles E. Curran. Indeed, when I showed it to him, Professor Factor advised against reading its revisionist perspective. Although I heard him, I didn't listen to his warning. And I now consider myself much more in that camp of theological ethics, even as Lewis's book and others similarly recommended then and over the years continue to inform who I am and what I do.

An Asian Theology of Liberation (Orbis, 1988) by Aloysius Pieris, S.J.

A Double Baptism: Immersion into Asian Poverty and Asian Religiousness

Peter C. PHAN, *Georgetown University*

As an Asian who did graduate studies in theology at Roman pontifical universities in the decade after the Second Vatican Council (1962-65) Aloysius Pieris's book, first published in German [*Theologie der Befreiung in Asien: Christentum im Kontext der Armut und der Religionen*, Herder, 1986] and two years later in English [*An Asian Theology of Liberation*, Orbis Books, 1988] was, for me at least, an intellectual bombshell.

When I did my theology at the *Pontificio Ateneo Salesiano*, later upgraded to *Universitas Pontificia Salesiana*, in Rome in 1968-1972, the reform of theological studies mandated by the council was beginning to be implemented. However, very few of the professors, who had been trained in neo-scholastic Thomism, were willing or able to embark upon it. All classes were done in lecture format; students were provided with mimeographed copies of the professor's lectures, which made attendance unnecessary; and the material for the only test in the course, a half-hour oral examination at the end of the semester, was based on these *dispense* [handouts], as these texts were called. The overriding goal of the theological curriculum was to inculcate the truths of faith as these have been taught by the Bible and Tradition, and students were graded on their ability to accurately expound on them. For the degree of *licenza*, which then required four years of full-time study and qualified its holder to teach in a seminary or a pontifical school, a written comprehensive examination on over a hundred "theses," appropriately called *de universis* [about everything], and a *tesina* [small thesis] were required. Creativity and critical thinking were discouraged; orthodoxy and fidelity to the magisterium were highly prized.

In terms of theological orientation, the curriculum was largely based on the teaching of the hierarchical magisterium, papal and conciliar. Rarely were primary sources themselves, for example, the writings of Augustine and Aquinas, read; rather, students learned about their theologies through the professors' summaries. Among contemporary theologians, only Europeans, such as Henri de Lubac, Jean Daniélou, Yves Congar, Marie-Dominique Chenu, Karl Rahner, Edward Schillebeeckx and Hans Küng (though, curiously, not Hans Urs von Balthasar and Joseph Ratzinger) were considered. Rarely if ever was mention made of Latin American theology, even after the landmark meeting of the Conference of Latin American Bishops in Medellín, Colombia (1968) and the emergence of liberation theology. Needless to say, African and Asian theologians did not even appear on the theological radar. In short, there was only one kind of theology, namely, the European, and it was regarded as contextually free, culturally universal, and permanently valid.

I mentioned this theological background to help readers understand why my encounter with Pieris's book was a mind-and-life changing experience. Right after completing my *licenza* in 1972 I returned to South Vietnam, and it soon became painfully clear to me that the theology I had imbibed in Rome was worse than useless for my ministry, especially as chaplain to the only prison for women in the country at the time. Since there was neither opportunity nor resources (nor, I must admit, interest) for theological research, I could not follow the theological developments in Asia. After I came to the U.S.A. as a refugee in 1975, I left pastoral ministry to teach theology, frankly, not as a mystical quest for eternal verities, but as a job to support my family.

My earliest scholarly interests were Orthodox theology of the icon, patristics, and Karl Rahner's theology. Later, in the course of teaching and research, I became acquainted first with Latin American liberation theology, and then with Asian liberation theology. In connection with the latter I began researching the history of Christian missions in Asia and Asian theologies, especially the teaching of the Federation of Asian Bishops' Conferences (FABC). It was then that I "discovered" Aloysius Pieris, and my theological horizon expanded, with Pieris serving as inspiration and guide. I first read *An Asian Theology of Liberation* in 1991, and then *Love Meets Wisdom: A Christian Experience of Buddhism* (Orbis Books, 1988) and *Fire & Water: Basic Issues in Asian Buddhism and Christianity* (Orbis Books, 1996).

Like first love, however, it was the reading of Pieris's first book *An Asian Liberation Theology* that made a lasting and profound impact on my understanding and practice of theology. The German title of his book expresses better than its English one the four aspects of Pieris's influence on me: *Befreiung* [liberation], *Christentum im Kontext* [Christianity in context], *Armut* [poverty], and *Religionen* [religions]. First, liberation, not intellectual contemplation, is the goal of theology. Second, the context of the local church determines the method and themes of theology. Third, the social context of Asian Christianity is systemic poverty. Fourth, the religious context of Asian Christianity is religious plurality/pluralism. Interestingly, *An Asian Theology of Liberation* is not an organically planned monograph. Rather it is a collection of nine previously published essays, and happily it is a slim volume—a mere 139 pages—and highly readable. The essays are grouped around its central theme, namely liberation, and divided into three parts: "Poverty and Liberation," "Religion and Poverty," and "Theology of Liberation in Asia." Clearly, the core concern of Asian theology is liberation and the two areas in which it is to be achieved are poverty and religion.

The first lesson I learned from Pieris, one that is so obvious that at first sight it is not worthy of mention, is that theology is inescapably context-dependent. But imagine how intellectually destabilizing this simple truth was for someone like me, who had a vested interest in defending the "Roman theology" I was schooled in, the theology that presented itself—implicitly at least—as contextually free, culturally universal, and permanently valid. It takes humility and truthfulness to acknowledge the essential situatedness—read: limitedness, partiality, bias, incompleteness, provisionality—of all theologies, including the self-proclaimed authoritative ("authentic") teaching of the "ordinary magisterium" and even papal *ex cathedra* definitions, the infallible pronouncements of ecumenical councils, and the "definitive teaching" of the "universal episcopal magisterium." This acknowledgment of the essential contextuality of all church teachings and theologies—*Christentum im Kontext*—rejects both the "dictatorship of relativism" and the "dictatorship of absolutism," which are unacknowledged ideological cousins. On the one hand, by recognizing that one's *truth* is but one way of knowing what is true, one rejects the relativistic claim that there is no truth as self-contradictory since at least the proposition that "there is no truth" is assumed as categorically true. On the other hand, recognizing that one's truth is but *one* way among many of knowing what is true requires the abandonment of the well-nigh irresistible temptation of intellectual absolutism, imperialism and colonialism in claiming that one's "truth" is the *only* truth.

If the context of Christianity specifies the approach and themes of its theology, how can the distinctive context of Asia be discovered? Here lies the second lesson I learned from Pieris, namely, the necessity of the social-political-economic analysis for theology. Of course, Latin American liberation theologians have long practiced this type of social analysis in order to unmask the root causes of systemic poverty in their continent. But Pieris's insistence on its necessity for theology is highly significant, and this for two reasons. First, the use of social analysis in Latin American liberation theology had been condemned by Cardinal Joseph Ratzinger, then Prefect of the Congregation of the Doctrine of the Faith, in his Instruction *On Certain Aspects of Liberation Theology* (1984) as of Marxist provenance, and hence contrary to the Christian faith. That Pieris insists on its necessity for Asian theology is a direct challenge to Ratzinger's understanding of how theology should be done. Secondly, Pieris, while appreciative of Latin American liberation theology, argues that social analysis is necessary but insufficient for Asia. Given Asia's religiousness, another analysis is required in order to understand the indispensable role of religion, both "cosmic" and "metacosmic"—that is, popular and organized—religion for liberation.

The third insight I learned from Pieris is his characterization of the Asian context as marked by widespread poverty and deep religiousness. Of course Asia is extremely complex—even the use of "Asia" is contested—and any shorthand description of it can easily be challenged. But for theological purposes, Pieris's thumbnail sketch of the Asian context is as good as any. What is most significant is that from these twofold characteristics he derives the double task for Asian Christianity, and by extension, Asian theologians, which he terms the "double baptism," namely "the Calvary of Asian poverty" and "the Jordan of Asian religion." As mentioned earlier, this double baptism forms the core of *An Asian Theology of Liberation*. Without this simultaneous baptism into poverty and religiousness there can be no Asian liberation theology at all, and furthermore, and this is Pieris's astounding claim, no Christian theology *sic et simpliciter*.

Note that Pieris insists on the necessity of *both* baptisms *at the same time* and asserts that this double baptism constitutes the "primordial experience of liberation" given by Jesus of Nazareth, which the church's "collective memory" (Pieris's term for Bible and Tradition), mediates throughout the ages, and which theologians must constantly reinterpret for their contemporaries in dialogue with popular ("cosmic") religiosity, the collective memory of other ("metacosmic") religions, for the sake of liberation. The baptism on the Calvary of poverty is undergone by being voluntarily poor ("option to be poor") and by working for the poor ("option for the poor"). Without the former, theology is but an academic exercise for the leisurely elite class; without the latter, theology is but an irrelevant and sterile *theoria* ("contemplation"). The baptism in the Jordan of religion requires that theology in Asia be done in collaboration and dialogue with believers of other religions to find "homologues" (not parallel, much less identical concepts) for a common religious idiom to express the primordial experience of liberation. Theology, for Pieris, is not primarily *fides quaerens intellectum* (faith in search of understanding), a favorite definition of theology in the West, but *fides promovens justitiam* (faith promoting justice) or *fides promovens liberationem* (faith promoting liberation). Liberation of whom and from what? For Pieris, liberation of the rich from their riches (without detachment from which through voluntary poverty it is impossible to enter the reign of God), of the poor from their enforced poverty (which is enslaving oppression), and of both from "greed" (the worship of Mammon).

I must confess that doing theology the way Pieris recommends and does is hard. Hard in two senses. First, academically rigorous. Pieris never tires of insisting on the necessity of mastering the scholarly tools and linguistic skills to do theology properly. He leads by example: besides being fluent in several European and Asian languages, he has mastered classical languages such as Hebrew, Greek, Latin, Sanskrit, and Pali. Secondly, spiritual discipline. Theology *is* spirituality, and vice versa, spirituality *is* theology. No wonder that I for one will ever remain a beginner or novice in the Pierisian school, and a deeply grateful one.

A Bibliographical Note: Of the many books by Pieris I have chosen *An Asian Theology of Liberation* as one of the most influential books for my theological development. Pieris has authored some 20 books and hundreds of articles, most of which are published in Asia and not widely available in the West. For readers who want to understand Pieris's theology more fully, I most strongly recommend his *The Genesis of an Asian Theology of Liberation: An Autobiographical Excursus on the Art of Theologizing in Asia* (2013). All of his books are available from Tulana Research Centre for Encounter and Dialogue, 521/2 Kohalwila Road, Gonowala, Kelaniya, Sri Lanka (info@tulana.com).

Analogical Imagination: Christian Theology and the Culture of Pluralism (Crossroad, 1998) by David Tracy

A Classic in the Truest Sense

Edward FOLEY, Capuchin, *Catholic Theological Union*

It was over twenty-five years ago that I read John Irving's remarkable *A Prayer for Owen Meany*. I remember the book as the finest fiction I had ever encountered. Recently I had the opportunity to download it as an audio book. While I enjoyed it even more the second time, I was also slightly dismayed about how much I had forgotten, how many vivid characters had faded from memory, the horde of outrageous humor that had evaporated, and the profound human and spiritual insights that had been virtually erased from my memory banks.

Similarly, I have always remembered *Analogical Imagination* as a paradigm-shifting read, and have regularly referenced it in my teaching and writing. Aware of my faulty memory, in preparation for crafting this reflection I thought it wise to reread this classic in its entirety. Akin to my revisiting of *A Prayer for Owen Meany*, however, I was both chagrined at how much I had forgotten about this treasure, yet gratified that so many ideas that I instinctively hold so firmly can be anchored in Tracy's opus. There are three central tenets of my own theologizing that have distinctive roots in this amazing classic. While closely related to each other, we will examine them here—as Tracy advises—as distinct but not separate.

Human Experience

Already in *Blessed Rage for Order* Tracy asserted the critical role of "common human experience" in the theological enterprise, noting that Christian theology today is best understood "as philosophical reflection upon the meanings present in common human experience and the meanings present in the Christian tradition" (p. 34). He returns to this theme in *Analogical Imagination*, arguing that classic works flowing from the human spirit—be those in art or religion—are necessary resources for interpreting our world and beliefs.

Analogical Imagination was written in a period of eroding faith, when the tenets of Christianity were met with increasing skepticism in the academy and society. Thus Tracy's commitment to theologizing in view of shared human experiences allowed him to engage theologically with a common grounding in humanity. This contribution has become increasingly important as the number of those unaffiliated with any religion continues to expand in this country and abroad, as does the number of those who self-identify as agnostics or atheists. While not directly engaged in training agnostics, atheists or humanists—although they are populating our seminaries and divinity schools—I am training people who will need to collaborate with representatives of these belief-streams both on religious (e.g., chaplaincy) and social (e.g., homelessness) endeavors. Beyond pastoral or strategic collaboration, I wonder whether a Roman Catholic and Humanist chaplain at a hospital can actually share some kind of depth reflection on their work together without compromising their own form of believing. Can a Roman Catholic engage in what is traditionally called theological reflection with someone who has no "theology"?

My response to this ministerial quandary has been a form of meaning-making called "reflective believing."[1] The beginning point of this interpretive venture is shared human experience, especially as narrated through storytelling and ritualizing. It was Tracy's emphasis on the centrality of human experience for the theological enterprise that triggered this venture

---

1 *Theological Reflection across Religious Traditions: The Turn to Reflective Believing* (Lanham MD: Rowman & Littlefield, 2015).

into a type of interpretation that did not require theological categories but still could broach the transcendent.

Tracy's valuing of human experience finds a Christological parallel for me in his assertion that the one classic event and person "which normatively judges and informs all other Christian classics ... [is] the event and person of Jesus Christ" (p. 233). A classic is any event, text, image, symbol or person with an "excess of meaning" that provokes understanding in the present with a kind of "permanent timeliness" (p. 102). Considering Jesus Christ as a classic allows me to think about, preach about, teach about a Jesus deeply rooted in humanity. Just as the early disciples first experienced his humanity in order to discern his divinity, so can I employ the human stories, deeds and parables of Jesus as a resource in interfaith dialogue and meaning-making with non-theists without having to abandon my belief in his divinity. Tracy has enabled me to ponder how humanity is a valuable portal to transcendence, particularly in Jesus mode.

Analogy

Another central concept in *Analogical Imagination* that has become a regular part of my teaching and believing is his emphasis on the analogical imagination for theologizing in this pluriform age. Analogical language for Tracy is capable of recognizing and articulating similarity-in-difference, even to the point of theologizing about a God who—despite the infinite chasm between humanity and divinity—can be grasped as more like the created world than unlike it. Tracy does see the need for a dialectical perspective in theology that emphasizes the fundamental rupture between God and creation and considers it an important antidote to the tendency to confuse every human activity with the work of the Holy Spirit. At the same time, however, Tracy holds that analogical thinking and speaking is essential in this increasingly pluralistic world so that despite our differences we can engage in fruitful and public conversation.

As a Capuchin-Franciscan friar, I find Tracy's turn to the analogical resonant with central tenets of Franciscan spirituality. Francis of Assisi is celebrated for his perception of creation as kin, worthy of respect and praise. Multiple are the tales of Francis preaching to birds, talking to wolves, and even smearing the walls with meat so that they could join in the Christmas feast. Every creature was a gift from God, a generosity of vision that extended to the poorest and most marginalized of humankind. Francis's vision is summarized in his "Canticle of Creation" that claims sun, moon, fire, water, earth and air as siblings in God. More systematically, Bonaventure's *The Journey of the Soul into God,* demonstrates how the universe is marked with God's fingerprints. Ultimately, Bonaventure concludes that the God whom Genesis remembers as declaring each stage of creation "good," is best named as the Highest Good (*Summum Bonum*). All of creation has its origin in this ultimate Good.

Finally, I find Tracy's emphasis on the analogical useful when teaching sacraments. Since the mid-20th century theologians have attempted to restore something of the elasticity that the early church predicated of sacramentality. The so-called "sacramental principle" asserts that everything in the created world has the potential to reveal God. That concept is often daunting to those suspicious of contemporary culture. However, Tracy's similarity-in-difference reasoning embraces the dialectical as a necessary corrective to any instinct to consider every cultural manifestation or societal trend as coming from God. At the same time, it respects God's creation as sacramental at its roots. This enables students to forgo confining sacramentality to prescribed liturgical events, and provides a broad invitation to sacramental living.

Public Theology

Finally, I find Tracy's emphasis on the theologian as a public figure, and theology as a public event enormously useful. Having taught worship for almost 40 years, and presided and preached for an equal length of time, it is refreshing to reimagine worship beyond some private service to the baptized. Instead, our sacramentalizing broadcasts who we are and what we believe in this religiously skeptical world.

While Tracy focuses on systematic theology as public theology, the same should be said of worship. The *Constitution on the Sacred Liturgy* (1963) notes that the liturgy is the font and summit of the church's life (#10). That means that it is the font of mission, of upholding the dignity of all human beings and the integrity of all of creation. If, as Pope Francis asserted in his *Joy of the Gospel*, every activity of the baptized is ultimately an act of evangelization (# 18), then our central acts of worship must by definition be acts of evangelization.

Tracy contends that systematic theologians must address society, academy and the church. Similarly, liturgy as "public worship" must have the same centrifugal energy. This becomes increasingly important with the growing number of religiously unaffiliated in U.S. society. While their population continues to expand, they have not given up ritualizing. In times of personal loss, major life transition or natural or man-made disaster, human beings need to ritualize and often flock to our churches. Liturgy at such dynamic moments must have a capacity to transcend narrow doctrinal or rubrical parameters and speak to broad communities at such liminal moments. *Analogical Imagination*'s presentation of theology as a public act amplifies and justifies such an approach. Traditionally liturgy has been called first (or first-order) theology. If all theology is to be a public act, then the first of our enacted theologies in word and sacrament, ritual and music must also be public.

Concluding Thought

Central to the message of *Analogical Imagination* is the conviction that classics are necessary resources for interpreting our world and our beliefs. *Analogical Imagination* has attained the status of a classic for me. I am personally grateful that this exercise provoked me to reread *Analogical Imagination* in its entirety. It's something I will need to do again.

The Autobiography of Malcolm X (Random House, 1965) by Malcolm X with Alex Haley

A Novice Reading

M. Shawn COPELAND, *Boston College*

On February 21, 1965, Malcolm X (born Malcolm Little and known as El-Hajj Malik El-Shabazz) was assassinated in the Audubon Ballroom in Harlem, New York. His autobiography, written in collaboration with Pulitzer Prize winner Alex Haley, was published shortly after his death but without, as sociologist and historian Manning Marable has noted, his final revisions and approval.[1] Still, *The Autobiography of Malcolm X* holds a secure place in the canon of 20th century American literature and has become a staple in courses in African American Studies. *The Autobiography* lays out in raw, mesmerizing detail one man's struggle for his own subjectivity or personhood and his advocacy for beneficial change in the social conditions of black Americans.

From the mid-1950s and through the decade of the 1960s, the civil rights movement held the attention of the American public. These were years of intense cultural and social ferment as the nation grappled with the ignominy of segregation and the ambiguities of integration. The urgent and eloquent appeals of the Reverend Dr. Martin Luther King, Jr., along with freedom rides and sit-ins carried out by hundreds of black and white

---

[1] Manning Marable, *Malcolm X: A Life of Reinvention* (New York: Viking Press, 2011).

college students shamed the nation with an activism forged from nonviolent protest, a commitment to redemptive suffering, and neighborly love.

Still, there were other voices, including that of Malcolm X. In July 1959, the New York based television program *News Beat* broadcast a five-part series by Mike Wallace on the Nation of Islam (NOI), featuring Malcolm, among others. His scorching anti-white rhetoric gave weight to the charge that the NOI taught love's opposite—hate. Malcolm's participation in the program established him as a powerful spokesperson for the Nation and its version of black separatism. He soon appeared on national television and radio talk shows, conducted interviews with major magazines, and lectured on college and university campuses. He also came to the attention of the Federal Bureau of Investigation (FBI). By the middle of 1963, Malcolm had grown disenchanted with the Nation and the immoral behavior of its leader, Elijah Muhammad. In December of that year, Muhammad suspended him from NOI ministry: Malcolm had violated a direct order by commenting publicly on the assassination of President Kennedy. Within months, Malcolm repudiated the Nation, converted to Sunni Islam, formed the Organization of Afro-American Unity (OAAU), and made the pilgrimage to Mecca. He travelled and lectured widely in Africa, the Middle East, and parts of Europe; he also changed his views on race relations and cautiously endorsed the aims of the civil rights movement. On the cusp of the bright achievement of his humanity, Malcolm X was gunned down before the age of 40.

I first read *The Autobiography of Malcolm X* in 1968 as a second year novice or newly professed (*neo-professed*) sister of the Congregation of the Sisters of St. Felix of Cantalice, more familiarly known as the Felician Sisters. The four years spent in religious formation in Livonia, Michigan, have proved the most enduring influence of my life, rivaled only by my graduate school encounter at Boston College with Bernard Lonergan and his most brilliant student, Fred Lawrence.

I came to religious life after the Second Vatican Council concluded. During our formation, the Council's challenge to religious women to examine and renew their lives was a priority. Our novice mistress was young, perceptive, very smart, and held a master's degree in theology. In daily sessions with us, she advocated holistic human development and growth in the spiritual life through cultivating an intimate relationship with Jesus Christ, prayer, meditation, theological study, and reflection. She oriented us toward the future of a changing world. Still, old rules jostled against the new: visits from family, relatives, and friends were limited to once a month and not at all during the canonical year, but there were prudent exceptions (a visit to a gravely ill grandmother). There was almost no access to television or secular newspapers or magazines, but popular and scholarly Catholic periodicals along with the latest theological books were readily available.

I was a novice in more ways than one: I was a novice in "black matters." I was the only black woman in my group of 24 or 25, and there was another young black woman in the high school preparatory program. Out of the more than 3,000 Felician sisters in the United States, only one black woman from the Buffalo, New York province, had professed final vows. My formal introduction to social oppression and the social suffering it causes came from learning about the Nazi attempt to exterminate the Jewish people. Still, I did not grow up ignorant of racial discrimination: I could not attend the Catholic school nearest my home because, as the sister said, "We do not take colored children." Despite Detroit's cunning patterns of social segregation, youth and geography placed me on the sidelines of the organized black struggle for civil rights. Like the other postulants and canonical novices, I was insulated from the day-to-day political events of U. S. society. But shortly before the retreat prior to first profession of vows, Detroit exploded. On July 23, 1967, a routine police raid on an after hours drinking club ignited smoldering black resentment at systemic bias and discrimination. Five furious days of rebellion left more than 40 persons dead and hundreds injured, more than 7,000 arrested, and more than 2,000 buildings destroyed. When the news reached us, a world away in suburban Livonia, I was stunned, apologetic, and very sad. I now know I was naïve. I was a novice in "black matters."

In September of that same year as second year novices, we went back to classes at Madonna College. With permission, I met monthly with other black women religious, seminarians, and the lone black priest in the Archdiocese of Detroit. We wrestled with meanings of race and identity in relation to religious vocation; we studied and discussed books by black authors. Taking cues from *Gaudium et Spes*, we too sought to "scrutinize the signs of the times,"[2] to analyze and interpret the social condition of black people in light of the Gospel and to situate that interpretation within the context of the renewal of Catholic theology. During this period, someone loaned or gave me a copy of *The Autobiography of Malcolm X*. I was galvanized and could not stop reading: I read after completing homework assignments, during study hall, after my chores, in my spare time. After we retired for the evening, I sat up reading in the glow of the exit light and our novice mistress coughed ever so discreetly before climbing the stairs to our dormitory to bless us. I will be forever grateful to her; she helped me immensely as I navigated uncharted waters.

The person and voice of *The Autobiography of Malcolm X* were unlike anyone and anything I had ever met or read. I was shocked at his criminal past, drug use, exploitation of women, and the rage he spewed at white people, but I agreed with his attack on institutional racism and its lethal impact on black life. I admired his ability to lead and maintain a separate sphere for Black Muslims, even as I disagreed with his theology, which breached everything I believed about the Gospel. Still, I admired his discipline and courage to change his life; indeed, through his self-transformations, he made of his life a radical, complex, and beautiful work of art.

Malcolm X was the first revolutionary I ever "met" and I wanted to be one too—a revolutionary black nun! Under the direction of our novice mistress I first tried writing theology and Malcolm gave me something to theologize about: nothing ought to be more sacred than the liberation of my people. Malcolm taught me seriousness of purpose, black pride, love of black history, and love of black people. He taught me resistance, resolve, and daring. He led me to black consciousness.

I came late to serious study of King's thought, but as I read our contemporary theological landscape, he remains *the* consummate practical-political theologian of the American experiment in social democracy. Obviously, it is much too simplistic to set Malcolm as King's opposite, to constrict him to the field of black power nationalism and separatism. James Cone in his *Martin & Malcolm & America: A Dream or A Nightmare* cautions against

---

2   *Gaudium et Spes*, The Pastoral Constitution on the Church in the Modern World, #4, Promulgated by Pope Paul VI, December 7, 1965.

such an approach.³ To do so poses a Manichean vision of life in America: Martin *or* Malcolm, integration *or* separation, white *or* black. To do so flattens the ambiguity and contradictions as well as the joys and pleasures of human living, ignores the infinite circumference of divine grace, and dismisses the cost of struggle for a nation—*a world*—without racism.

I have taught and still teach *The Autobiography of Malcolm X* as well as his speeches and interviews. The first time was at Saint Norbert College in an undergraduate course on Grace. I structured the reading, mainly fiction, to help students discern the fitful responses we humans make to the gift and movement of grace. I still remember the student who, in a thoughtful and well-written paper, drew out connections between Malcolm's self-transformation and Lonergan's categories of intellectual, moral, and religious conversion. I was elated. Two very disparate men, each of whom was so important to my intellectual development, came together in *my* classroom.

Much has changed in American society, the church, and the global order since I was a novice tackling *The Autobiography of Malcolm X* and wrestling with the density of the black lifeworld. My life has changed and *not* changed: I am no longer a vowed woman religious, but I still ache to be a revolutionary, to bring about change in society and church; I still ache for justice for all creation in our broken world. Today I take up and read *The Autobiography of Malcolm X* with critical appreciation for the sharp organic intellectual Malcolm was and for his capacity to critique and shift, even change, his religious, cultural, and social horizons. But, *The Autobiography* still indicts the continuing Christian betrayal of the Gospel and its failure to effectively counter the myriad ordinary ways race and racism shape our thinking about ourselves and our interactions with one another.

In the last months of his life Malcolm X came to articulate the necessity of authentic relationships between human beings, to insist that the struggle against white racist supremacy is a human problem. All of us, whatever our racial-ethnic and cultural backgrounds, "as human beings [have] the obligation and the responsibility, of helping to correct America's human problem. … In our mutual sincerity we might be able to show a

---

3   James H. Cone, *Martin & Martin & America: A Dream or a Nightmare* (Maryknoll, NY: Orbis Books, 1991).

road to the salvation of America's very soul."[4] As a political theologian, my work interrogates the meaning of being human in cultural and social conditions that insult our humanity and mock our efforts at authentic solidarity. Malcolm's words water my hope: words from a man who lived through the brutal and brutalizing effects of the vicious and long reign of sin that structural racism is. Malcolm's example summons us to live in such a *way* that the truth, intelligibility, goodness, and beauty of our concrete social order might be manifest and nourish the flourishing of each and every one of us.

---

4   Malcolm X, *The Autobiography of Malcolm X* (New York: Random House, 1965), 383, 385.

Being as Communion: Personhood and the Church (St. Vladimir's Press, 1985) by Jean Zizioula

Learning about Relationality from a Greek

James F. KEENAN, S.J., Boston College

In 1982 I began my studies in theological ethics at the Pontifical Gregorian University in Rome. From 1982-1984 I took roughly 16 courses, did comprehensives, and wrote a licentiate thesis with Klaus Demmer on moral metaphysics. From 1985-87, I wrote my dissertation on Thomas Aquinas under Josef Fuchs.

I had an exciting roster of courses those first two years. Three courses with Josef Fuchs, four with Klaus Demmer, three with Louis Vereecke, two with Edouard Hamel, and one each with Wilhelm Ernst, Frank Sullivan, and Jared Wicks. For a budding moral theologian, wanting to learn the "tradition" and the contemporary European approach to theological ethics, I was in heaven.

In the spring of 1984, colleagues told me I should sit in Jean Zizioulas's class. I had never had a course solely dedicated to Orthodox theology. I enrolled in a class of about 200 students, most of whom were priests.

I remember thinking that listening to Zizioulas was like listening to a Martian! I had spent two years on casuistry, fundamental and final options, deontology and teleology. With Fuchs and Demmer I was at the heart of the European debate about the autonomous conscience and the magisterium. This was not at all the banal debate that happened in the United States, about whether we *could* follow our conscience instead of a church teaching. For European moralists, and particularly the Germans, the autonomous conscience arose from the ashes of war-torn Europe, indicting itself for the ravages of fascism, Nazism and the holocaust. Conscience was not an option; it was a haunting, divine reproach of vicious subservience built on fear.

There in Rome, I was reading everything by Demmer and Fuchs and their colleagues, as well as overseeing the English editions of Fuchs' writings for Georgetown University Press. I also was having class with Louis Vereecke, from whom I learned about the probabilists, the probabiliorists, the equiprobabilists, to say nothing of the laxists and tutiorists. In the world of theological ethics I knew my tradition, from the heights of German and American debates over metaethics down to the minute particularity of the casuistry of an ectopic pregnancy.

Sitting that spring listening to Zizioulas was like hearing a whole new language, an entirely new perspective, and an absolutely unexpected breath of fresh air. Fresh air, that's what it was. Zizioulas was lecturing on the Holy Spirit and relationality. In my other 15 courses, with the exception of Hamel, the Holy Spirit was rarely mentioned.

At the Greg, little reading was required for one's course work. Readings were always referenced and one *could* do the readings, but accountability for a course was based on whether one understood the lectures. Zizioulas's readings were mostly in French. He juxtaposed his early essays with subsequent debates with two Roman Catholic theologians who engaged him, Ignace de la Potterie, S.J., and Yves Congar, O.P.

At the heart of his lectures was his book, *L'Être ecclesial*, that appeared later in 1985 in English as *Being as Communion*.[1] I was mesmerized by the relationality that seeped throughout these pages.

In *L'Être ecclesial*, Zizioulas argues that the Fall shows us what our nature is when we creatures we are left to ourselves. The Fall was, above all things, a break with communion. Alienated humanity after the Fall is left looking for personhood, which denotes at once particularity and communion. The person we are looking for is Christ, who is fully relational: to the Father and the Spirit in the Godhead and to us in our humanity. In his person, Christ is constitutively relational.

By the Spirit we become relational, because by the Spirit we are constituted as church. Baptism is then a birth whereby we go from being

---

[1] Jean Zizioulas, *L'Être ecclésial* (Paris: Labor et Fides, 1981). This was later translated as *Being as Communion: Personhood and the Church* (Yonkers: St. Vladimir's Press, 1985).

an individual to becoming a person. We become one who is at the same time constituted by community. As God is constituted as three persons in communion, so are we constituted by the Spirit as persons in communion with the Body of Christ.

Inasmuch as by baptism we discover that our personal freedom is in Christ, our freedom is no longer the alienating practice of choosing between two, opting for one and declining the other. Freedom is found not in individuating practices but in relational ones.

We must therefore see that the church as communion is never an either/or. It is not local or universal, but at once, the church is both. For believers it is impossible to understand that the local church is not at once the universal church. The church united in Christ is the integrity, the plentitude of the body of Christ. The universal church is as present in the local church as the body of Christ is present in the Sunday Eucharist in one's parish.

Most early councils wrestled to understand that the one local church could not refuse a faithful member of another community: each community was in full unity, not imposed from beyond but realized within as it broke the bread. For this reason bishops were not ordained outside the context of Eucharistic communion. Within the Eucharist we ordain the one called to responsibility for the communion of the church.

The Spirit not only constitutes us as persons but also introduces the *eschaton* into history and changes linear history into the present; history is not simply identified as the past, but as the present and the future as well. For the Greek Orthodox, the *anamnesis* of the Eucharist includes a remembrance of all three: "Remembering, therefore, this command of the Savior ("to do this in memory of me,") and all that came to pass for our sake, the cross, the tomb, the resurrection on the third day, the ascension into heaven, the enthronement at the right hand of the Father, and the second, glorious coming."[2]

What Christ gives us in the Eucharist is the structure of the kingdom itself: in the Eucharist we can understand that in the local church we can find the universal church and similarly in the present we can witness salvation history. In communion all that alienates us disappears.

---

2   The Greek Orthodox Archdiocese of America, *The Divine Liturgy of St. John Chrysostom*, http://www.goarch.org/chapel/liturgical_texts/liturgy_hchc

The relationality that Christ brings us in the Eucharist is his oneness with the Father and the Spirit and with us. In turn, in the local church, the bishop ordained in the Eucharist must see that the bishop's very identity is not as an individual but as relational person whose function is fundamentally to promote communion.

All this gives you, I hope, an appreciation for Zizioulas's gift.

At the end of every course at the Gregorian, we would have a final exam, a ten-minute oral for each student with the professor. Oral exams at the Gregorian were, well, in a word, weird. You just got in a long alphabetical line: you had to make sure that you were the person the professor expected when he looked up from his roster as you entered the exam. The professor would ask any number of questions based on his lectures. It was all very predictable.

For my oral exams I decided that I wanted a conversation with each of my professors. For each exam, I presented the professor with a list of readings that I had done for the course. This always worked, and better, no one else did it! The professor invariably would want, in the midst of the monotony of the endless hours of asking the same question, a conversation too!

For Zizioulas, I read everything: the early essays, the debates with Congar, *L'Être ecclésial*. I gave him the list. He asked me a few questions to see if I understood his writings. Surprised and satisfied, he asked me, "May I ask, what do you think of my writings?" "I am becoming a Jesuit casuist in all the particularity that that means. I am, if you will, at the opposite end from you of the lively spectrum of theology. You let me imagine the vastness of theology and you stimulate my imagination. I expect that I will not use your writings, but I have been forever changed by realizing just how small my field of Catholic theological ethics is on the landscape of Christian theology."

As I look back on reading *L'Être ecclésial*, I can see that Zizioulas (or was it the Spirit?) both lured me out of my autonomous ethics and prompted me to ask about relationality and led me to look for a personal conscience and a normative ethics based, not primarily on acting, but on being, and therein, a virtue ethics based on the person, not as an individual, but as primarily, constitutively relational.

Beyond the Text: A Holistic Approach to Liturgy (Indiana University Press, 1987) by Lawrence A. Hoffman

Going to the Borderlands

Julia UPTON, R.S.M., *St. John's University*

Although I do not specifically recall what initially drew me to Rabbi Lawrence A. Hoffman's book, *Beyond the Text: A Holistic Approach to Liturgy*, knowing myself it was probably the title alone that first attracted me. As colleagues in the North American Academy of Liturgy, I knew Larry to be a charming, good-humored, faith-filled scholar who inspired many of us with his ideas and perspective. The book not only did not disappoint, but it has also influenced my scholarship, thinking and teaching ever since.

Inspired himself by liturgical scholars such as Robert Taft and Geoffrey Wainwright, Hoffman's thesis is that we need to study what he calls the borderlands of our discipline, drawing on neighboring academic disciplines such as sociology, anthropology, psychology, history, etc. in order to fully understand our own discipline. He calls the liturgical field a "holistic network of interrelationships that bind together discrete things, acts, people, and events into the activity we call worship—or better still, ritual."

Rather than seeing this as "merely … revamping a little-known discipline," Hoffman describes it as "opening a new window on the life of religious people the world over, a window that looks out on the very essence of religious celebration, the way in which a holy calendar takes its shape, a committed life unfolds, a community of faithful takes its stand. It is not the text, then, but the people who pray it, that should concern us." Although the case study Hoffman offers is the modern study of Jewish liturgy, it was not difficult for me to make other applications even while I read the text.

A decade or so after first reading *Beyond the Text*, I found myself frustrated while working on the book that became *A Time for Embracing: Reclaiming Reconciliation* (Liturgical Press, 1999). Several years into that research, having approached the topic not just from historical and theological perspectives, but also taking both sociological and psychological stances, I felt increasingly inadequate to the task, thinking that I needed to read more deeply into both sociology and psychology before risking to write further. Since Larry had set me on that trajectory in venturing beyond the text, I thought he might be willing to help me on the path. I called him one afternoon and his advice at that time continues to echo in my life and work today.

I shared with him, for example, my concerns that I felt as though I needed to become a psychologist before going further in my writing. Larry seemed to bellow through the phone, "No! You are an artist, not a scientist. Artists use the work of scientists without being required to engage in it themselves." Once again he gave me a new way of looking at things. Of course I still try to be a careful researcher and not a dilettante, but I have tamed those inner demons that would have me believe I need to know everything about every aspect of those approaches before proceeding. Hoffman reminds us that "artists and scientists who wish to apply their crafts to liturgy must learn to be at home in the arcane world that traffics in the coin of literary conceits, stratified pericopes and manuscript comparisons."

Although *A Time for Embracing* includes an analysis of the rites of reconciliation, it moves beyond the text to give a historical overview of sacramental practice, to report on, analyze and critique a study on pastoral renewal and Penance conducted by the NCCB Committee for Pastoral Research and Practices, reflect on the place of reconciliation in contemporary American Society, and make some suggestions for reclaiming reconciliation. Because it is almost two decades old itself, the examples used in the text are often somewhat dated, but its scope is still valuable.

This urge to go beyond the text has found its way into my teaching as well. The student body at St. John's University (NY) has always been very diverse and I try to draw on that diversity in the courses I teach. For a number of years we had several graduate students from Ghana in the Theology program and their description of liturgical practice back home always excited and engaged me. Tired of simply hearing about such amazing, participative worship, I wanted to experience it for myself. Although it took quite a few years for me to have the opportunity to do so, in 2002 I was finally able visit one of my former students in Sunyani, capital of the Brong-Ahofo region of Ghana—to travel with him and enter fully into worship services. Reality did not disappoint! Instead, I was left thinking that my students had actually underestimated the vitality and intensity of worship there. Worship in the United States in general is often more cerebral than embodied, whereas the opposite was more true of my experience in Ghana.

Sunday Mass began at 6:00 a.m. that July morning and the church was packed, which was my first surprise at that hour. Although Mass was celebrated in Twi, the indigenous language, I had no need for a translator. The singing, dancing and waving of white flags as the entrance procession began clearly expressed the spirit of the celebration. It was all repeated again while the Gloria was sung, and sure enough the white flags were out again and waiving over the congregation as the Alleluias heralded the Gospel procession. Although Mass was not quite a two-hour extravaganza, it came close and I left spiritually uplifted and exhausted.

After inviting parishioners to consider serving in one of the liturgical ministries in our parish a number of years ago I was approached by a gentleman who had recently moved to the New York City area from Peru. He told me how disillusioned he was with church worship in the United States because it had none of the vitality he experienced in worship back home. When I suggested he consider becoming part of the solution by signing up for one of the ministries, he took me up on my offer despite being concerned about his "accent." Not only did he become one of our most dedicated lectors, but he eventually became a permanent deacon as well.

Those experiences leave me wondering what it is about our worship that often makes it seem so disembodied. Perhaps anyone who is familiar with the work of Thomas Kane, C.S.P. on *The Dancing Church Around the World* (Paulist Press DVD) has had similar questions. Campus liturgies are so vibrant, but students are often disillusioned that most worship services back home by comparison seem lifeless. Engaging others in a conversation that goes beyond the text might give us all a better understanding of how to address this dilemma.

For several years I have been privileged to begin the spring semester with students in Paris for an intensive week of study. We always go to Ste. Gervais for Sunday Mass where the Monastic Community of Jerusalem leads a vibrant, welcoming liturgy complete with a four-part harmony sung by the entire congregation. Year after year student leave amazed that in a service where they do not know the language they find themselves welcomed and moved more deeply than ever before in their lives. Ritual is such a powerful force when it is used well.

Getting beyond the text is important in other disciplines as well. In the past two years I have begun studying for a degree in Public Health. Perhaps it was just time to nurture the scientist in me as well as the artist, but becoming more deeply engaged in another discipline has actually reinforced for me the importance of going beyond the "text," although in this case the texts are less often literal ones.

Atul Gawande, MD, a public health researcher and staff writer for *The New Yorker*, made a similar discovery while caring for his father, also a surgeon, during his final illness. Gradually Gawande became aware that nothing he learned in medical school had prepared him for the reality of caring for dying people. Medicine had taught him to attend to diseases, but not to the people who suffer with them. His research "beyond the text" resulted in the national bestseller, *Being Mortal: Medicine and What Matters in the End*, which should be required reading of every healthcare professional.

The recent Ebola epidemic in West Africa might not have been as devastating if healthcare professionals there had initially gone "beyond the text" they saw in Liberia, Sierra Leone and Guinea to understand how the lifestyle and religious beliefs of the population helped to fuel the epidemic. Because the Ebola virus is more virulent once the patient has died, it was actually the burial practices of the population that exacerbated the situation so quickly. Had medical personnel sought first to converse with, understand and then educate the religious leaders of communities, the contagion of disease and the fear it engendered might have been stemmed earlier and with more compassion.

Hoffman concludes his book by recommending that "the holistic study of liturgy may begin with the text but must eventually go beyond it—to the people, to their meanings, to their assumed constructs, and to their ritualized patterns that make their world uniquely their own" (p. 182). Having gone beyond that text myself, I recommend that this approach is applicable to many fields of study, but most importantly to those that involve the life and health of human beings and the environment in which we live.

The Christian Faith (Harper & Row, 1963) by Friedrich Schleiermacher

Appropriating Schleiermacher's *Christian Faith*

Roger HAIGHT, S.J., *Union Theological Seminary*

Friedrich Schleiermacher (1768-1834) completed the first edition of his dogmatic synthesis, *The Christian Faith*, in 1820-21, and a revised version in 1830-31.[1] It is one of those books that affected my conception of theology at a basic level. I am not a Schleiermacher scholar; I have read him only in English translation. Specific interests have motivated my frequent returning to him. Narrative provides the best way to show how Schleiermacher has shaped a Catholic theologian in ways that correspond with three areas of thought: religious epistemology, christology, and ecclesiology. In each case I will note what led me to read Schleiermacher, what I learned from him, and what I take to be classic dimensions in his Christian theology.

Schleiermacher's Philosophy of Religion

I encountered Schleiermacher's theology initially as a student at the University of Chicago in the late 1960s in courses on nineteenth and twentieth century theology with Langdon Gilkey and in two courses of Joseph Haratounian which compared analytically the systematics of Schleiermacher and the systematics of Paul Tillich. I came to those courses having already

---

1 Friedrich Schleiermacher, *The Christian Faith*, ed. by H. R. Mackintosh and J. S. Stewart (New York: Harper & Row, 1963).

read Tillich and Karl Rahner, and with a specific interest in fundamental questions such as religious knowing, the genesis and nature of doctrine, the grounds and methods of theology, and, from the perspective of Roman Catholicism of the time, the possibility within one church of a pluralism of theologies. I also had a missiological perspective and wanted to know how Christian doctrine could be inculturated in non-western cultures.

For a graduate student immediately after the Second Vatican Council Schleiermacher offered some promising paths. First of all, the turn to the subject as the place to begin understanding religion, faith, and theology was congenial. This rather basic move provided an imaginative framework for understanding the structure and logic of the discipline of theology itself. I found deep and pertinent analogies between the structure of Rahner's theology and what is going on in Schleiermacher. Those similarly schooled in Rahner did not read Schleiermacher's analyses of the human subject psychologically, at least not in *The Christian Faith*, but as transcendental phenomenological analysis of the knowing subject. This was attractive because one aspect of what was going on socially at the Second Vatican Council could be understood as a massive turn of a whole church to experience as, if not a source for reform, at least a catalyst for updating the church.

Schleiermacher's distinction and linkage between self-consciousness, world-consciousness, and God-consciousness was also impressive. I brought with me a strong distinction between faith and knowledge, between the content of Christian affirmations, on one hand, and, on the other hand, what could be called knowledge of the things of this world. Schleiermacher's differentiations of different levels of a religious consciousness, while at the same time explaining the interacting influence that each has upon the other in a single conscious experience, allowed me to make distinctions that resolved some obvious problems. For example, the inseparability and mutual influence of world-consciousness and God-consciousness helps to mediate a deep historical consciousness and to explain pluralism in any community sharing common teachings and values.

From Schleiermacher, then, I accepted what has been called an experience-expression framework for understanding theology and doctrine.[2] My

---

2   This distinction was formulated by George A. Lindbeck in *The Nature of Doctrine: Religion and Theology in a Postliberal Age* (Philadelphia: The Westminster Press,

allegiance to him, however, includes strong emphases on the receptivity of revelation and grace, and a realism of God's initiative in the event of Jesus Christ and in scripture.

In sum, I initially found that on questions of religious epistemology, doctrine, and theology Schleiermacher's presentation of religious subjectivity as differentiated is classic; religious experience is structured in levels so that faith in God is always in dialogue with self and world. As a result, religious experience can be both a realistic consciousness, that is, open to and receptive of the real presence of divine influence, and pluralist and subject to change. Schleiermacher's framework gives at least an initial explanation of the possibility of holding together unity and difference.

Schleiermacher's Christology

Although I read Schleiermacher's christology earlier, it was only ten years after graduate school when I began to teach christology that I came back to his christology in a more focused way. Let me simply enumerate four aspects of Schleiermacher's christology that I have either internalized from him or found reinforced by him.

First, Schleiermacher's is a christology from below. His *The Life of Jesus* shows that he had an interest in the earthly life and ministry of Jesus.[3] His christology has Jesus of Nazareth, the earthly figure, as its initial imaginative focus of attention.

Secondly, Schleiermacher's theory of salvation bears out his attention to Jesus. Salvation consists in appropriating Jesus' God-consciousness in such a way that people are united with God and receive God's forgiveness of sin and empowerment in their lives. Schleiermacher broke the hold of the mythological views of redemption in which something was accomplished between God and God, or Jesus and God, and then extrinsically received by human beings. By contrast, Christian salvation begins historically in each person who absorbs Jesus' message and person in such a way that this consciousness becomes internalized.

1984), *passim.*

3   Friedrich Schleiermacher, *The Life of Jesus* (Philadelphia: Fortress Press, 1975).

Thirdly, Schleiermacher's formal christology, that is, his construal of the humanity and divinity of Jesus, has been called a "consciousness" christology. And so it is. But that is often construed in a thin or shallow psychological sense of consciousness. Schleiermacher, however, insists that the cause of Jesus' exalted God-consciousness and consequent sinlessness was the presence of God within him and to him. For this reason it seems more correct to think of Schleiermacher holding a Spirit christology, even though in *The Christian Faith* this category is not developed. The phrase "Spirit christology," that is, the "explanation" of Jesus' divinity through the presence and action of God as Spirit within him, fits his construction of Jesus' divinity.

And, fourthly, I accept the view of Schleiermacher that, in a systematic representation of Christian faith, the doctrine of the trinity should come at the end. The doctrine of the trinity is not the premise of christology but a doctrine that derives logically and historically from the development of the doctrine of Jesus as the Christ. The doctrine sums up "economically" the Christian story of how God has dealt with humankind through Jesus Christ. And the doctrine of the immanent trinity leads the Christian mind into absolute mystery.

In sum, what I take to be classic in Schleiermacher's christology consists in a dynamically tensive understanding of Jesus Christ, one that holds together an existential consciousness christology with a realist, ontological grounding. He roots the ultimate explanation of Jesus' exalted God-consciousness in the real presence and operation of God within him. The symbol of God as Spirit captures this. The economy of salvation thus consists in historical mediation of this God-consciousness to others. What Jesus mediates is God as Spirit as an effective presence and operation in human lives.

Schleiermacher's Ecclesiology

I was not deeply influenced or impressed by Schleiermacher's ecclesiology until I had the occasion to focus my attention on it and compare it with other ecclesiologies from Christian history. Here I will point to five characteristics of his understanding of the church that make sense today.

First, Schleiermacher takes the church seriously. His doctrine of the church is tied closely with his christology and salvation theory: the role of the church is intrinsic to the historical communication of Christian God-consciousness. It is not that an individual can only go to Christ through the church; it is rather that the force of Christ reaches out to humanity historically through the church community.

Second, Schleiermacher's is an ecclesiology "from below." Although there are invariable elements to the church and scripture prescribes certain features of the church, still the church as organization is conceived as having emerged genetically and developed historically out of the corporate consciousness of the original disciples.

Third, Schleiermacher's ecclesiology is historically conscious. This is reflected in his view of the doctrines of the church, which are accounts of religious experience set forth in speech at any given time.[4] His presentation of the organization of the church around elements that are essential and invariable and elements that are mutable and variable shows his awareness of historical context and change.

Fourth, Schleiermacher's ecclesiology is ecumenical. He explicitly designed it to meet the exigencies of different churches in a way that preserves the differences on the basis of higher principles that they share and a generalized organizational form that admits variations. In this way Schleiermacher conceives the church as an intrinsic and constitutive element of Christianity and at the same time introduces pluralism into its very structure. Some of his axioms illustrate this. There should be no separation on the basis of doctrine if practice is the same. No separation on the basis of practice if doctrine is the same. Divisions or divisive institutions, if they are justified by distinct traditions, cease to be divisive by mutual recognition. Without principles analogous to these the ecumenical movement that started less than a century later would not have been possible.

Fifth, Schleiermacher's ecclesiology includes an intrinsic orientation outwards in mission to the world. This feature too flows logically from his christology and soteriology. A number of adjustments in the theology of religions and mission theology are required in our post-colonial situation, but Schleiermacher's stress on a fundamental facing outwards into the world and history remains a Christian exigency.

---

4   Schleiermacher, *The Christian Faith*, #19, pp. 88-93.

Where does the classic dimension of Schleiermacher's ecclesiology lie? What is the over-arching insight or perspective that characterizes his approach to the church and remains consistently generative? I find it in what can be called a "whole-part" tension that characterizes the churches and the church. This combines a fruitful consciousness of being in a particular church or denomination and at the same time belonging to the wider whole church that includes other churches and ecclesiologies. The whole church is in each church; each particular church is but a part of the whole. This means simultaneously recognizing invariant Christian institutions in variable forms, defining specific offices of ministry and recognizing others in other churches, taking the church with absolute seriousness but one's own church with relative seriousness because it is a part of the greater whole. Schleiermacher was one of the first to do this and few if any do it better than he.

Conclusion

I am tempted to conclude with an exclamation: "Schleiermacher lives." But some might say, "That's not Schleiermacher, but a creature of your own making." Such is the ambiguous nature of interpretation and appropriation. But whether or not this particular reconstruction has merit, I take it that all can agree that Schleiermacher continues to speak to current theological discussion and that he poses these three challenges: on the question of religious epistemology he proposes to give experience a role in theology. Despite the ambiguity of the imperative, it requires theology to connect with people's actual lives and problems. On the question of Jesus Christ, he presents the option of a consistent christology beginning with Jesus, not as an exclusive option but as an encompassing framework that can include other methods and insights. On the question of understanding and organizing the church, he challenges local churches and denominations to transcend their narrow perspectives and embrace the whole Christian movement, a move that is particularly relevant in a time when we are conscious of Christianity as a whole being one religion among many others.

Editor's Note: This essay was written fifteen years ago as a presentation at the American Academy of Religion.

The Confessions by St. Augustine

A Turning Point in My Life

Gregory BAUM, *McGill University*

AUTHOR'S NOTE: *The Confessions of Saint Augustine initiated a profound transformation of my life. In* The Oil Has Not Run Dry: The Story of my Theological Pathway, *brought out by McGill Queen's University Press 2016), I wrote several pages*—"The Impact of *The Confessions* of St, Augustine," pp, 18-20, Chapter 3—*reflecting on this life-giving event, pages which I publish here with the publisher's permission.*

EDITORS' NOTE: Given the historical significance and classic nature of this work, two contributors reflected on this book. See also Wendy Wright's contribution following.

While a student at McMaster University [in Hamilton, Ontario, from 1942 to 1946], I was vaguely interested in religion. I thought of myself as a believing Protestant, attended Sunday worship in different churches and was an active participant in the McMaster Christian Union, a student organization associated with the international Student Christian Movement. My closest friend, Walter Hitschfeld, whom I had met in the internment camp [in Canada], was a student at the University of Toronto. Walter was a Catholic from Vienna.

Through him I met an older German refugee, Egbert Munzer, a Catholic, who had worked for the German government under Chancellor Heinrich Brüning. Since Egbert Munzer had refused to take the oath of loyalty to Hitler, an obligation imposed on the members of the administration in 1933, he decided to leave Germany. He now taught courses at the

University of Toronto. He regarded me as a young friend, and I enjoyed his company and learnt a great deal from him. He married a lovely woman, Margo, a refugee from Berlin, with whom I developed a great friendship that lasted several decades.

An important event in my life took place on January 1, 1946, the day I began to read a famous book Walter had given me for Christmas, *The Confessions* of Saint Augustine. This made a powerful impact on me. It made me recognize God's presence in my life and urged me to cultivate the interior life in which God deigns to address believers and their communities. It was a turning point in my life.

What was it that impressed me so profoundly in this book written in North Africa at the end of the 4th century? Young people are often deeply touched by special persons, their ideas or their actions, without being able at the time to analyze the reasons for their enthusiasm. I felt that *The Confessions* assigned new meaning to the Gospel, lifted me to a higher world and gave me the taste for the spiritual life: "Taste and see that the Lord is good" (Ps 34: 8). God's presence became more real to me than ever before. Reflecting 65 years later on the religious enthusiasm that *The Confessions* engendered in me, I observe four themes that touched me at the time and much later became guidelines in my theological thinking.

1. Augustine lived in the late Roman Empire, a pluralistic society, where people were exposed to a variety of religious and philosophical currents and had to make up their own mind about what they believed. This plurality of beliefs and values, very much like the pluralism of modern society, made the life of individuals, particularly among the educated, into a spiritual adventure—searching, discerning and committing themselves—that assigned priority to personal convictions, lifting them above tribal loyalties and cultural pressures. Beliefs and values were not inherited; they were chosen. Among the educated, each person had his own story to tell, very much like seekers in modern society. Even if Augustine's story of his conversion dealt with religious currents of the 4th century, he spoke to me in my own situation in the 20th century. He was my contemporary.

When I studied the *Summa theologica* of St. Thomas in the 1950s, I noticed that this great thinker presented his theology without referring to his personal history. He had never wrestled for his faith since it had been given to him by his Catholic culture. By comparison, Augustine was 'modern.'

2. *The Confessions* reveal that the God in whom Augustine came to believe was for him an inexhaustible source of vitality. Reading the Christian message as a series of moral obligations easily creates the impression that God is the great restrainer, the superego in the sky, limiting personal freedom and frowning upon our moments of happiness. For Augustine, finding the God proclaimed by the Church was the opening of doors and the starting point of a life of endless creativity.

He found in his faith both peace and passion. He left behind the failings that had marred his life until then, escaped from the prison of self-centeredness and became a free man deeply in love with God. In reliance on this God, he became a bold thinker, inventing new ways of proclaiming the Gospel to his society. As a gifted writer, Augustine was able to persuade many readers that God was the Really Real, the invisible redemptive mystery, unique source of life, truth and love. Turning to God in faith was the beginning of a spiritual adventure.

3. St Augustine was troubled by the cosmological images of the Bible that placed the throne of God in the heavenly kingdom above the earth. Heaven and hell were here spoken of as cosmic spaces. Following the Platonic tradition, Augustine came to think of God as eternal Truth, Goodness and Beauty beyond human comprehension, in which the world and more intimately human beings participated in some measure. This God was not enthroned in a space called heaven; this God had created space and time, transcended the world and was at the same time immanent in it. St. Paul had already moved beyond these cosmological divine images when he quoted with approval the Hellenistic aphorism, giving it new meaning: "In God we live, and move and have our being" (Acts 17: 28).

In *The Confessions*, Augustine also admits that he had been troubled by biblical passages that made God appear violent and vengeful. He was greatly relieved when he listened to the sermons of Bishop Ambrose in Milan who gave to these passages a non-literal, allegorical meaning. Augustine was not a literalist.

4. Augustine wrote *The Confessions* to give thanks to God for the spiritual gift that opened his eyes to the truth and made his heart capable of love. He recognized that his urgent religious quest had been a response to a divine summons, that he had been able to find God because God had found him first. According to Augustine, the Good News preached

by Jesus and explained by the Apostles reveals that people enter into the light not as a result of their own effort, but in response to a gratuitous divine call addressing them in their lives.

Already in *The Confessions* Augustine is the doctor of grace. The good things of significance that happen to us are unmerited gifts. Intelligence and will power alone do not allow us to discover the meaning of our existence. Faith is the response to God's Word. Augustine held that operative within us is a mystery, a hidden presence, a divine word, that allows us to find the way and see the light. For Augustine God was savior, rescuing us from our self-destructive propensities.

Under Augustine's influence I came to look upon my short personal history as a series of rescuing events granted me out of the blue, that made me marvel and be grateful. These included my wonderful mother, my flight from Germany, the internment that made me a student and brought me to Canada, the university education sponsored by a generous woman, and the encounter with God through Augustine's *Confessions*. The conviction that God is my rescuer has never left me. In English, we call Jesus Savior; in German we call him Heiland, a beautiful constructed word referring to his power to save and to heal. Many years later, as I shall report, I became deeply troubled by the question, "Why me and why not others?"

At the end of his life, Augustine wrestled against the theology of Pelagius, a spiritual guide in Rome, who held that personal will, aided by grace, is the source of holiness, hinting that by trying hard one could be saved. Augustine believed that this interpretation, subsequently named Pelagianism, contradicted the message of the New Testament. Salvation was a free gift of God, surprising and unmerited. He recalled the words of Jesus: "You have not chosen me, but I have chosen you" (John 15: 16) and "I am the vine, you are the branches, ... without me, you can do nothing" (John 15: 5). St. Paul also wrote that God had loved and redeemed us while "we were still his enemies" (Rom 5: 1). Augustine won the argument. In reliance on his writings, several church councils condemned Pelagianism and affirmed the gratuitous divine initiative present in the acts of faith, hope and love.

While I did not know this history when I read *The Confessions*, I caught Augustine's message that all good things begin in God. This conviction has remained with me. I have always been uncomfortable with sermons that scold people for breaking the commandments and urge them to become more obedient, without reference to the Good News that we are enabled to do good by a power not our own. Troubled by certain sermons I heard in church, I would go to my room, open the *Denzinger*, the collection of official church documents, and read the ancient conciliar texts that condemned Pelagianism (*Enchiridion Symbolorum*, # 373). Even when my theology become socially concerned and action-oriented, I never abandoned the Augustinian emphasis on the divine initiative. Here is a paragraph from my book *Religion and Alienation* that expresses this:

> Social engagement is not deprived of the mystical dimension that is part of the Christian life. According to the ancient teaching, especially of St. Augustine, the good we do is God's free gift to us. In this Christian perspective, action equals passion. While we see, we are being enlightened; while we act we are being carried forward; while we love we are being saved from selfishness; and while we embrace all people in solidarity, we are being freed inwardly to cross one boundary after another. Every step towards greater humanization is due to the expansion of a new and gratuitous life in us. We are alive by a power that transcends us" (p. 211).

The Confessions by St. Augustine

Listening to the Cry of Our Heart: A Story of Self-Awakening

Wendy M. WRIGHT, *Creighton University*

It had to have been 1971 or '72. Augustine's *Confessions* had been assigned alongside other primary sources as required reading in an early medieval history class at California State University at Los Angeles. The professor, a shaggy-haired, somewhat distracted middle-aged fellow uniformed in the ubiquitous elbow-patched tweed coat, had introduced all the required course texts with a social historian's dispassionate drone. For my part, I had no context with which to assess what he described as the western world's first autobiography. Augustine of Hippo was a name unknown to me, as was Suetonius, author of the gossipy, scandal-riddled history of the Roman Emperors, another of those texts that presented themselves to me as an allotted number of pages I must plow through in the coming quarter's short weeks.

I was in my mid-twenties, a not atypical student at Cal State L.A., a sprawling commuter school that served a diverse non-traditional population. This was not my first foray into higher education: in keeping with the free-floating seeker ethos of my generation, I had fleetingly attended several other local institutions after high school, wending my way through departments of music, musical theatre and dramatic arts, finally leaving academe's hallowed halls to pursue a professional career in show business. Hollywood was, after all, my hometown. For several years I was actually gainfully employed and donned quite a variety of costumes as my serial jobs required: as a singing and dancing Disneyland Kid of the Kingdom (preppy white uniforms matched with orange patent leather Mary Janes), touring the US with an industrial show for Pure Oil (alternately gold lamé draped with black ostrich feathers and a royal blue service station worker jumpsuit that slid off to reveal a bright yellow bathing suit), performing with L.A.'s multi-cultural Intercity Repertory Company in *West Side Story* (colorful immigrant Puerto-Rican flounces), and doing a stint in a Gay Nineties musical set in Paris in its pre-Broadway out-of town run at the Thunderbird Hotel in Las Vegas (the innocent ingénue's lowly chambermaid garb—one of only two non-topless female costumes in the show).

Somewhere along the way, in between trips to the unemployment office and auditions for TV commercials in which the suitability of one's leg shape was more a hiring requirement than one's ability to deliver a Shakespearean soliloquy, I burned out the back of the show business grind and returned to school, switching from theatre to history.

Augustine had not shown up on my pre-show biz reading list. Nor would he have been tucked away among the many tomes my parents kept on the shelves in the homes in which I grew up. As the only child of what my father used to describe as an upper-middle class bohemian couple—a jewelry designer and a writer—I was exposed to classic literature but not of the religious kind. The direction of my moral compass was oriented by my parents' non-religious pacifism and engagement in non-violent political activism. At the same time, I had experienced from an early age what might be described as a spiritual sensibility, a sense of God present that, in retrospect, I can only attribute to the continual presence of a deeply soulful older African-American nursemaid who nurtured me during my first pre-verbal years of life. My family did not regularly attend worship services, although I had some grade-school exposure at Hollywood First Congregational whose pacifist pastor my father had come to know.

Once my mother discovered I had a singing voice and had been advised that the best vocal training for one so young was a church choir, I was duly enrolled at Hollywood First Presbyterian, reputed for its tremendous choral program. My innate, or perhaps nanny-formed, spiritual sensibility was then honed in the lift and loft of hymnody. Church attendance was not the point of my enrollment but it came with the musical training. My parents only ventured in annually for choir festivals and, despite my love of song, I drifted away from the program during my high school years when new musical opportunities presented themselves.

By the time I arrived in that early medieval history course I had long been away from any formal religious formation. I began my foray into the *Confessions*—the Penguin Classics edition with translation by R.S. Pine-Coffin—as I would have any college text. Soon, the first person narrative arc carried me along, embroidered as it was into the fabric of Augustine's plaintive prayerful cries: "Hear me O God," "What then is the God that I worship?" "Who will grant me to rest content in you?" "Why do you mean so much to me?" The remembered childhood thievery of pears, the Latin student lamenting over the death of Dido, the passionate youth awash in the delights of fornication, the voracious theatre-goer applauding the ersatz tragedy that did not impinge upon his own life, the thirsty aspiring seeker drinking the dualistic liquor of Manichaeism to the dregs, the errant son fleeing the entreaties of his importunate mother, the companionable friend wrestling the imponderables with his philosophical companions, the awakening adult casting off his beloved mistress and mourning the deaths of friend and child.

Evil, eternity, materiality, spirit, guilt, grace, volition: Augustine's churning, restless ponderings swept me through the narrative to the point where, teetering on the verge of conversion, he flung himself down beneath a fig tree and cried out, "Why not now?" and the dramatic tension gave way. My history class assignment had been to read the entire book and so, although part of me felt that the story was in some way finished, I continued through Augustine's retrospective musings about free will, pride, memory and the pious death of his reconciled mother. Yet, unbeknownst to me, my truest point of encounter with the *Confessions* was yet to come: in Book X, chapter 27 to be exact.

> I have learnt to love you late, Beauty at once so ancient and so new! I have learnt to love you late! You were within me, and I was in the world outside myself. I searched for you outside myself, and disfigured as I was, I fell upon the lovely things of your creation. You were with me, but I was not with you. The beautiful things of this world kept me far from you and yet, if they had not been in you, they would

have had no being at all. You called me; you cried aloud to me; you broke the barrier of my deafness. You shone upon me; your radiance enveloped me; you put my blindness to flight. You shed your fragrance about me; I drew breath and now I gasp for your sweet odour. I tasted you, and now I hunger and thirst for you. You touched me, and I am enflamed with love of your peace.[1]

What had been until then an arresting read, a compelling storyline, a fascinating glimpse into an earlier world, was now a jolting self-awakening, a recognition of the cry of my own heart.

Several days later I found myself knocking hesitantly on the office door of our tweedy professor: in a random casual aside he had indicated the times that he might keep office hours. Seated across the desk from him I carefully opened my by-now dog-eared, penciled copy of the *Confessions*, then promptly laid my head down on his desk and began to sob. He paused, shifted in his chair and sighed wearily. "It affects some people that way," was his dry response.

**

During the decades that have elapsed since then—which included my own conversion, marriage, an M.A., three children, a Ph.D., and a tenured professorship—I have had Augustine placed before me any number of times. As a Religious Studies graduate student I learned to interpret the Bishop of Hippo's interior confessional transformation through the lens of *superbia* and *humilitas*. As a fledgling adjunct professor I was enlightened by a student's observation that the *Confessions* is a "story about two trees." As a Christian spirituality scholar I have been taken aback by the number of recorded instances of historical figures who have requested that the *Confessions*, often that same Book X, be read at their deathbeds. On occasion, a spiritual guide or confessor, even though thoroughly ignorant of my relationship to the book, will assign the fateful paragraph for my prayerful reflection. In addition, I frequently find myself annoyed when the fourth century saint is blamed for the short-sightedness of his utterances on themes that have subsequently indelibly shaped Christian theology:

---

[1] Saint Augustine, *Confessions*, translated by R.S. Pine-Coffin (Middlesex, England: Penguin Books, 1961): 231-232.

original sin, misogyny, predestination. He was just trying to figure it out as he went along, I want to say, asking the right big questions and struggling to come up with a plausible perspective in his limited context: that's what we all are and should be doing. Don't reify his answers. Come up with your own. Through it all, and even as newer editions of the classic autobiography have appeared on my office shelves, I have kept that original, now fraying, yellow-paged paperback copy with my loopy penciled notes running up and down the margins. It is the one I turn to when prayer, rather than academic inquiry, is my motive for returning to the source.

Certainly there are other spiritual books and authors that, when asked, I might reply have been more obviously formative for me over time. Brother Lawrence's *Practice of the Presence of God* was daily personal nourishment over the course of a decade after I joined the Catholic Church. And the inspired common sense embedded in Francis de Sales' varied writings has shaped and challenged me for over thirty years as I have applied my scholarly skills to analyze, translate and disseminate the rich heritage of that seventeenth century "Doctor of Divine Love."

But no other passage has ever leapt off the page, catapulted across sixteen centuries and vast tracks of historical and geographical distance, stopped me in my tracks, or spoken to my heart in quite the same way as did those words, captured in that euphonious Pine-Coffin translation, that emerged from Augustine's own confessing heart.

I have learnt to love you late,
Beauty at once so ancient and so new!
I have learnt to love you late!

The Communist Manifesto (with an Introduction by A.J.P. Taylor, Harmondsworth, Penguin, 1967) by Karl Marx and Friedrich Engels

Realized Eschatology

Gerard MANNION, *Georgetown University*

I grew up in an Irish family in a town in the East Midlands of England, about 67 miles north of London with Cambridge and Birmingham a little over 50 miles away either side. Many of my formative years were during the harsh Thatcher-Reagan era. The most popular music then was still very idealistic and transformative in nature. I sometimes have since wondered if perhaps I did not belong to the only generation still around who really believed the world could be changed for the better by our own efforts. We grew up in the aftermath of both post-World War II and post-Vatican II idealism. An era of the turn to rights and the turn to an unwavering commitment to radical forms of transformative social justice. The hymns we imbibed at primary school were about social transformation. We were getting liberation theology with our free school milk.

Socialism was not a dirty word in Europe and people were proud to be socialists. Class struggle was still very real and a privileged establishment and world of business were reviled more than aspired to.

In summer, 1987, I passed my O-Level exams and spent the summer working on construction sites. I would continue to for many summers, two gap years and the occasional weekend after that. It provided both an insight into the realities of a class-ridden society and an incentive to keep up with studies. Later in 1987, I embarked upon A-Level studies at my high school. During this time, I purchased a book, parts of which I had read before and about which I had read a great deal. It was the Penguin Classics edition of *The Communist Manifesto* by Karl Marx and Friedrich Engels. My time working on construction sites, alongside my studies and the political climate and debates of the day, as well as my engagement with movements such as liberation theology, fired me to read more about this "classic."

Marx and Engels wrote and acted in a world challenged by political turmoil. They passionately believed in helping to build a better society. One very different from that in which only a very few prospered thanks to the labors and turmoil of the many. In the century that would follow, many would explore Marx's and Engels' ideas. Others demonized them. Others exploited and distorted them.

The issues that *The Manifesto* deals with, as well as much of the social and political discourse that would be inspired by and follow from it, are factors that relate to and, indeed, helped set much of the context of theology and church mission and life in the nineteenth and twentieth centuries. It is not a long book. The core idea of the *Manifesto*, as Engels would later say in that 1883 Preface, was due to the genius of Marx alone and was as follows:

> "[T]hat economic production and the structure of society of every historical epoch necessarily arising therefrom constitute the foundation for the political and intellectual history of that epoch; that consequently (ever since the dissolution of the primeval communal ownership of land) all history has been a history of class struggles, of struggles between exploited and exploiting, between dominated and dominating classes at various stages of social development; that this struggle, however, has now reached a stage where the exploited and oppressed classes (the proletariat) can no longer emancipate itself from the class which exploits and oppresses it (the bourgeoisie), without at the same time for ever freeing the whole of society from exploitation, oppression and class struggles…' (p. 57, outlined in the body of the *Manifesto* itself on p. 93).

Of course, there are various pockets of historical narrative that would not conform to the sweeping implied historical determinism suggested here. We also know that what the following century and a half of history would bring would pose further questions for the deterministic assuredness of much of what is said in the *Manifesto*. But, nonetheless, the key ideas are instructive and illuminating and have been ever since: the clash between the oppressed masses and the few who essentially are the engineers of their exploitation and who profit greatly from such oppression. This remains a very real struggle, in differing forms in differing societies, down to our very day. Anyone who doubts this has simply to witness the Occupy Wall Street movement (*ca.* 2011) in the aftermath of the bailing out of the irresponsible banks and financial institutions at the expense of those very same oppressed masses.

But Marx (and Engels) did not quite mean what they said to sound so sweeping and deterministic in any case–their rhetoric was of the day and age. Rather they were trying to state that history was working toward a pivotal moment whereby a better world could be possible. And their *Manifesto* was a call to oppressed working people around the world to be part of building that world. This has multiple theological resonances but none moreso than with the doctrine of eschatology.

Back in my earlier high school years, little did I realize how much eschatology had already come to, and would increasingly continue to, preoccupy my faith. Multiple connections were made between Christianity and socialism and, indeed, interactions between theology and Marxism. We learned about liberation theology, Oscar Romero and the struggle for justice in Religious Education classes. Our textbooks from the early 80s were no doubt pulped soon after 1986 when the Vatican began its crackdown on liberation theology. I read about Teilhard de Chardin, Gustavo Gutiérrez and how Hitler had once said Marxism was "the illegitimate child of Christianity."

We studied a great deal of biblical theology, including the social setting and issues of the New Testament world and the social issues dealt with in the gospels and epistles. We learned a great deal about eschatology and the churches' engagement in the nineteenth century struggles against social injustice. And this in an ecumenical sense: from the free church commitments to abolishing slavery and establishing education for the poor, to the (Anglican) Christian Socialists, the Cooperative movement and the emergence of modern Catholic Social Thought, as well as Vatican II. So did we learn still more about liberation theology.

I was increasingly making connections across the disciplines and it was concerning issues of social justice that the greatest areas of commonality were to be found. So in engaging with the *Manifesto*, I learned a great deal about an age of passionate commitment to the belief that another world—a better world *is* possible and that people across different religious and political divides, as well as social settings, could and must be united in seeking to make that better world a reality.

Realized eschatology, then, was something that could unite many groups. For what else was the *Manifesto* than a call to build the kingdom of justice and righteousness on earth? *Laissez-faire* economics that privileged a few at the expense of the many was as much a social evil in the late twentieth century as it was in mid-nineteenth century as it was for the very first followers of Jesus. The Latin American liberation theologians fully understood this. As Pope Francis was later to say when questioned about his own statements *contra* capitalism, he was not a Marxist, but he knew a lot of people who followed such ideas who had achieved a lot of good.

I had, since being young, been a firm believer that theology and the church could and should partner with others in building a better world. This was shaped both by my own interaction with the social and political world of my youth and by the great legacy of Vatican II in regard to such partnerships.

One of my favorite films of all time also came out during this era—*The Mission*, about the Jesuit reductions in Paraguay. The pragmatic cardinal, wonderfully played by Ray McAnally, visits one of the missions where he is astounded by the beautiful voices of the Guarani choirs and then sees their violin workshop. He asks what happens to the proceeds raised when the latter are sold and is informed by one of the Jesuit missionaries that they are divided up equally and shared among the whole community. The cardinal snorts and says, "Ah, yes, there is a radical French sect that teaches such a doctrine." To this the Jesuit replies, "Your Eminence: it was the doctrine of the early church." One of the most hauntingly evocative and beautiful pieces of Ennio Morricone's movie score from that movie is entitled "On Earth as it is in Heaven." It never fails to move me profoundly.

Having further delved into the classic writings of the first generation of Latin American liberation theologians throughout my BA degree and having been trained in the multi-disciplinary approaches of the social scientific and anthropological study of religion, I knew that liberation theology was about much more than Marx or Marxism. Rather it employed various tools of social critique and analysis in order to help bring about a vision of social transformation (inspired by the gospels, Vatican II and political theology more than anything else). Yet I also learned that my church had set about trying to de-politicize the Latin American (although not the Polish) church. And I came to be horrified by the full frontal assault on liberation theology and its theorists and practitioners at the hands of Cardinal Ratzinger and the Vatican in the 1980s and beyond, making for depressing ecclesiological realizations.

Among the many revolutionary ideas the *Manifesto* develops further is the notion that capital is a collective product and therefore has social and not only personal power. As opposed to advocating that all private property becomes social property, the work rather argues for the abolition of the "class character" of capital: what is actually transformed is its "social character." Responding to critics and anticipating the caricature of communism from later years, it firmly denies that what is advocated is the "abolition of individuality and freedom." Rather, in all cases, it is the bourgeois notion of capital, property, individuality and freedom that are challenged. In these statements, we see many parallels of Catholic social thought, which explicitly states that private property is not an absolute right but must be utilized for social ends.

The concept of alienation is one of the most powerful ideas developed (though not originated) by Marx. This brought back to me my many hours spent toiling and socializing alongside manual laborers and construction workers—horrendously lengthy shifts, long travelling to and from the site of work, their distinct lack of rights or adequate representation, their low wages and exploitation and the total absence of job security.

As the *Manifesto* draws to a close, it states that the oppressed people of the world have "nothing to lose but their chains," ending with the famous rallying cry to overcome the social conditions that cause such oppression: "workers of all countries unite." I used a version of this paraphrase for a talk for CAFOD at the World Forum on Liberation Theologies in Belem, Brasil in 2009, which was entitled "We *Still* Have Nothing to Lose but our Chains." By 2010 I was living in the US, just sixteen miles from the Mexican border in San Diego. Now I live in the nation's capital city, Washington, D.C., where the stark contrast between rich and poor is evident everywhere. Thanks to such experiences, I believe as firmly as ever that our faith calls us to transform the world, to build a kingdom of justice, equality and freedom. Without the redistribution of the goods of the earth, this cannot happen. Pope Francis has already denounced capitalism in various ways. His call in *Laudato Si'* and elsewhere for a new politics and economics that are interrelated and which serve the whole community, but especially the poor, for an "integrated ecology" is a clarion call to build a better world for our own troubled times.

And what is the *Communist Manifesto* but a call to realized eschatology, to build a better world. If commentators are right that we now live in an age where liberal democracy and free-market capitalism have become incompatible, and the latter is destroying the former, then the ideas of Marx and Engels and of the radical Christian tradition that begins with the teachings of Jesus himself have never been more relevant. Nor, then, has the cry at the end of the *Manifesto* for the working (read oppressed and subjugated) peoples of the world to unite diminished.

As we see now with Francis, the dream that a better world is possible and that people of differing creeds, colors and perspectives need to unite to build it has never been more necessary. Marx and Engels dreamed of such a world too. And theology will always and should always remain in dialogue with secular perspectives on how to make the world a better and more just and egalitarian place

Our present century, then, shows the continued relevance of the issues and ideas outlined in the *Communist Manifesto*. Yes, the issues take on different forms and strains, but much of the underlying social analytical framework remains informative and inspiring. Theology and the church can and should, indeed must, learn new ways to partner with others in building a better world.

Cry of the Earth, Cry of the Poor (Orbis, 1997) by Leonardo Boff

Making the Connections: Poverty, Ecology, Mutuality, St. Francis and Pope Francis

Dawn NOTHWEHR, O.S.F. *(Catholic Theological Union)*

Leonardo Boff's *Cry of the Earth, Cry of the Poor*, appeared in English in 1997. It defined what are now primary pillars of Catholic ecotheology and environmental ethics: justice for the poor and justice for the earth. It followed the first United Nations Stockholm Conference on the Environment (1972), and the Rio Earth Summit (1992), which first conceptualized "sustainable development." Already a corpus of Catholic Social Teaching on ecological ethics was emerging from Catholic Bishops' conferences and Pope John Paul II's 1990 World Day of Peace Address.

Those That Cry Out

Boff's landmark work broadened liberation theology's gaze to include the natural environment, and closed breaches between and within liberation theology and environmentalism. It reasserted people's place *within* creation and their moral obligation to be its guardian. Boff stressed foundational biblical and doctrinal sources for Christian perspectives on ecological issues, and linkages to social, political, economic, or ecclesial structures. He drew deeply from the Franciscan classics (incarnation, trinity, poverty, Holy Spirit) constructing a revolutionary ecotheological synthesis. But significantly, Boff's work also bears the marks of a pastor among the poor. Boff holds:

"Liberation theology and ecological discourse have something in common: they start from two bleeding wounds. The wound of poverty breaks the social fabric of millions and millions of poor people around the world. The other wound, systematic assault on the earth, breaks down the balance of the planet, which is under threat from the plundering of development as practiced by contemporary global societies. Both lines of reflection and practice have as their starting point a cry: the cry of the poor for life, freedom, and beauty…and the cry of the Earth groaning under oppression" (p. 104).

The same logic drives dominant populations to oppress the marginalized and plunder the earth. A strong interconnection binds the ecological, human, social, and spiritual aspects of life. Boff argues that this evil has deep roots in the spiritual malaise that characterizes socialism and capitalism.

Hearing the Cries

Leonardo Boff was born in Concordia, Santa Catarina, Brazil, in 1938. His father was a school teacher who identified with the poor blacks in Concordia. Leonardo was ordained a Franciscan priest in 1964. He studied theology at the University of Munich, Germany, was Karl Rahner's research assistant, and Joseph Ratzinger directed his dissertation. For 22 years Boff was a Professor at the Franciscan Institute at Petrópolis, becoming an internationally renowned liberationist. After painful censor by Rome, in 1992 Boff resigned from the priesthood and the Franciscan Order, but he did not abandon Franciscan theology and spirituality. Like other transformative figures he saw connections other missed. He articulated the radical theological and ethical linkages between ecology, poverty, spirituality, and systemic violence against all creation—including humans—in terms consistent with modern realities. His detractors failed to distinguish basic terms (**_pan_**theism/pan**_en_**theism; Marxist analysis/Stalinist communism; Bonaventure's Trinity/Aquinas' Trinity).

Analysis and Method

Two life-changing experiences led Boff to embrace ecojustice and social justice within liberation theology. First, as pastor in a slum of Petropolis, near Rio de Janeiro, he encountered people forced to scavenge for food in garbage dumps, but who drew hope and self-worth from their Base Christian Communities. In the lush Amazon jungles of the diocese of Acre-Purus, Boff saw the raping of the Amazon rainforests by developers that threatened people's very survival. There, faith and life, God and suffering, all were one.

Boff insists that the poor must be "the point from which one attempts to conceive of God, Christ, grace, history, the mission of the churches, the meaning of the economy, politics, and the future of societies and of the human being" (p. 107). Concern for the poor provokes concern for the whole of creation, precisely because the poor are the most harmed by both capitalist and socialist abuses of the earth.

Cry of the Earth, Cry of the Poor begins with an in-depth analysis of the human-wrought ecological illnesses of Earth. Influenced by Jan Smuts, Boff then articulates a holistic ecological model. Using the "new physics," evolutionary biology, and environmental science, Augustinian, Bonaventuran, Pascalian, and existentialist traditions, Boff calls for merging ecological and theological concerns.

Boff finds theological warrants for protecting the poor and the earth in Christian panentheism ("everything in God, God in everything"), the sacramentality of creation, and a doctrine of the Holy Spirit ("God's absolute passion, absolute love"). This all supports an ecology-based cosmology, rooted in evolutionary processes, and a definition of sin as "breaking connectedness." Informed by Brian Swimme, Thomas Berry, Meister Eckhart, and Teilhard de Chardin, Boff finds God within the "cosmogenic process of the universe." Further, the liberation vision of the just society is modeled after the social relations of the persons of the Trinity following the Cappadocian and Victorine traditions. Fulfillment of this vision requires spiritual conversion.

Boff offers living "cardinal ecological virtues," as exemplified by St. Francis of Assisi as the pathway forward. Prayer was St. Francis' entrée to his self-understanding as an ontological poet-mystic, able to grasp the sacramentality of all things. He reveled in religious erotic enchantment, wonder, fascination, and desire for and with all things in the universe (love). Francis's radically related God compels humanity to care for their kin in all creation as God cares for them (obedience). Francis experienced his own dignity bound up with all creation insofar as everything originates in One Creator (humility). From this stance, Francis encountered all relationships as one utterly available to the need of others (poverty). Through penance, poverty and prayer Francis lived securely and passionately, grounded in his relationship with God and all creation—especially the poor.

Connecting with Brother Leonardo

Leonardo Boff's *Cry of the Earth, Cry of the Poor* changed my life by strengthening my insights and convictions about self-identity as a person, a Christian, a life-committed Franciscan, and a theological ethicist. Often my worldview is *"contra la corriente"* larger than most of my peers. I first read this book in 1997 during a retreat marking the 25th anniversary of my profession of faith as a Catholic; the 20th year since entering the Franciscan Novitiate; and 13th year as a life-professed Franciscan Sister, and the 3rd year as a theological ethicist, having completed the Ph.D. in 1995 at Marquette University.

My doctoral dissertation in feminist liberation ethics, *Mutuality: A Formal Norm for Christian Social Ethics*, sang in harmony with Boff's sources and claims concerning power. "Mutuality" with its four-fold manifestations (gender, generative, social, cosmic) would place limits on power destructive of human and planetary life. Like Boff, my work utilized the models, metaphors, and perspectives available to theology from the "new physics," Franciscan sources, and social analysis done "from below." I immediately identified with Boff intellectually, and I found synergy with his passion for justice.

I was gifted with wise, well-educated, committed Lutheran parents who modeled a profound respect for the dignity of each person and who delighted in the wonders of creation. My mother was a teacher, and later a proofreader for the local weekly. She delighted in her large garden and prize-winning hybrid roses. Family camping trips were settings for interdisciplinary lessons in theology and natural sciences. In that atmosphere,

I was seduced—heart and mind—into a profound awareness of the compassionate Presence—God.

But I rejected the sin-centric theology of the Missouri Synod Lutheran tradition. As a "Seeker," I discovered Catholicism through a Franciscan lens—a compassionate approach to sin, forgiveness, "baptism of desire," the "call and response" to God, and agapistic virtue ethics. Providentially, I received a scholarship to a Franciscan women's college. There I read theology and the social sciences with Franciscan educators using an integrative approach.

With a B.A. in Social Work and Psychology, I joined the Volunteers in Diocesan Action program in Pueblo, Colorado. As a community organizer/youth minister among newly immigrated Mexicans, I learned firsthand about the lethal combination of war, poverty, ecological destruction, racial prejudice, and the blind unyielding power of the white wealthy majority.

Retuning to Minnesota, I became the Chief of Group Living in a JCAH accredited psychiatric hospital for abused and neglected children. With Mayo Clinic psychiatrists we strove to heal the wounds inflicted by parents, who themselves were so injured. There I frequently witnessed grace-filled moments when the beauty and wonder of the hospital's small forest soothed wounded children.

As a Franciscan Sister, I earned an M.A. Degree in Religious Studies at Maryknoll School of Theology, 1981-85. My teachers were the "Who's Who" of the liberation theologies of the day—including Leonardo Boff. Spring Term of 1985 I was in war-torn Sandinista-ruled Nicaragua with Maryknoll sisters; then with Penny Lernoux and Franciscans in Colombian "peace communities" threatened by drug lords.

Later, as a Field Organizer for NETWORK—A Catholic Social Justice Lobby, based in Washington, DC, I frequently entered the halls of Congress. Experiencing the palpable power present there was like facing the mouth of a dragon. One could not predict when it would spit fire or simply purr. I saw that raw power, used for both harming and helping the poor.

Then, as Education Consultant for the Division of Social Ministry in the Roman Catholic Diocese of Rochester, NY, my work with Bishop Matthew H. Clark focused on drafting his pastoral letter on HIV/AIDS and then implementing an action plan in the diocese. Many encouraged me to study for the Doctorate—and the rest in history!

The wisdom of Boff's inspired liberation theology—where ecology and theology are partners, not rivals—confirmed truths I learned among the poor and my immersion in Franciscan spirituality and theology. These moved, shaped, motivated and impassioned me with a kind of sacred energy still palpable today. The intense awareness of—our incarnational God, the awesome humility of God in Christ, the image of God as overflowing Fountain Fullness (Bonaventure), the penetrating particularity amid wildly creative diversity of the panentheistic expression of God in the material world (*haecceitas* Duns Scotus)—all found their home delightfully within every fiber of my being. Certainly, the virtues lived by St. Clare and St. Francis of Assisi—now knowable through models of the "new physics"—outline a theological framework and moral vision that, deep in my bones, I *know* can transform human hearts—the world.

My life and Boff's influences have crossed paths again. His work was integrated into Pope Francis's encyclical *Laudato Si'—Care for Our Common Home* (See especially §49 and Chapter 4 Integral Ecology). It has been my pleasure to be able to do a variety of presentations on the document in numerous venues, and to serve as an ethics consultant on several committees supporting Archbishop Blaise Cupich's efforts to fully implement the encyclical in the Archdiocese of Chicago. Indeed—"The Lord hears the cry of the poor. Blessed be the Lord!"

The Diary of a Country Priest
(The Thomas More Press, 1983)
by Georges Bernanos

All is Grace

Elizabeth A. DREYER, *Fairfield University*

"Does it matter?" Grace is everywhere…" (*Qu'est-ce que cela fait? Tout est grâce*). These are the final words of the Curé d'Ambricourt, a thirty-year-old priest, dying of stomach cancer. He is in Lille to see a doctor. This happens not long after being assigned to his first parish in Ambricourt, a forlorn parish in rural France. He takes his last breath in the dingy apartment of a seminary classmate and former priest, now fallen on hard times. Such is the story of *The Diary of a Country Priest* (*Journal d'Un Curé de Campagne*) written in 1936 by Catholic novelist, Georges Bernanos. These three words—"all is grace"—have echoed in my consciousness, prodding me to plumb the theological and spiritual meaning of the world's holiness—Incarnation—one third of an inseparable trinity of doctrines that includes creation and Holy Spirit.

As a French major in college in the 60's, I first read *The Diary* in a course on 20th century French literature. I recall a pall descending on me that term, darkening otherwise cheerful days. Reading Albert Camus, Jean-Paul Sartre, Eugene Ionesco, Jean Genet, Samuel Beckett, André Gide, and François Mauriac was a heavy load for a twenty-something. It was also the birth of important questions about the human condition.

A close re-reading of *The Diary* undertaken for this essay reminded me of the critical ways in which fiction and poetry inform my theology.

Jewish author and critic, Cynthia Ozick, describes literature's goal: "to light up the least grain of being, to show how it is concretely individual, particularized from any other." *The Diary of a Country Priest* sheds such light on one particular world, built around Christianity's call to love others and trust in the divine presence in history. The literary conceit of a journal orients us toward the very "stuff" of everyday life, the daily round of concrete events and feelings.

Bernanos's life (1888-1948) was marked by creativity, intense commitment to ideals, and puzzling contradictions. He was a Catholic monarchist, who, until 1920, supported the ultra-nationalist movement, Action Française. In his pro-royalist, impassioned youth, he fought in the streets, manned barricades, and defaced public monuments. He was a crusader in search of a cause worthy of self-sacrifice. Surrounded by the devastation of war, he deplored what he saw as the empty rhetoric of religion and politics. Bernanos was wounded and decorated in World War I. He witnessed from close range the suffering of the Spanish Civil War and World War II. Due to financial problems in the 30's, he moved his family to Majorca, Paraguay and then Brazil. After 1940, he spoke out against the evils of totalitarianism and the wealthy Catholics who opted instead for their own social preservation. At de Gaulle's request, Bernanos returned to France in 1945. In much of his writing, he railed against the eclipse of the glories of a Catholic France. He saw secular society—indeed, the church itself—as propagating empty, abstract rhetoric and pseudo-intellectualism, fueled by the illusions of money, science and progress. Lost in the fray was awareness of God's radical incarnational activity in the world. He labeled these developments a kind of reverse incarnation or "disincarnation"—a process against which we must be on guard to this day.

On one level, the story of the Curé is simply depressing. The unnamed Curé ministers to a wretched parish—"miserable little houses huddled together under the desolate November sky" (p. 2)[1]—whose indolence and

---

1   Page numbers refer to *The Diary of a Country Priest* by Georges Bernanos. Trans., Pamela Morris. Chicago, IL: The Thomas More Press, 1983. See also Michael Robinson Tobin's *Georges Bernanos: The Theological Sources of His Art* (Montreal: McGill-Queen's University Press, 2007) and Robert Bresson's superb film, *Diary of a Country Priest* (1950).

cruelty provide a sterling argument for original sin. He writes in his journal: "I still do not know my parish and my parish have pretended not to see me" (p. 91); "Sometimes I fancy the village has nailed me up here on a cross and is at least watching me die" (p. 40). Bernanos compares the aura of boredom in the village to a persistent, cancerous growth, a leprosy of despair, Christianity in decay. The playing field for a cosmic battle between good and evil is level. On page after page Bernanos describes the "thin steady rain which gets sucked in with every breath, which seeps down through the lungs into your belly" (p. 1). Stomach pain and human cruelty relentlessly erode his physical, emotional and spiritual strength.

As an author, Bernanos was drawn to social outsiders, individuals who were not at home in their own skins, much less in society. Shame, self-hate, feelings of inferiority, and suicide are frequent motifs in his fiction. The Curé contrasts his poor peasant upbringing with the social pretensions of his fellow priests. He describes himself as awkward, inept, clumsy, poor of speech—a foolish idiot who never knows what is *really* going on. He lives in constant, realistic fear of being mocked (p. 26). "As usual, my inexperience and foolishness, combined with a kind of absurd bad luck, always seem to complicate the simplest matters" (p. 37). By most measuring rods, he was a "loser."

But once again, I was drawn into the compelling, elusive world of Bernanos's art and theology. The novel presses readers to confront the dark underside of humanity in psychological and theological terms. Through the daily struggle to pray and be faithful to self-sacrificing love, and in spite of his tortured self-condemnation, the Curé discovers, and eventually applies to himself, the truth that God wants us to be merciful to ourselves as well as to others (p. 173). It is hard-won enlightenment. No "cheap grace" here. The final grief for Bernanos is to stand impenitent under the merciful eyes of God (p. 192).

Bernanos strove to recover the concrete, historical, active, embodied substance of the language of faith and holiness. He saw bourgeois Catholic piety as empty and lukewarm. Instead, he proposed an all-or-nothing commitment to *become* Christ by loving the "other"—no matter how insignificant or repulsive. Thérèse of Lisieux hovers in the background. In strange, yet compelling ways, *The Diary* lays out a blueprint for incarnational living—no matter your state in life.

Bernanos reminds us that through Incarnation, divinity enters the physical, making them one. *The Diary* chronicles a journey that leads the Curé to a humble embrace of his own humanity. At the end, he reflects: "I have not lost my faith…I have found it again, though not in my poor brain…nor in my feelings, nor even in my conscience. It sometimes seems to me that it has withdrawn, that it lives on in a place where I certainly would not have looked for it, in my flesh, in my miserable flesh, in my blood and in my flesh, in my perishable, but baptized flesh" (p. 104).

The Curé's life is marked from childhood by isolation and estrangement. In spite of his deep suffering, he carries on, often in doubt and confusion, because of his sure, yet elusive, conviction that we are loved by a God who also suffered rejection and loss. Incarnation points him toward community and the world—love, kindness, and respect for everything and everyone. In a transforming dialogue with the Curé, Mme la Comtesse, the wife/mother in a powerful local family, is able to abandon her lifelong resentment and hate of God. She had lost her only son as a child and had never forgiven God for the loss. The Curé convinces her that the state of her soul matters because it affects others for good or ill. He tells her that we could not live if God had given us clear knowledge of how closely bound we are to one another in good and evil (p. 166). The Christian vocation to love is a universally inclusive community affair. His flirtations with despair alert him to the true meaning of hell, which is to give up on love (p. 171). And so he chooses love—over and over again—in daily concrete ways in the face of pain, rejection, and despair.

Bernanos lamented that the church had lost its way, abandoning the trenches of everyday life for abstract empty words devoid of concrete embodiment. For him, the ideal church is not afraid of sin (her own or that of others) but takes it upon herself as Christ did (p. 18). The church's central work is to preach the miracle that everyone is a blessed child of God; to keep the soul of childhood alive by offering—for free—joy, candor and the freshness of youth. The risen Lord is "a marvelous and living friend, who suffers our pain, takes joy in our happiness, will share our last hour and receive us into His arms, upon His heart" (pp. 27, 29, 20). The real tragedy of sin and evil lies in ignorance of this one essential reality of the Christian life. The childlike Curé looked forward to teaching catechism to the children, a setting in which he hoped to be able to be himself and speak honestly of God and joy. But the children are already filled with cynicism and malice. Love, he experiences, is something to ridicule. They play cruel jokes on him, rank with sexual innuendo. And yet he is incapable of responding in kind and refuses to give up on them.

The Diary of a Country Priest was conceived and created by a French artist, in a pre-Vatican II world. There the meaning of clergy, laity, church and holiness was markedly different from our own. On the surface, it is not a book likely to resonate with the twenty-first-century American Church. The dark world of Ambricourt is calculated to baffle and shock (as was Flannery O'Connor's). But by painting evil in its quiet, depraved starkness, Bernanos lifts up the sheer power of God-with-us in the ordinary and extraordinary events of life; the alarming call to become other Christs; the possibility of genuine trust and hope rooted in divine presence. The story is an antidote to cynicism. A reminder of the childhood gifts of simplicity and trust. A window onto the difficult, beautiful, elusive presence of grace in the concrete, physical, "real" world.

In *The Diary of a Country Priest*, Bernanos imagines the Christian life as a story of innocence and vulnerability; death and loss; fidelity to loving action; and surrender to good so that evil might be transformed. While I would not have shared Bernanos's politics, I am moved and enlightened by his theology—in Christ humanity becomes the essence and vehicle of divinity. *The Diary of a Country Priest* is more than a carefully wrought work of art, a probing analysis of human psychology, or a moving, life-out-of-death meditation on the cross—although these it certainly is. It is, above all, a novel about the mysticism of everyday life. It is a reminder that holiness comes through our humanness not in opposition to it. Flesh as well as spirit is made glorious in Christ. *The Diary of a Country Priest* is an important way station on the road to ever more radical understandings of Incarnation. "All is grace."

Faith in History and Society: Toward a Fundamental Practical Theology (The Seabury Press, 1980) by Johann Baptist Metz

Substantiating the Nexus for Liturgy and Ethics

Bruce T. MORRILL, SJ, *Vanderbilt University*

In fall, 1991, as a two-time alumnus of American Jesuit higher education (B.A., religious studies, Holy Cross; M.Div., Jesuit School of Theology at Berkeley), I entered doctoral studies at Emory University imbued with the foundational theology of Karl Rahner. Emory's formidable theological studies faculty had looked favorably on my stated purpose of pursuing liturgical theology, interested in better understanding the church's sacramental practices as graced experiences in human ritualizing, a deeper grasp of symbolism as the divine means of human transformation.

Describing sacrament in terms of grace and experience rings of the German Jesuit Rahner's fundamental method—an effort at articulating everyday life as the locus of God's presence to humanity, of God's ongoing revelation through Christ in history. The appeal of Rahner's theology both to the American Jesuits who'd taught me and to myself, who by then had completed a decade of Jesuit formation, was due in no small part to a common spirituality, a renewed appropriation of Ignatius Loyola's practices for discerning God's active presence in the story of one's life with others. Jesuits are formed for "finding God in all things," a motto drawn from Ignatius's rules that more than two generations of U.S. Jesuit leadership had been promoting among our members and as a guiding principle for our colleges and universities.

Another motto had likewise emerged from the reforming mid-1970s General Congregation of the Society of Jesus: "The service of faith and promotion of justice" realized vigorous adoption as the new mission-mandate for the U.S. Jesuit provinces. Rahnerian theology, focused as it was on the individual believer (the "subject," in modern philosophical terms), provided limited scholarly support for applying the biblical and doctrinal content of Christianity to persistent and newly erupting social struggles—whether public or ecclesial, local, national, or global. At the extreme, "faith and justice" Jesuits and colleagues derided what they considered widespread self-absorbed spirituality among American Catholics, often targeting liturgical practices.

On that point I was sympathetic, for I was disheartened by the extent to which I largely found Catholic celebration of Mass adapting its symbolic elements, seasonal cycles, and biblical content either to the popular customs comforting their middle-class lifestyles or, conversely, to the social causes agitating them. Experience and study to date had convinced me that the rites, by then completely reformed in the wake of Vatican II, should form us, not the other way around. Likeminded Catholics, however, were to my knowledge seemingly few, making me suspicious that something was amiss in Catholic and wider Christian culture.

My first semester of doctoral coursework at Emory quickly confirmed my decision to study with faculty and students broader than my Catholic circle. Two of my seminars entailed extensive reading of the formidable Karl Barth. Theological ethicist James Gustafson had us studying huge portions of Barth's fourteen-volume *Church Dogmatics*, but it was philosophical theologian Walter Lowe's advice that for his course I concentrate on Barth's early breakthrough book, *The Letter to the Romans*, that had an explosive impact on my thought. Such an effect was, in fact, Barth's very intention in writing some seven decades earlier. His was a clarion call to the churches in the wake of the human devastation wrought across Christian Europe in World War I, against which liberal, transcendental-idealist Protestant theology had proven impotent. In *Romans* Barth elicits images from that catastrophe to interpret Paul's message, likening the gospel, most bracingly, to a bombed-out crater. Into that void on earth's broken surface God's Word comes as alien to humanity, an empowering, *because completely other*, message for living toward a new creation, out of hope that in this age remains ever on the distant horizon.

Barth's resolute emphasis on otherness and distance from human capacities and inclinations he pressed as a damning corrective to experience-expressing theologies, the very type of method North Atlantic Catholic theology had largely come to embrace several decades later. Still somewhat youthful, I found myself carried away with enthusiasm for the Barthian critique of modern Christianity's institutionalism and social conformity. And yet, in passionate conversations with generous classmates I could not help but realize that the Swiss Protestant theologian's aversion to any sacramental efficacy through the church's symbolic ritual in its members, along with his meager offers for positively explaining *how* the gospel reaches humans *as humans*, severely limited his resourcefulness to my project.

In a further course with him in my second year of studies, Professor Lowe again proved a solicitous guide for shaping a theological project in service against the malaise I (with many others) perceived in U.S. Catholicism. The common work of the seminar was our poring over writings by early critical theorists, especially the "Frankfurt School" (Adorno, Horkheimer, Marcuse), while the professor individually assigned each of us a theologian in our particular traditions engaging such philosophy in their own work. To me he assigned Johann Baptist Metz, a German Catholic priest-theologian whose methodology and argument had most comprehensively come together in his *Faith in History and Society*.[1] Metz's critique of late-modern Catholic theology and practice, as well as his constructive proposals reorienting fundamental theology, spoke compellingly to my observations, questions, and concerns.

Metz develops his practical fundamental theology on the thesis "that the widely discussed crisis of identity in Christianity is not primarily a crisis of the Christian message, but rather a crisis of its subjects and institutions. These are too remote from the undeniably practical implications

---

1 Johann Baptist Metz, *Faith in History and Society: Toward a Fundamental Practical Theology*, trans. David Smith (New York: The Seabury Press, 1980). The German original, *Glaube in Geschichte und Gesellschaft* (1977), has realized multiple revised editions, as well as a completely new English translation by J. Matthew Ashley (New York: Crossroad Publishing, 2007). Citations here will be from the 1980 edition, the English version contemporaneous with my autobiographical narrative.

of the message and so tend to destroy its power" (pp. ix-x). Against the mistaken popular explanations of Christianity's slide into increasing social and personal irrelevance, namely, that the Bible and traditional doctrine are incapable of addressing the needs and interests of modern humanity, Metz counters that such institutions as the theological academy and internal church structures have failed in their reactions to secularity.

Thereupon Metz constructs what he calls a "theological enlightenment of the Enlightenment," a reexamination of Enlightenment history arguing for how the rise of the privatized individual has precipitated crises for religious tradition and authority. Such analysis of religion's reduction to a private middle-class affair opens into a fundamental theology addressing the practical conditions and possibilities for emancipating people ("the human subject") by means not of abstract principles but of the practical categories of memory, narrative, and solidarity.

Metz develops his "political theology of the subject" as a corrective to the transcendental fundamental theology of his mentor and friend, Karl Rahner, whose theological anthropology he extols as the finest exercise exploring the *formal* subject produced by the Enlightenment. In reflecting upon existence, person, subject, or the human, Rahner achieved the pinnacle of Roman Catholic theology's belated response to Kantian transcendental philosophy. The problem, however, is the level of abstraction. Modern theology has failed to ask whether such a religious subject actually exists, that is, whether or to what extent actual people in modern society approach their personal and societal lives on the basis and priority of *Christian* concepts of reason, freedom, and autonomy.

As a privatized affair, Christian religion functions as affirmation of values the middle-class subject attains elsewhere in society, and in the public sphere, is reduced to providing customs for holiday celebrations. For a growing majority, Christian faith becomes a "religious paraphrase" of how they already perceive and practice their lives in the world, thereby making participation in liturgical worship expendable. Meanwhile, a much smaller minority, in contrast, seeks refuge in a rigid "pure traditionalism" that threatens the church with sectarian isolation.

In establishing the concept of political theology, Metz analyzes the threatening socioeconomic conditions of late modernity in order to argue that the Christian message can realize its salvific import today only if recognized as a "dangerous memory," the *memoria passionis*. Relying extensively on the Frankfurt School critical theorists, Metz describes the threat that the instrumental, "evolutionary" reason of technology and the market poses to humanity and ecology at this juncture in history. To the extent people accept the rationality of capitalism's exchange-principle and technology's instrumentalism, the logic of inevitable (evolving) progress amounts to "a new form of metaphysics" or "a quasi-religious symbol of scientific knowledge" (pp. 171, 6), often with negative social consequences.

Far from generating the sort of optimistic view of history and nature that characterized the nineteenth century, the present valorization of technical reason has produced deep measures of fatalism and apathy. People find themselves part of an anonymous, inevitable, timeless technological and economic process. The need to conform for success in these systems depletes people's imaginations, inhibits dreams for the future, and ultimately threatens the loss of their subjectivity and freedom. In its now near universality, the exchange mentality inherent to market capitalism integrally influences not only politics but also the foundations of spiritual life in a culture of the makeable, replaceable, and consumable, eroding commitments, attitudes of gratuity, and capacities to sit with sorrow or feel profound joy. The strains on personal and social relations overlap. Frustrations, especially economic hardships, in the face of the inadmissible limits of the instrumental reason of technology, the market, and political bureaucracies, can foment hateful fanaticism, for which Auschwitz stands as the haunting witness.

With that powerful symbol of modernity's disastrous turn, Metz articulates the current danger to humanity, as well as the emerging social and political movements confronting the suffering that technological and economic processes have caused. Anonymous progress is interrupted by questioning *whose* progress, at what cost to the freedom of *others*, and with increasing awareness, to the ecology. Remembrance of the victims of these social processes constitutes an interruption of the abstract arguments for progress. Metz then turns to the memory of Jesus, the narrative of whose passion, death, and resurrection reveals God's identification with and promise of redemption for all victims of humanity's inhumanity.

The pattern of Jesus' life and death, one of service to the oppressed, constitutes the pattern of life that can be salvific for Christians now, a pattern that promises an authentic subjectivity and freedom. Metz thereby recovers the tradition of the *imitatio Christi*—an imitation dangerous both in the conversion it requires of its practitioners, away from a privatized view of salvation, and in the threat it poses to the conventional (evolutionary) wisdom of society. This praxis of mysticism and politics, liturgy and ethics, likewise becomes the means for believers to know, in an experiential or practical way, deep joy and hopeful consolation, freedom lived in the presence of God, the God of Israel and Jesus, the God of the living and the dead.

Such is a brief rehearsal of Metz's fundamental theological project. In his comprehensive book, as well as subsequent essays, he cites the Eucharist as the mystical source of the "remembrance-structure" for a social ethics true to biblical faith and tradition. With the details of the history, theology, and practice of liturgical tradition having remained beyond his purview, Metz has placed me in his debt, orienting the work of my doctoral dissertation and now two decades of sacramental-liturgical scholarship as an ongoing dialogue between political and liturgical theology.

Gitanjali by Rabindranath Tagore (Chiswick Press, 1912)

Wisdom Lost and Found Again

Francis Xavier CLOONEY, S.J., *Harvard Divinity School*

I had just turned 23, and had just come several months before to Kathmandu, to teach at St. Xavier's School, a Jesuit boarding school for Hindu and Buddhist boys in the Valley. I was figuring out how to teach, how to supervise teenagers in games and recreation and in study hall in the evening, and asking myself what I was doing so far from home. One evening in September, 1973, I was sitting at the front desk of a classroom of some thirty boys, and to pass the time had before me a book I had selected at haste from the Jesuit library shelf. It was *Gitanjali* (Garland of Songs), just a little book of 103 poems by Rabindranath Tagore (1861-1941), a Bengali Hindu writer, written and rewritten in a time of loss, as he lamented the death of his wife and daughter and son. I did not then know that this was the book, published in 1912 in the West, that won for Tagore the Nobel Prize for Literature in 1913, the first non-Westerner to win any Nobel Prize.

I remember that night in study hall, reading the opening verses with some astonishment, recognition, and a sense of being at long last in contact with the great traditions of the East:

> Thou hast made me endless, such is thy pleasure. This frail vessel thou emptiest again and again, and fillest it ever with fresh life.

> This little flute of a reed thou hast carried over hills and dales, and hast breathed through it melodies eternally new.

> At the immortal touch of thy hands my little heart loses its limits in joy and gives birth to utterance ineffable.
>
> Thy infinite gifts come to me only on these very small hands of mine. Ages pass, and still thou pourest, and still there is room to fill. (p. 1)

I turned the page, and found the second to be nearly as beautiful:

> When thou commandest me to sing it seems that my heart would break with pride; and I look to thy face, and tears come to my eyes…
>
> Drunk with the joy of singing I forget myself and call thee friend who art my lord. (p. 2)

And every poem after that made its own mark on me.

Gitanjali actually became a way of introducing myself. Any number of times when I talk about my initial experience of India and all that followed from it, I quote this song:

> Thou hast made me known to friends whom I knew not. Thou hast given me seats in homes not my own. Thou hast brought the distant near and made a brother of the stranger…
>
> Through birth and death, in this world or in others, wherever thou leadest me it is thou, the same, the one companion of my endless life who ever linkest my heart with bonds of joy to the unfamiliar.
>
> When one knows thee, then alien there is none, then no door is shut. Oh, grant me my prayer that I may never lose the bliss of the touch of the one in the play of many. (63)

And I also appreciated Yeats' amazement in discovering these songs, evocative of "a world I have dreamed of all my life long." For him, *Gitanjali* was a "work of a supreme culture" wherein "poetry and religion are the same thing." In Tagore's poetry Yeats—and myself at age 22—found encounter possible: "A whole people, a whole civilization, immeasurably strange to us, seems to have been taken up into this imagination." Yeats, toward whom my Irish-American soul was already well disposed, confirmed my hope that Tagore was indeed the very Indian, very Hindu, very universal poet who could convince us that the borders between cultures and religions were indeed crossable. I was on my way to what would become a life-long study of Hinduism, a love of its literature and a sharing of some of its deepest emotions and insights.

And it was that I was in love with these poems, and found in them a validation of my trip around the world, from New York to Kathmandu. All of this convinced me, more than texts like the Bhagavad Gita that I had already read, that I had not come East in vain. *Gitanjali* had become famous in Ireland and Britain, but it was there for me in Kathmandu. In those two years in Kathmandu, I would gradually discover many other bonds to connect me to the students I taught, the culture of the Valley, and to Hinduism. I would, later on, read much Hindu literature in the Sanskrit and Tamil languages, and find many holy and beautiful temples in the deep south of India. My link to India would soon enough not depend entirely on Tagore. Yet it was in reading *Gitanjali*, beginning that night in September, 1973, that the possibilities of a Catholic realization of Hindu wisdom moved from possibility to actuality.

But later on, this early glow was eventually to fade. After my years in Katmandu (1973-1975) and after ordination as a priest (1978), I did my doctoral studies at the University of Chicago (1979-1984), in the Department of South Asian Languages and Civilizations. There, among many other things, I learned about Orientalism, the fatal temptation of the West to remake the world in its own image, "the Orient" re-used and misused to confirm and reinforce ideas "the Christian West" already had about itself. I learned the complexities of translation, the inevitable betrayal of the original in a new language.

I read much more of Tagore's vast corpus of drama and novels, poetry and songs, criticism and philosophy; he painted; he founded Shanti Niketan, a school with novel ideas about how children learn; he resisted the intellectual hegemony of the Raj. This strong-minded public figure was no fragile mystic hovering between this life and the next. He was a flesh and blood person with a booming voice in a specific time and place, not a cipher standing in for the eternal East. Broadly opposed to British rule in India, he was not willing to be shaped and re-shaped in accord with even well-meaning Western views of him. He kept the Nobel Prize, but in protest against British rule, he returned his knighthood to the king.

And I learned that *Gitanjali* in the Bengali (a language I do not know) is quite different from the 1912 version known to most of us. I learned that in his introduction Yeats had conjured a fictional Tagore, who confirmed what Yeats was looking for in rediscovering his Irish soul in counterbalance to the British, their empire, and their Church. I heard the rumors that Yeats may have "fixed" the poems of *Gitanjali*, to suit the tastes of the West, so that it was a really a Tagore-Yeats *Gitanjali* that won the Nobel Prize in 1913, a work rather distant from Tagore's Bengali original. Scholars and translators like William Radice, Brother James Talarovic, and Joe Winter created new translations that showed me how differently the poems collected as *Gitanjali* could be translated, received, experienced. I came to understand why his other works (other than an essay here or there, such as those collected in *Sadhana*) never appealed to me as did *Gitanjali*, since the Tagore of 1912 perhaps had never really existed.

And so, like many a Westerner who had come to love India and Hinduism through works such as *Gitanjali* but then learned too much more, I was forced to step back, putting aside sentiment in deference to scholarship. *Gitanjali* had slipped away, reduced for a time to just one more book on my shelf, remembered but little read. While I did not abandon my intuition that Catholic and Hindu sensitivities could be deeply intertwined, I realized that my scholarship, like that of Radice, would in part serve to surprise readers, getting them to see that interreligious learning is hard work, never what we had first expected. India is not the mystical East, the comforting Other, but a world as complex and real, stubborn and other, as our own.

But now, some thirty years later, I have learned still more, how to distance myself also from the disenchantments of a post-Orientalist age. I've found the grace of Paul Ricœur's "second naïveté," a surprising recovery of what had been lost, and so a chance to reconnect with Tagore too, as that little English *Gitanjali* has come alive once more. When I look back now, and review the singular translations Tagore made of his poems, placed in an order that does not replicate the Bengali, and when I read about the intensity he brought to this particular work of translation, when I consider how Yeats was consciously and unconsciously bringing this Indian soul-mate into his Irish soul—I am no longer a romantic, nor a skeptic. Where in life has bias not been operative, something lost in translation, the Other reconceived in our own terms? The miracle is not the fact that simple things happen in a simple way; it is simple things arising in the midst of confusions, errings, manipulated and taken apart, taken apart but then put back together again.

Just as my original encounter with Tagore was too simple, I learned that it was also wrong to allow the miracle of that 1912 *Gitanjali* to slip away entirely, erased by the cuts of sharper scholarship, historical detective work, alternative translations, and suspicions of motives. The prize-winning *Gitanjali* was, after all, Tagore's work, even if Yeats was a figure in its reception in the West. Tagore worked intensely on the book, as he never would again on a single small book. Though not telling us everything of Tagore, it stands as a monument composed in a time of personal loss that was also the moment when he rediscovered the West. Flawed, singular, complicated, in need of footnotes, *Gitanjali* is still, I think, a meeting point of East and West, Hindu and Christian, potent in an age of disenchantment but also beyond it.

This tale of my discovery, loss, and rediscovery of *Gitanjali* is consoling in a personal way. Much of my own scholarship stands in-between on that uncertain yet wondrous edge between the Hindu and the Christian. Yes, I have written Indological essays and a whole book on Hindu ritual theory; and yes, I can with some effort write simply as a Catholic theologian. But for the most part my scholarship, my "comparative theology," falls in-between, poised as a Catholic's reading of Hindu texts (largely poetry), going deep inside a Hindu tradition here or there, but then returning, changed, to a now changed Christian tradition. My work does not prove that India and the United States, or Christianity and Hinduism, are the same or essentially belong together; there probably is no hidden stream of perennial wisdom. But the moments of insight and understanding, where Hinduism comes alive in my work and sets afire my own Catholicism, are worth all the trouble.

Perhaps Yeats was right in his introduction: even as Tagore lamented his personal losses, and gave us something quite different from his Bengali songs, he really was communicating something "so much a part of himself" that it became universal, so much so that we cannot be "certain that he is not also speaking of the saints" when he writes,

> On the seashore of endless worlds children meet. The infinite sky is motionless overhead and the restless water is boisterous. On the seashore of endless worlds the children meet with shouts and dances...
>
> On the seashore of endless worlds children meet. Tempest roams in the pathless sky, ships get wrecked in the trackless water, death is abroad and children play. On the seashore of endless worlds is the great meeting of children. (p. 60)

God for Us: The Trinity and Christian Life (HarperSanFrancisco, 1991) by Catherine Mowry LaCugna

"The Trinitarian Shape of Christian Life"

Richard GAILLARDETZ, *Boston College*

It was as a lay minister that I first came to a decision to pursue a Ph.D. in theology. I had already worked in the church as a pastoral minister in a variety of capacities. The opportunities to teach and write that these ministries offered me are what led me to pursue further graduate studies. I applied to a number of doctoral programs and was accepted at the University of Notre Dame. At the time, I was interested in exploring the intersection between moral theology and ecclesiology and looked forward to the opportunity to study under Richard McCormick, S.J., Richard McBrien and Thomas O'Meara, O.P. It was only after arriving at Notre Dame that I was introduced to a young but rising star on the Notre Dame Faculty, Catherine Mowry LaCugna.

Soon after my arrival in South Bend my academic advisor encouraged me to register for LaCugna's doctoral seminar on the Trinity. I signed up for the course only reluctantly. LaCugna was brilliant and could be quite intimidating at the personal level and my first encounter with her at a departmental event had not gone well, with my committing a social *faux pas* too embarrassing to share. More to the point, I had very little interest in Trinitarian theology, which I associated at that time with a more abstract, metaphysical mode of theological reflection far removed from my interests in moral theology and ecclesiology. Fortunately, I took the course anyway and experienced an exhilarating world of theological insight open up before me. Over the course of the semester LaCugna rehearsed the main themes that would appear in her most important work, *God for Us*, a volume that was published the year I completed my studies at Notre Dame, 1991. The book established her as a major figure in Catholic theology but her great promise would only be partially realized, as she succumbed to cancer in 1997 at the age of 44.

Her book, which I read soon after its publication, only amplified the themes that had so captivated me in her seminar. Looking back, my engagement with her thought effected nothing less than an intellectual conversion as I re-discovered the most "practical" doctrine of the Christian faith. Like so many Christians, I had long dismissed the Trinity as one of the most arcane of church doctrines, an unsolvable arithmetic problem (how can 3=1?). As Karl Rahner had famously put it,

> [D]espite their orthodox confession of the Trinity, Christians are, in their practical life, almost mere 'monotheists.' We must be willing to admit that, should the doctrine of the Trinity have to be dropped as false, the major part of religious literature could well remain unchanged.... One has the feeling that, for the catechism of the head and heart (as contrasted with the printed catechism), the Christian's idea of the incarnation would not have to change at all if there were no Trinity.[1]

At a more basic level, when the Trinity did inform the popular religious imagination, it functioned at a rather simplistic level, suggesting "two men and a bird" in heaven. In more academic circles the marginalization of the doctrine of the Trinity was less obvious; nevertheless, the power of the doctrine was often obscured in an arid neo-scholastic tradition that worked through an abstract fog of Trinitarian notions, processions, missions and relations.

LaCugna's book punctured both the misleading tendencies of popular catechesis (e.g., using the shamrock or the three states of H_2O to explain the doctrine) and the intellectual esotericism of the neo-scholastic tradition. For LaCugna the Trinity named how God is God *for us*. It reminded us that

---

[1] Karl Rahner, *The Trinity* (New York: Herder and Herder, 1970), 10-11.

while we experience relationships as something that we are always either moving into or withdrawing from, God does not enter into relationships. Indeed, God does not *have* relationships at all; God *is* perfect relationship. "God is *essentially relational*" (p. 289). Moreover, if God is perfect relationship, and we are created in the image of God, then the doctrine of the Trinity is concerned with *our* life as well. We are called by divine grace to enter into that mode of loving relationship which defines God's very being.

The first half of her magisterial work represented a rich exploration of the Christian tradition, East and West, as she demonstrated how over the centuries the Trinity receded from its early Christian centrality to the theological margins of the Christian tradition. Yet she insisted: "the Christian doctrine of God originated as the theological justification for the idea that the events of the economy of salvation, notably redemption through Jesus Christ and the sending of the Holy Spirit, reveal the nature of the ineffable God" (p. 209). It was the early Christian experience of God's saving action through Christ and in the Spirit that gave rise to Trinitarian doctrine. The Trinity evokes a God whose being is characterized by an eternal movement toward us, if you will, in redeeming love. Yet LaCugna also insisted that the Trinity names our graced movement toward God. In other words, LaCugna claimed, the Trinity was as much about doxology (the praise of God) as it was about soteriology (salvation). It is the Holy Spirit at work in our hearts that moves us to prayer and worship as we unite ourselves with Christ in offering praise to God. This doxological dimension of the Trinity is not limited to formal, public worship. Liturgy is a ritual performance of a doxological way of life. We give glory (*doxa*) to God by living in right relationship with God and God's creatures. Praise is what allows us to get over ourselves, to enter into the logic of "overflow" (p. 338), a dynamic movement toward God and others characterized by a kind of self-forgetfulness. Within this theological horizon, sin is revealed as a perversion of right relationship or, as LaCugna provocatively put it, "sin...is the absence of praise" (p. 343).

Finally LaCugna's work has helped me think about my own field of study, ecclesiology, with fresh eyes.

> Just as the doctrine of the Trinity is not an abstract teaching about God apart from us but a teaching about God's life with us and our

life with each other, ecclesiology is not the study of an abstract church but a study of the actual gathering of persons in a common faith and a common mission (p. 403).

Baptism is initiation into the triune life of God "which is indistinguishable from God's life with every creature throughout time, past, present and future" (p. 382). Participation in that triune life is mediated through the life of the church. LaCugna was herself influenced by the work of Yves Congar and the Eastern Orthodox theologian, John Zizioulas, both of whom articulated a deeply Trinitarian theology of the church as a communion of persons. The church is called, even though it so often fails to live up to that call, to be the new "household of God's reign" that offers a radically new form of human existence in Christ (p. 388).

LaCugna appreciated the extent to which the Second Vatican Council had recovered the Trinitarian foundations of the church. "The church on earth is by its very nature missionary," the council taught in *Ad Gentes* #2, because "it has its origin in the mission of the Son and the holy Spirit." LaCugna saw this Trinitarian dimension in the church's sacramentality; the church is to be a visible embodiment before the world of life in the Risen Christ (p. 401). Her commitment to a thoroughly relational vision of the church has implications for our understanding of church ministry. For centuries the Catholic Church has struggled with an overly juridical understanding of such ecclesial realities as ministry and power. We have tended to imagine ordination as the conferral of discrete "powers" on an autonomous individual, who then could wield those powers over other believers. Yet, LaCugna's commitment to a Trinitarian understanding of personhood led her first to present Christian baptism as a ritual that introduces the believer into a fundamental ecclesial relationship, Christian discipleship. Ordination, in turn, draws the believer into a new ecclesial relationship within the ecclesial communion, one dedicated to public service in the church. It is only when ministerial leadership is understood in this way that we can hope to overcome the sin of clericalism.

Catherine Mowry LaCugna offered the church a profoundly contemplative, moving account of the triune God who comes to us as Word and Spirit and draws us into divine communion through the life of the church. Hers is a vision of God who is, at the heart of the divine being, God for us.

God's Presence in History: Jewish Affirmations and Philosophical Reflections (New York University Press, 1970) by Emil Fackenheim

Deepening the Question

Mary Jo LEDDY, *Toronto School of Theology*

In the early 70s, I was in danger of becoming another graduate school dropout. In the philosophy department at the University of Toronto, linguistic analysis and logical positivism seemed to reign supreme. I was bored, unable to see the relevance of philosophy to the causes for justice and peace that I was getting involved in. And then I attended Emil Fackenheim's graduate course on the Philosophy of Religion.

The first day of class, Professor Fackenheim offered two maxims for our consideration: first, that good philosophy does not necessarily have to be boring and, secondly, that if you really understand something you can say it simply. I was interested. I actually felt I was beginning to think, as if for the first time. He took us through the long history of encounters between faith and Western philosophy. By that time, he was a recognized expert on Modern German thought – Kant, Fichte, Shelling and Hegel. He spoke with a heavy German accent and often had a twinkle in his eye as he puffed on his cigar.

Then one day, as he introduced 20th century philosophers of religion, he began to reflect on the Holocaust. He faced us and asked, "How can we go on thinking in the same way after what has happened?" I thought it was the first real question I had heard in the course of my graduate studies.

It would shape my ongoing interest in the exercise of historical judgment, i.e., how can we think about events in our own time? Philosophers often seemed to have a lot to say about events that happened in the past, but seem more unable to think through the world as it is happening around them.

Emil Fackenheim had just published his book *God's Presence in History* and I purchased the first edition, reading it through the night. It was a powerful and gripping reflection that invited the reader to think dialectically. In his view, Hegel's dialectical thought had often been reduced to the formulaic thesis-antithesis-synthesis. Fackenheim presented the dialectic in a dynamic way, insisting that the thesis encompassed but did not obliterate the distinctions. Reading this book taught me how to think dialectically and to consider the dynamic relationship between history and philosophical and theological reflection.

He argued that the Jewish identity is grounded in significant "root experiences" that manifest God's presence in history. However, he also recognizes that events in history can conceal God's presence in history. He situates his reflections in the faith that God is revealed in history while remaining faithful to the victims of the Holocaust. This reality of the Holocaust shatters any easy faith in God or in humanity. In this book he laid out the foundations for considering revelation as ongoing in history and that the historically grounded faith (of Jews and Christians) make them vulnerable to what had happened in the Nazi era.

The Holocaust, by the time I met him, had become the focus of much of Fackenheim's reflections. He himself, a young Jewish rabbi, had been imprisoned for a few months in Sachsenhausen and had escaped to England and Canada where he was interned in a Prisoner of War camp. For a long time he had been unable to think about the Holocaust and had completed his philosophical studies by focusing on the notion of creation in medieval Arabic philosophy.

However, his friendship with Elie Wiesel and his marriage to the feisty Rose gave him the courage to think about what had happened during the Holocaust. The Six Day War, in May and June of 1967, which seemed to threaten the existence of the State of Israel, was a further impetus.

Fackenheim first articulated the oft repeated phrase "Jews are forbidden to hand Hitler posthumous victories" in his article "Jewish Faith and the Holocaust," *Commentary 1967*.

He quotes that article almost verbatim in the concluding chapter of *God's Presence in History* because "I am unable to express it better now than in my earlier statement."

> Jews are forbidden to hand Hitler posthumous victories. They are commanded to survive as Jews, lest the Jewish people perish. They are commanded to remember the victims of Auschwitz lest their memory perish. They are forbidden to despair of man and his world, and to escape into either cynicism or otherworldliness, lest they cooperate in delivering the world over to the forces of Auschwitz. Finally, they are forbidden to despair of the God of Israel, lest Judaism perish. A secularist Jew cannot make himself believe by a mere act of will, nor can he be commanded to do so.... And a religious Jew who has stayed with his God may be forced into new, possibly revolutionary relationships with Him. One possibility, however, is wholly unthinkable. A Jew may not respond to Hitler's attempt to destroy Judaism by himself co-operating in its destruction. In ancient times, the unthinkable Jewish sin was idolatry. Today, it is to respond to Hitler by doing his work (p. 84).

During the early 70's I was privileged to hear him thinking out the challenges of the Holocaust. I listened to him in the courses and over the Passover meals at the home of Rose and Emil. He argued forcibly that there was such a thing as what Kant called "radical evil," evil done for the sake of evil. He gave reasons why the Holocaust was a unique event in history. I agreed with him, then and now.

His description of the Commandment to endure dialectically is related to the differences between religious and secular Judaism. All Jews, he wrote, must have the courage to bear Jewish children in a post-Holocaust world. His description of the dilemma of a Jewish parent was poignant:

> A Jew today is obliged to retrace the road which led his brethren to Auschwitz. It is a road of pain and mourning, of humiliation, guilt, and despair. To retrace it is living death. How to suffer this death and also choose Jewish life which, like all life, must include joy, laughter, and childlike innocence? How to reconcile such a remembrance with

life itself? How dare a Jewish parent crush his child's innocence with the knowledge that his uncle or grandfather was denied life because of his Jewishness? And how dare he not burden him with this knowledge? The conflict is inescapable, for we may neither forget the past for the sake of present life, nor destroy present life by a mourning without relief—and then there is no relief (p. 90).

In *God's Presence in History* Fackenheim speaks of "the Commanding Voice of Auschwitz," a bracing thought given the more liberal thinking of the times. Yet the Command, although not clear, has implications for how Jews and Christians are to live in the world as it is.

The book outlines five considerations, which he calls "fragmentary responses" to the "shattering reality" of what had happened. In this book, Fackenheim had taken up the summons to think about an event that shattered the faith of the biblical people and the optimism of the modern worldview. I finished my graduate studies with the conviction of the importance of recognizing the significant questions in life, in faith, even when the answers were not clear. "The important thing," said Fackenheim in one of his lectures, "is to deepen the question."

This was the first book of Fackenheim's that I read. Although it is not a long book, it is dense and demanding. I stayed up most of the night reading it. Since then I have read almost all of his other books and essays and I learned a great deal from him as he supervised my doctoral thesis, which focused on the exercise of political judgment in the reflections of Hannah Arendt. He did not like Arendt much (not critical enough of Heidegger!). However, I actually came to think that Arendt had insights to offer that filled in some of the gaps in Fackenheim's thought.

I still struggle with his interpretation of the Commandment to endure and to survive, so that Hitler would not be granted posthumous victories. Having been involved in some struggles against injustice, I have become more aware of how we can become like what we fight against. In facing the fires of injustice, the fires of Auschwitz, we can begin to mirror in our minds the very patterns we are resisting. There were times in the 70s and 80s when Fackenheim seemed more aware of what he was against than what he was for. After he moved to Israel he tended to interpret any criticism of the State as a threat to the survival of Judaism.

Nevertheless, his reflections summoned me to think about what was happening in the world of my times and to take the risk of thinking about this world, albeit in a provisional and fragmentary way. I had the privilege of meeting and reading someone who taught me that thinking is a way of acting in the world, that writing is a way of acting in the world.

Gyn/Ecology: The Metaethics of Radical Feminism (Beacon Press, 1978) by Mary Daly

Righteous Anger and the Sin of Sexism

Susan A. ROSS, *Loyola University Chicago*

In the late 1970s, the feminist movement was in full flower in the church and society. The first women were ("irregularly") ordained to the Episcopal priesthood in 1974 (made "regular" in 1976). The first Roman Catholic Women's Ordination Conference was held in Detroit in 1975. And, in the winter of 1977, the Vatican issued *Inter Insigniores*, declaring its "inability" to ordain women because women lacked a "natural resemblance" to the male Jesus. At the University of Chicago Divinity School, where I began graduate studies in 1975, women students were in the minority, but we had begun to find our voices. Some of the more advanced students organized a Women's Caucus. I eagerly joined them.

I was a product of women's education and strong women role models. Unlike many women my age, and even younger, I had had a quite a few women teachers in high school and nearly all of my Religion professors in my women's college were women (religious) with Ph.Ds. My mother and grandmother both worked to help support their families when it was clear that my grandfather's or father's paychecks would not cover all the bills, at times when this was decidedly out of the ordinary. The Religious of the Sacred Heart, who ran my high school and college, placed a high value on educating girls and women. They and I never doubted my ability to accomplish what I had set out to do.

After college, I worked for a few years in an investment banking firm in New York, and was the assistant to one of the first women portfolio managers. She and the other (male) portfolio manager I worked for considered it their responsibility to train me to move up, gave me additional responsibilities and both encouraged me to get my MBA. When I announced that I was going to the University of Chicago, they were delighted until I told them that I would be studying across the quad from the Business School; even then, they were encouraging and said they would welcome me back as a business ethicist, although my own path led me elsewhere. It would seem that I was a born-and-raised feminist (or, "women's libber," as we called ourselves then) who knew what sexism was.

But at one of the first Divinity School Women's Caucus meetings, I came to realize how much I was influenced by patriarchal society. A group of a dozen or so women, we went around the room, saying a bit about ourselves and responding to the inevitable question a graduate student is asked: what do you want to write your dissertation on? I can't recall all the answers, although I do remember the late (and great) Nancy Hardesty sharing her work on women and American Protestantism. When it came to me, I remember saying something like, "I am interested in feminist theology, but I really want to write on systematic theology." There may have been a collective gasp in the room—there should have been—and I left the meeting wondering whether my idea that I was interested in women's issues, but what I really wanted to work on was the "real stuff" of theology, needed to be reexamined.

I went about the business of a graduate student in theology, studying the history of Christian thought (Origen, Augustine, Anselm, Aquinas, Scotus, Luther, Calvin, Schleiermacher, etc.) and contemporary theology (Moltmann, Niebuhr, Rahner, Gadamer) under some of the school's great scholars: David Tracy, Brian Gerrish, Langdon Gilkey, Bernard McGinn, Paul Ricœur. Anne Carr had joined the faculty the same year I came as a Master's student, and I took her course on Rahner, the theologian on whom she had written her dissertation. Yes, women's issues were interesting and important, but first, I needed to learn (real) theology.

Then, sometime in 1978, my friend Anne Patrick gave me a copy of Mary Daly's *Gyn/Ecology: The Metaethics of Radical Feminism*. Anne had been asked to write a short review for a journal, but she had a full plate of other things to work on, so she asked me if I were interested. I agreed; I was familiar with Daly's *The Church and the Second Sex*, which made a strong but "balanced" (i.e., non-threatening) argument for the full inclusion of women in all of the church's ministries, and I knew about *Beyond God the Father* and the famous "walkout" at the Harvard Chapel. But nothing had prepared me for *Gyn/Ecology*.

Perhaps because I was taught to try and enter the mind of the author with empathy, I did not immediately respond to Daly, as many of my undergraduate students have, with shock, horror, and especially denial to her many charges: that Christianity is inherently necrophilic because it worships a dead man on a dead tree, that Shel Silverstein's classic children's book *The Giving Tree* is really about how men destroy women with their greed and selfishness, that American gynecology and psychiatry need to be understood in the same category as the burning of witches, Chinese footbinding, Indian suttee, and African genital mutilation. Rather, in reading Daly, I began to realize that the religion and culture in which I had been raised—even as a privileged, upper-middle-class white woman from the suburbs—were profoundly, deeply, and utterly riddled with sexism.

I read Daly's book not so much as a literal description of reality but as a radical exercise in the implications of misogyny. I remember sitting in my apartment with the book, feeling as if my head had been taken off my neck, turned upside down, completely shaken up, and put back on. Everything I had been taught to believe was challenged: the tradition I was studying, the church that I had been raised in, the society that had even given me so many opportunities—all of them were infected, riddled with the sin of sexism. I did not then and do not now go as far as Daly did in her critique—that is, to find all institutional religions hopelessly patriarchal and destructive to women—and I appreciate the critiques made by Audre Lorde and others of her descriptions of African, Indian, and Chinese traditions as culturally imperialistic and insensitive. Nevertheless, Daly devastatingly exposed the slimy underbelly of religion's treatment of women over the centuries and its present implications. For me, there was no turning back to an innocent or even "balanced" understanding of women and religion.

Feminist theology was just emerging in the late 1970s, and after reading Daly I began to read everything on the topic I could get my hands on. And although I did not write my dissertation on an explicitly feminist topic—I wrote on the connections between Catholic theologies of revelation and theological aesthetics—I soon came to see how this topic had many feminist implications. My Madeleva Lecture and book, *For the Beauty of the Earth*, drew out some of them.

A year or so after I read Daly, I was preparing for my first teaching job, and was assigned two introductory courses in Theology and one course of my own choosing. When I told my new department chair that I wanted to teach a course on Women and Religion, he protested that I was hired to teach systematic theology. I asked Anne Carr what I should say in response, and she said, "Tell him that feminist theology *is* systematic theology: it asks what difference it makes if women as well as men are taken into consideration." I remembered my own words from a few years before and I credit Mary Daly's book with helping to move me towards this point.

Many years later, I had the opportunity to talk with Daly. I was coediting an issue of *Concilium* on the topic of Women's Voices in World Religions and I had written her to ask if she would contribute a short article. She wanted to talk about it and so we did. At one point, she asked how I could survive being a faculty member at a Jesuit university, and I responded by saying that if she could, I could too! We both laughed. Although she declined to contribute, I valued her candor and thanked her for her contributing to my own growth in feminism.

Daly is difficult to teach to undergraduates; her radicalism can turn off students who have never been exposed to feminist ideas. Students learn that she excluded men from her classes since she wanted her women students to feel free to speak. Even though I explain that she would meet with male students separately, for many she seems to embody all of the stereotypes of the man-hating feminist. Her brilliant and often wickedly humorous twists on redefining words, her refusal to bend to convention, and her laser-like focus on every kind of injustice to women can alienate students who are wary of feminist ideas that sound "angry." But without righteous anger, there would be no feminism. Thomas Aquinas famously argues that if one is not angered by injustice, there is something wrong, and Daly, with her classical education, would agree. Daly taught me that one cannot smooth over or excuse misogyny, that it must be exposed and named, and that one must use everything in one's power—one's intelligence, wit, and yes, anger—to overcome it.

On occasion I have found myself labeled as a "radical feminist." I am sure that Mary Daly, were she still with us today, would object. I have spent my entire teaching career of over 35 years in colleges and universities run by religious orders of men. I have learned to get along with them, to befriend some of them, to watch my language, to make compromises. I insist that my students not reject theologians solely because of their views on women. But sexism and misogyny still exist, religions still have not done enough to condemn them, and powerful statements against these sins are needed more than ever. Daly's central role in the development of feminist theology cannot be overstated and I for one am grateful that she had the courage to be radical and to inspire me.

Hearers of the Word
(Herder & Herder, 1969) by Karl Rahner

The Human Person:
Fundamentally Open to the Transcendent

William MADGES, *St. Joseph's University*

The first edition of Karl Rahner's *Hörer des Wortes* appeared in 1941. It was the compilation of 15 lectures that Rahner (1904-1984) delivered at the Salzburg Summer School in 1937 concerning the "Foundations of a Philosophy of Religion." The 1941 text, revised by Johannes Baptist Metz, was published in German in 1963 and in English, as *Hearers of the Word*, in 1969.[1] As Metz observed in his preface to the revised edition, the book's original publication during the early years of World War II was a major reason that its contribution to the philosophy of religion did not receive the attention it deserved until decades later. I encountered Rahner and this work in the year before my graduation from college, four years after its publication in English.

Hearers of the Word is a work of fundamental-theological anthropology. In it Rahner presents the human person as the possible hearer of the possible, free revelation of God in history. As with his previous major

---

1 Metz's revision shortened the original text by removing lecture material that was repeated at the beginning or summarized at the end of each chapter. This led to the removal of one chapter entirely (the original chapter 14). Metz incorporated what remained of new material into the previous chapter (13). He also inserted some corrections and expanded certain aspects of the original's content. Rahner approved of Metz's editing.

philosophical work, *Geist in Welt* (*Spirit in the World*), Rahner's approach to his subject matter was influenced both by Thomistic metaphysics and Heideggerian phenomenological ontology. *Spirit in the World* and *Hearers of the Word* together provide the philosophical underpinnings of Rahner's theological thought.

One of the fundamental ideas that Rahner develops in *Hearers of the Word* is *potentia oboedientalis*, the idea that human beings are oriented by their very nature toward the self-communication of God. Rahner made this assertion and attempted to demonstrate its cogency in a social and intellectual context that questioned the reality of God and the meaning of existence.

Although serious questions about belief in a theistic God had been raised since the Age of Reason, by the mid-twentieth century doubt and skepticism had descended from the ether of educational elites and had begun to permeate broader segments of the general population. The horrific human toll of the Second World War contributed to a growing sense of the absence of God. The question about life's meaning became more urgent.

In *Le Mythe de Sisyphe* (1942), published one year after Rahner's *Hörer*, Albert Camus described the absurdity of our continually asking the question about the meaning of life when, as he claimed, there is none. The absurdity of this paradox is embodied in the image of Sisyphus, who repeatedly pushes a rock up the mountain, only to see it roll back down, requiring him to begin the process of pushing it uphill again and again. By contrast with Camus, Rahner argued that this unquenchable questioning was not absurd, but rather a constitutive feature of human nature, drawing us toward that holy mystery named God.

But for many people in the 1960s, God—at least God as traditionally conceived—needed to be rejected so that human freedom and life could flourish. Three years before the publication of the English translation of Rahner's *Hörer des Wortes*, the cover of *Time* magazine (April 1966) asked, in large red letters over a black background, Is God Dead? Thomas J.J. Altizer, a leading figure in the death-of-God theological movement, had affirmed in a 1964 essay, reprinted in book form in 1966, that "God has died in *our* time, in *our* history, in *our* existence. The man who chooses to live in our destiny can neither know the reality of God's presence nor understand the world as his creation; or, at least, he can no longer respond—either interiorly or cognitively—to the classical Christian images of the Creator and the creation."[2] Drawing on Nietzsche and Martin Heidegger, Altizer explained: "a No-saying to God (the transcendence of *Sein*) makes possible a Yes-saying to human existence (*Dasein*, total existence in the *here* and *now*)."[3]

In *Hearers of the Word*, Rahner affirms not only the reality of transcendence, but also the reality of God, who nonetheless always exceeds being fully grasped by humanity. " ... God is not a datum which can be directly grasped in his true self by man and his experience," Rahner wrote. God "is revealed every time man enquires into anything which exists, but who remains knowable only as the remote cause of that which is."[4] While atheistic thinkers asserted the absurdity and meaninglessness of existence, Rahner appealed to human experience, in which he claimed to discover the "openness of being and man" and transcendence toward God. Unlike those who concluded that God must die for human freedom to be (fully) actualized, Rahner showed how our fundamental openness to Being—to God—grounded and enabled our freedom, not curtailed it.

Drawing upon Heidegger's notion that the question of the meaning of one's being is preceded by a "pregrasp" (*Vorgriff*) of the world's horizon of meaning, Rahner wrote: "Of necessity . . . the question about being is part of human existence, because it is a concomitant of every proposition that man thinks or utters. He would not be human if he did not so think and speak. Every statement is a statement about some specific existent thing and is made against the background of a previous although implicit knowledge of being in general" (p. 35). As Rahner develops this thought, he comes to the conclusion that the human person is "absolute receptivity for being pure and simple." Rahner called this basic constitution of the human person spirituality. He continues:

---

2   Thomas J. J. Altizer and William Hamilton, *Radical Theology and the Death of God* (Indianapolis: Bobbs-Merrill, 1966), 95. The original essay first appeared in *The Centennial Review* in 1964.
3   Altizer and Hamilton, 98.
4   Karl Rahner, *Hearers of the Word*, trans. Michael Richards (New York: Herder & Herder, 1969), 7-8.

Man is spirit, that is, he lives his life in a perpetual reaching out towards the Absolute, in openness to God. This openness to God is not a contingency which can emerge here or there at will in man, but is the condition for the possibility of that which man is and has to be, even in the most forlorn and mundane life. The only thing which makes him a man is that he is forever on the road to God whether he is clearly aware of the fact or not, whether he wants to be or not, for he is always the infinite openness to the finite for God" (p. 66).

Encountering Rahner as a young adult, the appeal of his work was multiple. First, there was his method. Instead of arguing for the truth of Christian beliefs about the reality of God and human nature on the basis of scripture or magisterial teaching, Rahner sought to establish their truth by directing attention to human experience. His method asked me to turn inward and to reflect upon the process of acquiring knowledge, to ponder why we humans are creatures who ask questions and who, despite any answers we might get, always have more questions—questions in search of an answer that might quench this seemingly unquenchable thirst. Rahner's method opened up for me the possibility of grasping the intelligibility of Christian convictions on the basis of experiences that I could correlate to the teachings of the church, rather than simply accepting those teachings solely upon the authority of another. A second reason is related to the first. Rahner gave a strong example of how one could be a believing Catholic Christian, while also having a questioning intellect.

The acceptability of asking critical questions—even experiencing occasional doubt—was a most welcome message to me in my young adulthood. But Rahner's example carried and supported me beyond my younger years. As I pursued graduate studies and then a professional theological career spanning more than three decades, I frequently found myself returning to Rahner for inspiration. Insofar as the human person is constituted by transcendence and freedom and insofar as God is Holy (and wholly) Mystery, Rahner encouraged theologians to exercise their freedom to explore this Mystery creatively. He inspired me and many others not to be afraid of interpreting and applying the Christian tradition in new ways in the different contexts of our world. As he made clear in *Free Speech in the Church* (1959), Rahner extended this right to voice one's responsible views to the entire people of God, even if those views did not always elicit official ecclesiastical approval.⁵

Although Rahner's theological work played a major role in my decision about a future career, his was not the only influence. The Second Vatican Council, at which Rahner was a theological expert (*peritus*), was the other defining factor. The Council's pastoral orientation, Saint John XXIII's message of the "medicine of mercy" in place of words of condemnation, the Council's open dialogical stance with regard to the modern world, and its desire to build bridges of understanding with other Christians and other religions—all of this supported my decision, having attending Catholic elementary school and a Jesuit high school and college, to continue my education at a non-Catholic institution. When I began my graduate studies in the Divinity School of the University of Chicago in 1975, the Rahnerian and conciliar spirit of dialogue and openness was palpable. The faculty included theologians and scholars of religion from different Christian churches and other religious traditions. The Catholics among the faculty included David Tracy, Anne Carr, and Bernard McGinn, and Catholic students actually constituted the majority of the student body in what had begun as a Baptist seminary. The Divinity School offered the stimulating environment in which the creative questioning that Rahner encouraged could flourish.

Hearers of the Word is not an easy book. It is filled with concepts and terminology drawn from transcendental Thomism, ontology, and modern phenomenology. Although *Foundations of Christian Faith: An Introduction to the Idea of Christianity* (New York: Seabury, 1978) subsequently provided a more accessible introduction to the philosophical underpinnings of Rahner's theology, it was my encounter with those ideas in *Hearers of the Word* that gave definitive shape to the trajectory of my professional life and offered me deep existential meaning.

---

5   See, for example, Karl Rahner, *Free Speech in the Church* (New York: Sheed & Ward, 1959), pp. 38-39.

The History of Black Catholics in the United States (Crossroad, 1990) by Cyprian Davis, O.S.B.

"That Our History Bring Hope"

Sandra YOCUM, *University of Dayton*

"That our history bring hope." So Father Cyprian Davis, O.S.B., wrote just above his signature on the title page of my now well-worn copy of *The History of Black Catholics in the United States*. True to his historian's craft, Father Cyprian included the date, "2007." The inscription and signature appear in three lines of elegant calligraphic print with the tail of history's "y" reaching out but not quite touching the ascending middle line in hope's "e." That visual space between history and hope seems somehow emblematic of the story of black Catholics, which in Father Cyprian's telling, is as elegant as the inscription he chose to commend his book.

The History of Black Catholics in the United States is an amazing witness to hope and more. Since its publication in 1990, I have read it with students every time I teach a course related to the history of U.S. Catholicism, and that is a lot. Like most of my students, I had little awareness of a black Catholic community in the United States. My first introduction to it came at the University of Notre Dame (I was a faculty member at St. Mary's College across the street) where Father Cyprian presented his work-in-progress, detailing how he combed colonial baptismal records to locate family names of community members. The power in the completed narrative often seems palpable in our class discussions—the power of the faith and faithfulness of black Catholics in a church whose words and actions too often reinforce the racism endemic in American society.

None other than John Tracy Ellis, the dean among twentieth-century historians of American Catholicism, had previously told Davis such a history was impossible. Sources did not exist. Davis proved him wrong. His concluding sentences of the final chapter are his rejoinder. "Too long have black Catholics been anonymous. It is now clear that they can be identified, that their presence has made an impact, and that their contributions have made Catholicism a unique and stronger body" (p. 259). Yes! Thank you, Father Cyprian! Your long labor of love makes those contributions quite clear.

Davis challenges black Catholic anonymity with the preface's opening paragraph where readers encounter a "nameless black teenager," a slave in sixth-century Carthage, whose Catholic owner had enrolled him in the catechumenate. The young man received baptism despite an illness that left him paralyzed, unable to speak his assent as he entered the waters of resurrected life. He died shortly thereafter. This unnamed young black man stands as the principal witness in a theological treatise on "the power of baptism and solidarity with the church" (pp. ix-x). Father Cyprian then tells us "this book is about him" (p. x) and describes his "task" as a historian "to make the past speak, to highlight what has been hidden, and to retrieve a mislaid memory." As a historical theologian, I say, "Yes! Of course! That is why I got into this work!" Every time I read that near perfect description of the historian's vocation, I am moved, inspired, and not a little intimidated.

Father Cyprian then continues to display his enormous historical skills in so many ways. I share with my students how Father Cyprian's work taught me about writing histories of those "too long . . . anonymous." I put this complex task perhaps too simply: one can write a history from the vantage point of what has been done to a community, for a community, or by a community. Davis certainly does all three but his major emphasis is on that last preposition, what has been done individually and collectively by black Catholics in the United States. His first chapter, "African Roots," lays the historical foundation with its first sentence: "All black history begins in Africa." This opening line surprised me when I first read it and continues to surprise most of my students. They, like me, expect a history of Black Catholics in the United States to begin with Africans' forced migration and enslavement. Now it seems so obvious to me that the black

Catholic community's history must begin with Christianity's beginnings. Davis not only demonstrates that black Catholics' history begins in Africa but that Catholic origins have their deepest roots in faith among Africans, beginning with Philip's baptism of the unnamed Ethiopian eunuch whose conversion precedes even Paul's, not to mention the God-fearer, Cornelius.

Davis certainly lays bare the sins of racism within the Catholic Church, particularly in the U.S. He does so in the spirit of true charity so aptly described in Matthew 18:15: "If your brother [or sister] sins [against you], go and tell him [or her]…." Davis has much to tell, and in the telling prepares the reader to learn the central story, the existence of a thriving black Catholic community in the Americas from colonial times to the present. Chapter titles illustrate Davis's emphases. A sampling will have to suffice here—"Christ's Image in Black: The Black Catholic Community before the Civil War"; "Builders of Faith: Black Religious Women before and after the Civil War"; "Shepherds with Black Skins: The First African American Catholic Priests"; "'A Humble Experiment . . . An Entering Wedge': The Emergence of the Black Catholic Laity"; and "Black and Catholic: A Testimony of Faith."

Each chapter details episodes that move between inspiring and disheartening. I never tire of reading Davis's account of a precious discovery—every historian's dream. In the Sulpician Archives, he came across "a small notebook, 8" x 6 ½,'" the oldest extant written record (1843) of a black Catholic organization, "the Society of Colored People." Sadly, the 270-member society was short-lived when, in 1845, their meeting space was given to another group (non-black)—a variant of that story line appears at regular intervals throughout the book. Reading the chapters dedicated to "Black Women Religious" and "The First African American Priests" evokes wonder in me about the faith-inspired tenacity of black women and men who pursued their vocations in the face of skepticism and downright hostility. Davis also acknowledges support from non-black clerics, like the Bavarian Redemptorist, Thaddeus Anwander, who knelt before Baltimore's Archbishop begging permission to serve as spiritual director of Baltimore's Oblate Sisters of Providence and thus ensuring the community's survival then and, as a consequence, now.

Father Cyprian includes those who met with less enduring success, like the remarkable Mathilda Beasley. Her marriage brought her to Savannah,

Georgia, where she "risked imprisonment by instructing black children, slave and free, in antebellum Savannah." Using some extant letters, Davis then pieces together her efforts, after her husband's death, to found a community of Franciscan sisters. Having little ecclesial support, her small community and its orphanage were eventually suppressed. Davis offers a judgment whose standards are drawn from the heart of the gospel. "By all accounts the work of Mother Mathilda Beasley was a failure. Her foundation did not succeed. Yet the witness of her life . . . leave[s] one with the impression that here was a woman of extraordinary faith. She has earned an honored position in the history of African American religious women" (p. 114). His subsequent remarks on black sisters' communities emphasize their "witness to the existence of a vigorous black Catholic community even prior to the Civil War. Vocations come from a community, from a milieu in which faith is shared and spiritual values passed on" (p. 114). His concluding remarks offer more than historical perspective; they provide a challenging theological standard for judging the vitality of any Catholic community.

I could enumerate many more inspiring examples from Father Cyprian Davis's *The History of Black Catholics in the United States*, but I will allow those who have not read it the pleasure of discovery for themselves. Yet, I need to convey what else this book has taught me. It is by far the most important treatise on ecclesiology that I have ever read. I thought long and hard before writing the preceding sentence, not out of fear of offending ecclesiologists, but black Catholics, who might find this claim as one more attempt to reduce their community to anonymity under the broad heading, "Catholic church." That is far from my intent, and I hope not the end result. In his account of the courageous fidelity of black Catholics in the United States, Father Cyprian displays the reality of Christ's Mystical Body. It is the particularities of these black Catholic lives individually and collectively that matter here. Their words and deeds testify to the church's sacramental life as real and empowering as well as its too frequent failure to be the truly "Catholic Church" it professes to be.

One example must suffice. Beginning in 1889 and through the nineteenth century's end, black Catholic laymen, leaders in their local faith communities, held five national meetings. In the fourth black Catholic congress, convened in Chicago, 1893, eight participants signed a final written statement. Addressed to all Catholics, the statement called the church to task, clearly denouncing discrimination within the faith community and demanding greater commitment from the church to its social mission. Their reasoning is thoroughly ecclesiological. "With thorough confidence in the rectitude of our course in the enduring love of Mother Church, and the consciousness of our priesthood, we show our devotion to the Church, our jealousy of her glory and our love for her history" (p. 189).

Perhaps, Father Cyprian had this statement in mind when he wrote: "That our history bring hope." Appealing to the virtue of hope seems apt when one recalls that Thomas Aquinas in the Summa identifies hope's object as "a future good, difficult but possible to attain." Father Cyprian's *The History of Black Catholics in the United States* testifies that hope is indeed an audacious virtue, a gift from God ever-present in that space between our history and our hope.

History of the Council of Trent (translated by Ernest Graf, 2 vols., London: Thomas Nelson, 1957-1961) by Hubert Jedin

A New Orientation for Church History

Massimo FAGGIOLI, *University of St. Thomas*

When I was working with a colleague on a small book on the sources for the research on the Second Vatican Council (Massimo Faggioli – Giovanni Turbanti, *Il concilio inedito. Fonti del Vaticano II*, Bologna 2001), Giuseppe Alberigo, the general editor of the *History of Vatican II*, the five-volume standard work for the most important Catholic theological event after Trent, managed to convince a young doctoral student (it was back in 2000-2001, in the Bologna Institute that was much inspired by German historiographical and theological tradition) that a small book on the sources was the way Hubert Jedin started his own volumes on the history of the Council of Trent.

The last of the four-volume *History of the Council of Trent* by Hubert Jedin (1900-1980) was published 40 years ago and it is still one of the most important works of Church history published in the 20th century. Jedin's work was given new light by the more recent (2013) and brilliant book by John O'Malley, *Trent. What Happened at the Council*. O'Malley reminded us not only of the importance of Trent to understand Vatican II and Catholicism today, but also that only the first two volumes of that prodigious work have been translated into English (Hubert Jedin, *A History of the Council of Trent*, translated by Ernest Graf, 2 vols., London: Thomas Nelson, 1957-1961. Original German: *Geschichte des Konzils von Trient*. 4

vols. in 5. Freibur i.Br.: Herder, 1949-1975). True, Jedin's work was difficult to translate into other languages (all four volumes were translated into Italian, but not one volume was ever translated into French), also because of the sheer number of pages (more than 2,700 pages). It is nevertheless one of the paradigm-changing works in Catholic historiography ever. All historians of modern Catholicism are indebted to Jedin.

The first of the four volumes, published in the early days of post-war Germany, in 1949, (opens with a most audacious *incipit* for a series of volumes focused already on a big event: an entire volume on the pre-history of Trent, introducing what Jedin called "the victory of the papacy over the councils" of the 15th century. The Catholic historian Jedin was breaking a taboo very much present in Catholic culture in the mid-20th century (still trying to figure out the implications of the definitions of the papacy approved by Vatican I in 1870) about the relations between the papacy, conciliarism, and the conciliar tradition itself. Jedin explained the difficult and uneasy relationship between the pope and the bishops gathered in a council not in terms of theological necessity, but in historical terms and with a sense of historical development. For Jedin, the Council of Trent (1545-1563), the most defining moment of early modern Catholicism, did not stand alone in Church history, but was part of the long and tense history of the Catholic Church, and especially of Catholic ecclesiology. In a sense, it was the result of the end of 15th-century conciliarism. The second part of the first volume addresses the history of the attempts to call the council after Martin Luther's call for Church reform that eventually became the Protestant Reformation. Volume one ends with a chapter devoted to the opening of the council at Trent with just a handful of council fathers—25 bishops and 5 superiors of religious orders, just a tiny minority within the Catholic episcopate, not at all representative of what back then was the Catholic world.

Volume two (published eight years after the first one, in 1957) focuses on the first session (1545-1547) and the transfer of the council south of Trent, that is to Bologna; a period with key debates on justification, original sin, the number of the sacraments, and the decision on the obligation for bishops to reside in their dioceses. Volume three (published in 1970) analyzes the sessions in Bologna (1547-1548) and the second period in Trent (1551-1552), which solidified the fracture between Rome and the Protestant reformers. Volume four, parts I and II (published in 1975) is about the last period at Trent with the debates on ordination, the Eucharist, indulgences, the saints, and the role of images in devotional practices. In the conclusion of the work Jedin analyzes the last three sessions (including session XXIV, with the deliberations on the decree on marriage) and draws a final assessment of the contributions made by the most important event in the history of Catholic theology and culture between the 16th and the 19th century.

Jedin's "opus magnum" on the history of Trent is indeed one of the monuments of Catholic historiography, and in a sense the highest moment in 20th-century historiography of the councils of the Church. Jedin was the most important historian in a Church that after World War II—but still before Vatican II—was finally accepting the historical-critical method as the approach necessary to understand the Church as a historical subject, and in a Church slowly coming to terms with the limits of conceiving Church history still in theological terms, as a "sacred history." Jedin's *History of the Council of Trent* was indeed the culmination of his historiographical contribution that changed the way Catholic historians would look at their profession: abandonment of a strictly confessional and apologetic historiography, the awareness of the limits of the historiographical positivism strictly limited to the publication of sources, and the claim of new spaces opened up by the end of the persecution of "modernists" in the early 20th century. This shift was made possible in Jedin by his important teachers and intellectual references in Germany (Joseph Wittig, Leopold von Ranke, Sebastian Merkle, and Albert Ehrhard), his contemporary colleagues in Italy (the philosopher Benedetto Croce and the historian of heretics Delio Cantimori), and his encounters with the characters and historical events that emerged from the pages of history, starting with Girolamo Seripando, superior general of the Augustinians and a member of the Council of Trent. Jedin's outstanding historiographical contribution was the result of the application of the historical-critical method in the period that followed the liberalization of historical studies with the opening of the Vatican Archives by Leo XIII in 1881, but still characterized by apologetics and theological controversialism. Until Vatican II, Jedin's work was considered not Catholic enough by some guardians of Catholic intellectual orthodoxy.

The decision for Jedin to write a history of the Council of Trent is intimately linked with his path of life. Jedin's mother was Jewish, and that meant for him the withdrawal of the *venia legendi* (permission to teach in German universities) and the banning from state universities in Nazi Germany. That had brought the young lecturer only the poor position of archivist of the diocese of Wroclaw (back then still in Germany, now in Poland after the post-war boundaries). After the *Kristallnacht* of November 9, 1938, it was not safe for Jedin to remain in Nazi Germany. So he decided to return to Rome, where he had lived already, to be the editor of one of the volumes of the prestigious series *Concilium Tridentinum*, the edition of the historical documents of the Council of Trent. On September 1, 1939 the Second World War broke out, and Jedin succeeded, thanks to fortunate circumstances, in reaching Rome with a suitcase full of material he had collected on the history of the Council of Trent. He stayed in Rome during the course of World War II (including the German occupation of Rome) until the liberation of the city by the Allied forces in June, 1944. Jedin kept working—even in those difficult conditions during the war—in the Vatican Archives on his history of the Council of Trent, whose first volume was published in 1949.

Jedin's work gave us—four centuries after the end of the Council of Trent in 1563!—the first reliable and definitive history of the most important event in the history of the Catholic Church between Martin Luther and Vatican II. This four-volume history put an end to the controversies between the two polar opposites dominating Catholic scholarship on Trent until Jedin: the anti-papal and polemical history of the council by the Venetian Paolo Sarpi (published in 1619 and immediately put on the *Index of Prohibited Books*) and the official, apologetic history by the Jesuit Pietro Sforza Pallavicino (published in 1656-1657). That was possible because, as his first step in the work toward the history of the council, Jedin wanted to take a look at the archival sources and their use. This prepatory part of the work, originally conceived as an introduction to the *History*, became a self-standing book published in 1948: *Das Konzil von Trient. Ein Überblick über die Geschichte seiner Erforschung* (*The Council of Trent. Overview of the History of the Research*). Interestingly, Jedin called this little introductory work to the history of Trent "my best book."

The ramifications of Jedin's work go well beyond the field of specialists of Trent and the Tridentine era. If we have the standard *History of Vatican II* directed by Giuseppe Alberigo (1995-2001, in five volumes, published in seven languages, English edition by Joseph Komonchak), it is because there was Jedin's *History of the Council of Trent* before. Not just because Jedin's work was brought to Italy largely by his student Alberigo (1926-2007), but because the approach to Vatican II by the international team of scholars gathered by the so-called (often insultingly) "Bologna school" consciously followed Jedin's methodological choices: a wide-ranging attention paid to many different kinds of sources (official *acta*, diaries, theological treatises, correspondences, political history of the council); the reconstruction of the history of the council starting with the long pre-history; and a historical study of "what happened" without relying on the mantras of the absolute continuity of Church history.

A History of Theology
(Garden City, NY: Doubleday, 1968) by Yves Congar

God Talk in History

Catherine E. CLIFFORD, *St. Paul University (Ottawa)*

I received one of the most important introductions to theology and to the world of one of the great theologians of the twentieth century when I first opened the pages of Yves Congar's *A History of Theology*.[1] It was never a "bestseller" and may not be counted among the major works of the Dominican theologian's impressive collection of writings. Yet it opened the door to a set of questions on the changing role of theology—its ability to reflect upon the experience of God and to speak to contemporary people in every moment of history and in widely divergent social contexts—that have occupied my study and teaching ever since.

I was in a fourth year honors seminar of an undergraduate program, having changed my major to Religious Studies just a year earlier. The program was offered through the collaboration and shared resources of Catholic, Anglican, Mennonite, and United Church colleges. The Mennonite professor chairing the seminar asked me to prepare a presentation that would explain to my classmates—most of whom belonged to other Christian churches—how, since the Second Vatican Council, the Catholic Church could change so much yet remain the same church. Others followed these developments with rapt attention! Not knowing

---

1   Yves M.-J. Congar, *A History of Theology*. Trans. Hunter Guthrie (Garden City, NY: Doubleday, 1968).

quite how to respond to this challenge, I sought advice from one of my Catholic professors, who immediately referred me to *A History of Theology*.

A challenging read, *A History of Theology* is a revised and updated version of an article that Congar had published early in his career (1938-1939) in the *Dictionnaire de théologie catholique*, entitled "Théologie." Congar (1904-1995), a French Catholic priest, was born at the beginning of the last century. He contributed perhaps more than any single theologian of the twentieth century to the study of the church, including its structures and mission, called "ecclesiology." During Vatican II (1962-1965) he served as an expert advisor to several key commissions, making direct and at times significant contributions to the official texts of the council.

In six well-documented chapters, *A History of Theology* examines the changing definitions and approaches of theology through history. It begins from pre-Christian times when theology—a reasoned reflection on God—was a work of the metaphysical philosopher, to the views of early Christian writers, through the scholastic period of the early and High Middle Ages, the sixteenth-century Reformation, and from the Early Modern period to the late twentieth century. Variously understood, theology's methods evolved from the scriptural commentary of the church fathers (*sacra pagina*), to the more systematic and speculative works of the medieval theologians (*sacra doctrina*), and increased specialization in modern times. Readers today will be impressed by the dynamic and continuous evolution of theology. In the wake of Vatican II, Congar noted that "the theological situation, in fact, even the idea of theological endeavor" continued to evolve.

Congar deftly traces the historic shift in Western theology from an approach informed by the philosophical tradition of Aristotle and represented by the works of Albert the Great and Thomas Aquinas in the thirteenth century, to the more positivist system of the Franciscan Duns Scotus at the turn of the fourteenth century. Where Thomas and his followers proposed a distinction and continuity between our knowledge of the world and knowledge of God, Scotus' approach considers the revelation of God as something quite extrinsic to the order of creation, standing in the Augustinian line with St. Bonaventure. These developments, prefigured in the dramatic condemnations of the thought of Aristotle and Averroes at the University of Paris in 1270 and 1277, set the stage for the rise of nominalism and the decline of late medieval theology. His perceptive discussion provides clues to persistent tensions, which continue to manifest themselves in various currents of contemporary theology.

The medieval scholastics, in their quest for a coherent and logical system of thought, unwittingly made theology into an "instrument of specialists" that lost contact with the life of the church and the biblical tradition. In reaction, the sixteenth-century Reformers called for a return to the priority of sacred scripture and a reflection more attuned to the daily struggles of ordinary Christians. In the early Modern period, both Catholicism and Protestantism were influenced by more pietistic movements centered on encounter with Christ. In an age of social upheaval, peasants and the working classes easily identified with the suffering Christ and empathized with his mother. The theological renewal of the twentieth century was driven by the pastoral concern to proclaim the gospel to modern people and informed by a return to the Bible, to the early sources of the liturgy, and to theological insights of the earliest Christian writers.

In every age, theologians are concerned to engage with the intellectual currents of their time, and to inform the living faith of the community of believers as they encounter new questions. The living witness of the church, rooted in the same faith of the first followers of Jesus that is recorded for us in the scriptures, is necessarily transposed into the vernacular of new cultures and engaged in dialogue with new scientific knowledge. The human community changes and develops through history. The church learns from the developments of science and culture, and—with the assistance of God's Spirit—can grow in its understanding of God's revelation. In this way we can speak of "development" in Christian doctrine, which is more than a simple change in the language or expression of faith, but also involves a deeper penetration of the mystery of God and of God's boundless love for humankind.

While *A History of Theology* is not about Vatican II as such, it helped me to understand the council as a moment when the whole Catholic Church undertook a comprehensive self-examination when confronted by the historic social, political, and economic changes that were reshaping the human community. In a desire to proclaim the heart of the gospel message to modern men and women, it sought to update church teaching, governance, liturgy, forms of ordained ministry and vowed religious life, and the witness of the lay faithful. The perspective of history—or what we have come to call "historical consciousness"—led theologians and church leaders to understand that the church has adapted itself to changing social and cultural contexts and to the concrete pastoral needs of the people in every age.

Theology can never content itself to repeat blindly the formulae of the past. It has a critical and creative responsibility to appropriate the wisdom and meaning of faith in ways that will help contemporary people to encounter Christ and live as his disciples. Theology is charged with mediating the good news in ways that might inform the Christian community's response to new challenges and insights as they arise in human history. As a creature of history whose ultimate purpose is to inform the practice of Christian living, nothing escapes theology's concern: economics, questions of social justice, concern for the poor and the marginalized. To accomplish this task it must be in engaged in dialogue with other disciplines.

Over the years I have come to appreciate just how significant and transformative it was to introduce an operative historical mindedness into theological reflection and into the life of the church. The earliest version of *A History of Theology* was penned in the same period that Marie-Dominique Chenu, then Rector of the Dominican house of study, the Saulchoir, where Congar taught, delivered a programmatic lecture. That lecture sparked a controversy that stretched over more than two decades. Speaking on the feast of St. Thomas Aquinas in 1936, Chenu reflected on the historical method that inspired the study and teaching of theology at the Saulchoir,[2] an approach characterized by critics as a *nouvelle théologie*—a dangerous "innovation" and departure from an unchanging tradition. Chenu was largely inspired by the reflection of Thomas Aquinas, who carefully distinguished between the object of faith as such and the expression of faith which is conditioned by a particular cultural context. The Saulchoir taught the works of the "Angelic Doctor" prescribed by Pope Leo XXIII as the model for Catholic theology, but with an approach that was historically minded, not uncritical, and attuned to contemporary pastoral challenges.

---

2   The text of the original lecture was republished in 1985 together with insightful commentary by Giusepppe Alberigo, Étienne Fouilloux, Jean Ladrière and Jean-Pierre Joshua, in: Marie-Dominique Chenu, *Une école de théologie: le Saulchoir* (Paris: Cerf, 1985), 91-176.

In 1938 Chenu was obliged by his religious superiors to subscribe to a number of theses that amounted to a retraction of his reflections, which soon appeared on the index of forbidden works. Shortly after he was removed from his post as Rector and the Saulchoir was closed. Congar escaped censure during this period of the Second World War, when he served as an army chaplain and landed in a prisoner of war camp. But throughout the 1950s he himself would be subject to suspicion, incomprehension, and censure.[3] Who knew that taking history seriously could be so costly, or considered such a dangerous undertaking?

The insights of Congar, Chenu, and many others would only be widely received when John XXIII convened the Second Vatican Council. Pope John saw Christ as the center of history. In the Incarnation Christ entered into human history. The Risen Christ, through the Spirit, continues to act in and through the human community. While there is both good and evil in the world, history is a graced reality and a "the teacher of life" from which the church might learn.[4] Indeed, Pope John XXIII invited the bishops taking part in the Second Vatican Council to assume a renewed sense of responsibility for the mission of the church on what he called the eve of "a new era in the history of the world."[5] These themes are taken up in the council's Pastoral Constitution on the Church in the Modern World, *Gaudium et spes*, where the council calls upon all Christians, and indeed all people of good will, to assume their responsibilities as "artisans and authors of the culture of their community." The vocation of humanity, in an age where we have developed the capacity to shape the world in which we live—dangerously taxing the resources of the earth for future generations—is to act in accord with "our responsibility to our sisters and

---

3 See Thomas O'Meara, "Raid on the Dominicans," *America* (2 May, 1994).
4 John XXIII, "Mother Church Rejoices: Opening Address of John XXIII at the Council [*Gaudet Mater Ecclesia*, October 11, 1962]," in *Council Daybook: Vatican II, Sessions 1 and 2*, Floyd Anderson, ed. (The National Catholic Welfare Conference: 1965); also at http://conciliaria.com/2012/10/mother-church-rejoices-opening-address-of-john-xxiii-at-the-council/#more-2134.
5 John XXIII, "Pope's Address to the World Month before Council Opens [Radio Address of September 11, 1962]," in *Council Daybook, Sessions I and II*; also at http://conciliaria.com/2012/09/popes-address-to-world-month-before-council-opens/.

brothers and to history" (#55). Today, the task of theology continues to be to reflect on that responsibility in the light of the Gospel.

Reading *The History of Theology* opened up a door into the world of theology. It led me to Congar's other ground-breaking works—*Divided Christendom* (1937), *Lay People in the Church* (1950), *True and False Reform in the Church* (1953), *Tradition and Traditions* (1960-63)—and his many studies in ecclesiology. His example of persistent hard work in the face of great adversity and censure spoke to me of how the service of theology is sometimes met with great incomprehension. Shedding light on the hard truths of history and pointing up the way to conversion brings the cross. When I am tempted to be impatient with the slow pace of progress, it is helpful to take the long view of history. Stepping back helps to bring things into perspective, to discern the movements of God's Spirit.

That first challenging conversation as an undergraduate student was the beginning of a long apprenticeship in the habits of dialogue. I have discovered many more ecumenical companions along the way. More than conversation partners, they are fellow pilgrims from whom I have received much. The men and women with whom I had the privilege to study through my years of graduate school helped me to cultivate a passion for the church. Not because it is a perfect community, but precisely because the Spirit of God continues to work through this rag-tag gathering of humanity, with all of its failings and weakness. I strive to instill in my students today that same sense of confidence in the God of history and a love for the diversity of spiritual gifts that nourish and enrich God's pilgrim people.

The Imperative of Responsibility (University of Chicago Press, 1984) by Hans Jonas

Human Responsibility: The New Challenges

John T. PAWLIKOWSKI, *OSM, Catholic Theological Union*

As an emerging academician in 1972 I participated in a one-time gathering of learned societies of religion. That experience left a lasting impact on me as a person as well as on my future scholarship, largely because of the powerful keynote address delivered by Hans Jonas. Jonas, a refugee from Hitler's Germany, was then associated with the New School for Social Research in New York. Ethnically Jewish, but secular in terms of belief, Jonas' scholarly contributions focused primarily on developing a philosophically grounded ethic for the technological world of our generation and beyond. He also wrote on the significance of the Nazi Holocaust though he did not do much to relate these two areas of his concern. His best-known book, which is in effect a collection of essays written over a period of years beginning in 1959, remains *The Imperative of Responsibility.*

As I sat and listened to Jonas make the presentation, which basically serves as the opening section of this volume, my horizons were expanded and my sense of what is required of me as part of contemporary humanity and the rest of creation was enhanced in a way that had never occurred before or since.

Early on in his speech Jonas uttered a sentence that has become permanently implanted in my consciousness: "We are the first generation forced to ask the question whether there will be future generations." Never had I been confronted in such a dramatic fashion about the condition of the creation in which I shared as a human person. Never had I understood the depth of responsibility that I and the people of my generation now shared for the survival of planet earth and the life it sustains. I came to realize that many of the justice issues with which I had already been engaged, such as racism, economic justice and human rights, while still critical in their own way, nonetheless relinquished their primacy in the face of the challenge of creational sustainability. Even if we might prove successful in addressing these particular issues, such success would prove ultimately meaningless if we failed to take the immense steps necessary to preserve the life-giving capacity of the air and the water that surround and sustain us. In short, we will all be dead.

Jonas' Los Angeles address basically became chapter one in *The Imperative of Responsibility*. His argument begins with an analysis of the significant change in the nature of human action in the modern world. Prior to the onset of modernity human action was perceived as having a *neutral* relationship with the rest of creation. Humanity's actions in relation to nature were not deemed to be ethically significant. Ethics only came into play in the sphere of inter-human activities. In part this was due to a mistaken belief that human actions involving the natural world had no negative impact on that world.

For Jonas all traditional ethics was anthropocentrically grounded. They only affected people's relationship with themselves and with other human persons. And even within the human sphere ethics pertained largely to the immediate effects of a particular human activity. Discussions about ethics were basically focused on the impact of the activity as it was taking place. There was little or no consciousness of more remote effects of human conduct nor of possible future consequences of present-day activity. Or if future results were raised, they were relegated to chance, fate or providence—areas beyond human control and therefore beyond ethical discernment.

The operative maxims that guided and evaluated human behavior, such as "Love your neighbor as yourself," "Do unto others as you would wish them to do unto you," or "Subordinate your individual good to the common good" all reflect a concern with the impact of an action in the process of its actual occurrence. It is those presently alive and in some relationship with the doer of a deed who must be considered from an ethical perspective. In order to apply such a perspective some knowledge was required. But it was not technical or scientific knowledge, according to Jonas, but rather the knowledge of a kind readily available to a human person, the type of knowledge described by Immanuel Kant. And even in more sophisticated ethical discussions, such as those found in the writings of Aristotle, there is no need to probe the "science of things" in the process of coming to ethical conclusions.

For Jonas the extended implications of human action in a specific time constitute the most crucial dimension of the new ethical challenge. Ethics must become part of the fabric of the future as well as of the present. In the past no one was responsible for the long-term consequences of a particular act. While the particular act might in fact be well-intentioned, well considered and well performed from an ethical perspective in its time, down the road it may in fact produce disastrous results. This is especially the case with regard to acts that impact the world of nature. Hence the need today for an ethic that breaks through the immediacy of human action and creates moral criteria for far-reaching consequences. It is a challenge that no previous generation had to confront to the same degree as those of us living today.

In responding to the new ethical challenge, Jonas describes key components of the transformation of human consciousness that needs to be realized in our day. The sphere of "neighbor ethics" still commands importance today. But it must be incorporated into a wider ethical perspective that guides the cumulative effects of actions by the global community as a whole. These "cumulative effects" often take on a power unknown in the more proximate sphere of human activity, and hence, generate a level of human responsibility well beyond what previous generations were able to conceive.

The first of the new components of human responsibility for the present and the future is the recognition that humanity now has the capacity to alter nature itself. Nature is no longer seen as a static reality but as something that can be changed. Here Jonas stands very close to another writer of the same era, Victor Ferkiss, who in his 1974 volume *The Future of Technological Civilization* put the contemporary challenge to humankind in these words: "Man has achieved virtually godlike powers over himself, his society, and his physical environment. As a result of his scientific and technological achievements, he has the power to alter or destroy both the human race and its physical habitat" (p. 88). For Jonas and Ferkiss, as a result of the development of technology, human action has undergone a profound redefinition. The overall impact of many individual human acts in many different places on the biosphere has emerged as a prime ethical concern, for which previous classical ethics provides little or no answer.

Jonas then goes on to detail some of the profoundly new aspects of moral responsibility today. The first is the "vulnerability of nature" in the face of human technological capacity. The nature and extent of human action has changed. The human community through technology can now impact the entire biosphere. We have acquired new powers over the natural world that no previous generation could ever imagine. As a result, the extent of our moral responsibility has grown exponentially. As scientific research began to reveal even in the seventies, when Jonas issued this warning, human action has the ability to destroy the sustainability of the planet, a possibility that has been raised to a level of near probability over the decades since Jonas' address.

Secondly, contemporary ethics must begin to take the importance of knowledge far more seriously than in the past. Jonas acknowledges that we face an unprecedented challenge in this regard. It will prove increasingly difficult to acquire and integrate the scope of the knowledge required for the exercise of moral responsibility in our time, because it must include an element of prediction as to the ultimate impact of human action on a global scale, both now and in the far-off future, including the possible extinction of the human community. We have acquired an urgent need for a new conception of rights and duties for which there is little grounding in classical metaphysics.

Jonas confessed in his lecture that the view he was presenting still was rooted in an anthropologically-centered perspective on creation. But he did go beyond this to some extent by at least raising the issue of whether it is legitimate to speak of "rights" in terms of the rest of creation. He said in 1972 that it was important to begin asking whether ethics can remain anthropologically centered in an exclusive way or whether we must begin to reflect on moral obligation towards the entire biosphere. Has the entire biosphere now become a "human trust" not merely for our ulterior sake, but for its own and in its own right? Should this prove to be the case, though Jonas was not quite prepared in 1972 to commit to such an understanding, it would demand considerable rethinking of basic ethical principles. It would mean to seek not only the human good in our actions but also the good of extrahuman reality. The so-called "ends of human action" would need to expand beyond the human sphere and embrace all of creation. No previous ethics, and certainly not the dominant, scientific view of nature, has adequately prepared us for such an expanded vision.

Re-reading Jonas' 1972 address reminds me again of why I was so captivated by its original presentation. Jonas saw far more clearly than most that humanity had moved into a profoundly new situation in terms of moral responsibility. Ethics today needs to take on a global, even a planetary, dimension. So the starting point for ethical reflection today is quite unlike what is was in the past. And though Jonas remained uncertain as to how far our current starting point must move beyond the human to include all forms of creation, he at least opened the door for a deep-seated discussion in this regard. That discussion has now led to a widely accepted notion of an integrated web of creation, even though consensus has not been achieved as to whether such an affirmation of the web of creation entails the rejection of any notion of a pyramid in creation. I for one would not totally dismantle the pyramid in the manner of some associated with groups such as the animal liberation movement, in part because the human part of creation carries a special moral responsibility for creational survival not shared by the rest of creation.

As I indicated previously, Jonas addressed the question of moral responsibility on a global scale as a secular Jew. He never really discussed the question whether the classical religious traditions were so mired in a non-global, non-futuristic framework that it rendered them useless in terms of creating a base for the new expansive understanding of moral responsibility. That was largely the contention of a pioneer in the religious community on the ecological challenge, the late Thomas Berry, C.P. Jonas' Jewishness came through primarily in his writings on the Holocaust, though he never really brought this analysis to bear on his perspective on moral responsibility in the new global and technological age. In my judgment, Jonas missed an important opportunity here, because the Holocaust raises some of the same issues regarding the scope of moral responsibility in our time in light of greatly enhanced technological power. I also believe we must probe further whether the classical religious traditions can in fact still be mined as part of a constructive framework for contemporary moral responsibility.

Jonas set me on an entirely new path as an ethicist grappling with the meaning of moral responsibility. There is no possibility of moving backwards on this path if creational survivability is to be assured. For that I am forever grateful.

Infections and Inequalities: The Modern Plagues (Berkeley: University of California Press, 1999) by Dr. Paul Farmer

Personal Responsibility Must Be Combined with Social Responsibility

Emily REIMER-BARRY *(University of San Diego)*

I grew up very comfortable talking about sickness and health. My father is a physician and I have warm memories of seeing him working at the hospital. On special Sundays, my Mom would take my three siblings and me to church. Then we would go eat lunch with my Dad in the hospital cafeteria. Looking back, I realize now that it was because my father was *working on a Sunday*. But at the time, I remember thinking it was really neat to carry my own cafeteria tray and make my way to our family's favorite Sunday brunch spot: the round table in the corner of the hospital cafeteria. If we ate everything on our plate, we could even have Jello for dessert.

The older I got, the more I enjoyed talking to my father about his work. He'd share cases with us. I noticed that when family members or friends' relatives were sick, my dad was often asked to give advice or to check up on the patient in the hospital. At home, my dad encouraged us to take good care of ourselves: healthy food, daily exercise, no smoking, and absolutely no motorcycle rides. My dad saw a lot of people who were sick or injured because they didn't make good choices. He wanted his children to learn from his experiences treating those patients. Every case study had a clear moral lesson: don't dive into water unless you know how deep it is; don't do drugs; don't drink and drive; be careful on ladders; don't swallow magnets; and always have health insurance.

I grew up with my moral compass focused on personal responsibility. I felt a sense of control over my life choices, not only because of my family's value system but also because of the privileges I experienced as white and wealthy. At the same time, my parents taught us the importance of helping those less fortunate. My parents gave to charities. They participated in school fundraisers. And we always donated toys at Christmas to a poor family so that their kids could have a fun Christmas too.

When I learned about liberation theology—first as an undergraduate student at the University of Notre Dame and then as a graduate student at Weston Jesuit School of Theology—my worldview shifted in considerable ways. I continued to feel grateful for my hard-working parents and the values they instilled in me. But I also began to think critically about the world we inhabit. Why did my family have a room full of presents to open on Christmas morning, while other families did not? My father's advice of "never let your health insurance lapse" is good advice, but impossible to follow if you simply cannot afford health insurance. To my parents' emphasis on personal responsibility and the importance of helping the less fortunate, liberation theologians added the necessity of social responsibility and solidarity with the poor. The person who has most influenced my thinking on liberation theology is not a theologian at all. He is a physician, medical anthropologist, and co-founder of Partners in Health. His name is Dr. Paul Farmer.

For more than three decades, Dr. Paul Farmer has argued that health care is a human right. Drawing on liberation theology, Farmer explains that he is "on the side of the poor." But he doesn't just write about liberation theology. He lives it.

Farmer grew up in a working class family, the second of six children. Tracy Kidder describes Farmer's unusual upbringing in his 2004 biography, *Mountains Beyond Mountains: The Quest of Dr. Paul Farmer, A Man Who Would Cure the World*, noting how his family lived in Florida when he was young, first in a campground and then in a houseboat. Farmer earned a full scholarship to Duke University and earned his MD/PhD from Harvard.

He practices medicine both in Boston and in Haiti. He also travels frequently for lectures, conferences, and health care advocacy with Partners in Health, whose mission is to provide a preferential option for the poor in health care. Farmer's impact on global health has been enormous.

Farmer grew up Catholic, and Kidder describes how Farmer received the sacraments through Confirmation, but still did not feel engaged in church life as a boy and teenager. It was his encounter with Catholic nuns advocating for the rights of migrant workers that first drew him to the radical side of Catholicism's social justice teachings. Sister Julianna DeWolf, working with the Friends of the United Farm Workers, introduced Farmer to Haitian farmworkers on plantations in North Carolina. Farmer's curiosity was stoked. He began to read more liberation theology and traveled to Haiti to understand the plight of the poor. Eventually, Haiti became home.

I was drawn to Farmer's writings because of his passion for justice coupled with his irreverent attitude—which, as an undergraduate and then a graduate student, I found strangely liberating. For example, Kidder describes a conversation with Farmer about faith:

> "He would say, some years later, that he had 'faith,' then add, 'I also have faith in penicillin, rifampin, isoniazid, and the good absorption of the fluoroquinolones, in bench science, clinical trials, scientific progress, that HIV is the cause of every case of AIDS, that the rich oppress the poor, that wealth is flowing in the wrong direction, that this will cause more epidemics and kill millions. I have faith that those things are true, too. So if I had to choose between lib[eration] theo[logy], or any [-]ology, I would go with science as long as service to the poor went along with it. But I don't have to make that choice, do I?'" (pp. 85-86)

With regard to the church's teaching authority, Kidder notes Farmer's frustration with teachings that disregard solid public health strategies: "I'm still looking for something in the sacred texts that says 'Thou shalt not use condoms,'" Farmer told Kidder. Farmer focuses on the praxis of faith, not particular church teachings. Kidder explains that Farmer could have had a life of financial security, stability, and safety, teaching Harvard students and treating patients in wealthy US hospitals. But he felt his calling was to accompany the poorest of the poor and to bring excellent health care to them. His many books and articles provide an opportunity for him to share this vocation with readers. The book that had the most influence on my life is *Infections and Inequalities: The Modern Plagues.*

Infections and Inequalities: The Modern Plagues was published in 1999. I read it shortly after. I was a graduate student at Weston Jesuit School of Theology in Cambridge, Mass. Farmer's writing brought together a passion for justice, a method of listening to the poor through ethnography, and an interdisciplinary approach to understanding and solving problems. These ideas challenged me, inspired me, and shaped the direction of my doctoral work.

Infections and Inequalities focused on Ebola, Tuberculosis, and HIV. It demonstrates the blindness of a methodology that studies these epidemics solely from the perspective of infectious agents (be they viral or bacterial), without also studying the social inequalities that fuel the epidemics among human populations. Farmer tacks back and forth between the microscopic levels and the transnational levels. This is done in order to surface key questions about how to achieve universal access to health care and the goods necessary for each person to thrive. In what follows, I will offer an overview of the key themes of the book, showing how Farmer adopts a social lens for understanding disease, critiques practitioners' "immodest claims of causality," speaks with outrage at the "stupid deaths" people of privilege too often tolerate or ignore, and utilizes ethnography to help readers understand the life experiences of ordinary people who suffer from systemic injustices.

Understanding Disease through a Social Lens

A key theme in Farmer's writing is that diseases do not act "randomly." In *Infections and Inequalities*, Farmer explains that the 1976 outbreak of Ebola in Sudan "was anything but random." Contamination resulted from improper sterilization of syringes in a mission hospital and because social inequalities shaped the contours of the epidemic. Wealthy expatriates did not seek care in the same health care facilities and thus were not "at risk" to the same degree as poor refugees. Similarly, Farmer explained, "HIV has spread across the globe, often wildly but never randomly. Like tuberculosis, HIV is entrenching itself in the ranks of the poor and marginalized."

"Immodest Claims of Causality"

Farmer describes how the poor bear a disproportionate burden of disease in every context.

Farmer is not afraid to challenge powerful groups or to rebuke scholars for their "immodest claims of causality." He is critical of physicians who blame patients for their "noncompliance" when patients could not afford to eat, purchase medicines, or travel back to the clinic for follow-up care. Through descriptions of his work with particular patients and their life stories, Farmer helps the reader to see the complex threats that face the poor. In such cases, good medicine is important. But so are food, shelter, employment opportunities, and education. In Farmer's practice of medicine, he sees each patient in his or her full context. Instead of blaming a poor patient for being hungry and therefore "noncompliant," Farmer would assign blame to the structural forces that prevent that person from being able to have enough to eat. Farmer sometimes describes these broadly—poverty, gender inequalities, the legacy of chattel slavery or colonial power. But sometimes his blame is more direct: the Péligre Hydroelectric Dam in Haiti becomes a recurring symbol of corporate self-interest, government mismanagement, and the failure to protect the well-being of the families who used to live in the valley that was flooded.

"Stupid Deaths"

Farmer is an outspoken critic of those who argue that it is not "cost effective" to treat some patients. When someone dies of a curable illness, Farmer calls this a "stupid death." The problem, he says, is not that we don't have effective treatments. In the cases of tuberculosis and HIV, we do have effective treatments. But not everyone has *access* to those effective therapies. With regard to multi-drug resistant tuberculosis, Farmer argued in *Infections and Inequalities* that with the right design and implementation, it would be possible even in resource-constrained settings, to effectively treat multi-drug resistant tuberculosis. In chapter eight, Farmer describes in detail the Proje Veye Sante case study, in which two tuberculosis control programs were implemented side by side. Both offered medical treatments, but one of them also offered nutritional assistance, close follow-up by community health workers, including home visits, and payment of travel expenses for clinic appointments. The group who received the extra supplements and assistance had a cure rate of 100%, compared to the other group's cure rate of 48%. Farmer concluded that their project "suggests that high cure rates are possible in settings of extreme poverty in which hospital-based care is unavailable even for the critically ill." Farmer argues that "health policy is not a zero sum game." We do not need to choose between prevention and treatment. We must figure out how to do both. And he remains optimistic about that possibility, even as he documents his criticisms of the status quo.

The Importance of Listening

Farmer's use of ethnography and storytelling was particularly effective in *Infections and Inequalities*. In order to introduce readers to the issues at the heart of the book, Farmer tells the life stories of his patients. Borrowing a term from liberation theology, Farmer asks, "Who are these throwaway people?" As he tells the stories of Jean Dubuisson, Corina Bayona, and Calvin Loach, he contextualizes their experiences of tuberculosis by explaining their medical histories, family experiences, and the social forces that constrained their behaviors (the Péligre Dam in Haiti, flawed World Bank and IMF policies imposed on Peru, and the treatment of Vietnam veterans and people of color in the US). For Farmer, listening is a gateway into understanding the complex social worlds we inhabit. But listening alone will not solve his patients' problems. Listening must become an opportunity for conversion and action. Farmer calls this a move towards "pragmatic solidarity," which means listening to understand the burdens a patient labors under (e.g. hunger, bad harvests, leaky roofs, dirt floors), and attending to those problems. And, on top of that, seeking increased support to deliver the best possible therapies to every patient, even the poorest ones.

Infections and Inequalities raises moral questions about the way our world is structured and proposes health care solutions rooted in the claim that all persons have inherent human dignity and should have access to good medical care. Since the book was published, there have been some important gains in global health. New cases of HIV have fallen by more than 35% since the publication of *Infections and Inequalities*. But there have been significant challenges as well. The 2010 earthquake in Haiti, itself devastating, was made worse by a cholera epidemic that killed over 8,000 people. A new outbreak of Ebola in West Africa killed over 11,000 people before the World Health Organization declared Sierra Leone, Guinea, and Liberia to be Ebola-free in 2016.

From Farmer, I learned to ask big questions, to choose terminology carefully, to get the data, and to listen to and partner with the most marginalized. I chose to focus my doctoral research on women's experiences of HIV and AIDS in part because of the influence of Farmer's writings on my worldview. As a graduate student in Chicago, I worked at a social service agency on the north side of the city. There I came to understand the particularities of the HIV epidemic in Chicago through the people I met there. Many of them seemed to me to be doing the best they could in very difficult circumstances. *Infections and Inequalities* challenged me to recognize my own privileges and my own complicity in structural injustices, even as it also rejected "public health nihilism." In Farmer's writing I saw pragmatic and hopeful solutions to thorny complex problems. I saw the importance of ethnography in understanding social problems and in enabling readers to step into the shoes of another person and understand reality from another's perspective.

I have also enjoyed assigning Farmer's writings in some of my classes (most recently, in my HIV/AIDS and Christian Ethics class, and in my Christian Changemakers class). For over a decade, the writings of Paul Farmer have provided my students with examples of how to apply Catholic social teachings in the real world, without losing hope. His story also raises hard questions about self-sacrifice and the cost of discipleship. Readers of Tracy Kidder's biography of Farmer, *Mountains Beyond Mountains,* have to wrestle with the personal cost of Farmer's vocation to serve the poorest of the poor. Speaking personally, I find that every time I encounter his story I am invited to more deeply reflect on my own deepest values and my desire for a comfortable middle-class life. Can I really say that I am "in solidarity with the poor" when I am so well-fed, well-educated, well-connected? I am deeply appreciative, not only of Farmer's persuasive books, but also of the example of his life and how he continues to model what it means to serve the poor.

The Interior Castle
(tran. by Kieran Kavanaugh and Otilio Rodriguez, Mahwah, NJ: Paulist Press, 1979)
by Teresa of Avila

Discovering Teresa's God

Gillian T. W. AHLGREN, *Xavier University*

My "Take and Read" came from the hands of a favorite professor, just after I had finished my first course in church history. "Gillian," Grover Zinn said, placing a book in my hands, "you have to read this."

I was 19 years old, and I had been led to Grover soon after my first trip to Europe. That trip had been unexpected: a wonderful and thoroughly surprising odyssey that had taken me into the ethereal landscapes of the Benedictine monastery of Montserrat, Spain and then into the inner world of the choir sculptures and stained glass windows of the cathedral of Chartres. If God had ever wanted to capture the imagination of a young woman, that would have been the way. And now Professor Zinn, a specialist in the Christian mystical tradition, was handing her Teresa of Avila's *Interior Castle* after introducing her to a host of writers, all calling us to take life-giving relationship with God seriously, and the texts they had left behind: Antony and the desert dwellers, Bernard of Clairvaux's *On Loving God*, Bonaventure's *Soul's Journey into God*, Julian of Norwich's *Showings*. The road had been well paved.

As I lost myself in its pages, I was fascinated by both the inner landscapes that Teresa opened up and the navigational tools she offered in the complex journey toward the God who dwells within us. I was stunned by her capacity to speak, through *her* experience, to me. And I found it impossible not to try to locate myself in one of the seven stages she described on the journey toward union with God: Where was I? Teresa spoke to an unarticulated aspiration of mine: not just to *seek* God, but to *find* God and to be *found.*

For over 30 years now, I have taught and been taught by Teresa and her *Interior Castle*. And I have been taught not only by the content of the book but also by how the book touches and impacts people around me, by what they bring to the book and how their experience informs a continuing conversation about God, about the human journey, about growth as human persons, and even about the "new and universal solidarity" that Pope Francis recently called for in his *Laudato Si': On Care for Our Common Home*. In this reflection, I will try to capture some of these moments of encounter and describe the ways that this text and its reader(s) have made their way into my life.

I first read the text in English, of course. In fact, in that first moment of encounter, at age 19, I had just one year of Spanish under my belt, and was about to begin Spanish composition. Learning of my interest in Teresa and Spanish mysticism more generally, my Spanish professor introduced me to the poetry of John of the Cross, and helped me to see, at the outset of my journey into the Spanish language, the profound literary and linguistic impact of Teresa and John for Spanish-speaking peoples. I spent my senior year in college working through Teresa's corpus in Spanish and writing an honors thesis on how she used metaphors to communicate her experience of God. While my initial effort at capturing what Teresa accomplished in the *Interior Castle* was inelegant at best and reflected the typical clumsiness of undergraduate thinking, the process of research and writing convinced me that I belonged in the academy, and, although I didn't entirely know it at the time, a theological writer was slowly being born. I had no language for this yet, but I think that, even then, I sensed that Teresa was doing far more than simply relating to her readers her *experience* of God; she was teaching her readers how to sense the movements of God in their own lives, even as she was creating new forms of theological expression as a woman working in an inhospitable theological climate. What is more, Teresa teaches us how to grow theologically and how to become authentic theologians.

When I arrived at the University of Chicago, in 1985, there were two female professors at the Divinity School. Neither of them was in historical theology or the History of Christianity, so it was important for the words and methods of people like Teresa, Hildegard of Bingen, Catherine of Siena, and others to supplement the instruction that I was receiving at Chicago. They always showed me not only that women belonged at the core of theological discourse but also that women brought different questions to the table, as well as a broad set of experiences that needed careful and thorough integration into the theological arena.

After my first year of graduate work, however, I found myself weary and discouraged, and I sought advice from my advisor, Bernard McGinn. Schooled in Teresa's own melodious language of subjectivity, all I could say to him was that it felt to me that my studies were causing me "to lose the simplicity of my soul." I appealed to the example of St. Francis (who was rumored to have said, "Preach the gospel at all times; use words when necessary") and told him that I was considering taking a year off. Bernie wisely referred me to his wife Pat. And fortunately, I found out about the University's Tinker Field Research Grant for Latin American and Iberian studies.

Not six weeks later—God seems to work fast in these matters—I was on a flight to Seville, Spain, home of the manuscript of Teresa's *Interior Castle*. And even though I hardly knew what I was doing, on the afternoon of my second day in Seville, I was ringing the buzzer on the wall of a completely unremarkable building with a tightly locked doorway right up against the street.

"Ave Maria," came the voice through the speaker.

Lacking experience in such matters, I clutched. What does one say to such a thing? Fortunately, I came up with a spontaneous "Gratia plena." It seemed to work.

"Si?" responded the voice. I tried to explain who I was, feeling rather awkward through the speaker, and the voice then went through a series of instructions in Spanish: When the door opened, I was to walk across the central courtyard, through to a doorway on the right side, and in the back of that room I would find a wooden turnstile, in which I was to place my letters of presentation (one from the University of Chicago and the other from the local archdiocesan vicar of religious orders), and then pull the chain. My journey into Teresa's cloistered world had begun. It was, in fact, in this very same convent that Inquisitional officials had entered in 1576, to question Teresa about her unusual experiences of prayer.[1] I would be walking in their footsteps, as well, when I entered the inner courtyard.

The letters disappeared, and, as the turnstile turned all the way around again, they had been replaced by a set of keys, the largest of which was approximately one foot long. Now another set of oral instructions, this one even harder to follow: I was to use the largest key to open the central wooden door on another side of the courtyard, then I was to lock the door carefully behind me. I should then proceed through the chapel to the sacristy door at the right end and open it with a second key.

I think the first key weighed about three pounds. It was itself a historical artifact.

Again I followed what I thought were the instructions, only to be surprised, at the end of my journey, by two sisters awaiting me in the sacristy. The one presented me with my letters; the other invited me to sit down next to a tall glass of brilliantly cold, freshly squeezed lemonade. I commented on the latter immediately, as it was late July and about 105 degrees outside. We had a conversation that lasted nearly an hour. The sisters took a kind interest in me and were full of questions: what had brought me to them, what did I hope to accomplish, what books did I need access to, how long would I be staying in Seville? As the conversation wound down, we worked out a schedule that would allow me to work there in the sacristy, for three hours each afternoon over a period of two weeks.

Each day I would arrive at the Discalced Carmelite convent, pick up the key from the turnstile, walk back into the sacristy, and the book I had requested the day before would be set out waiting for me, along with another glass of that miraculous lemonade. I was never alone. Depending on the day, I might be accompanied by the 92-year-old librarian, who would slip into a siesta in her chair as the warmth lulled her to sleep; other times,

---

1   For a reconstruction of this moment in Teresa's life, see *Teresa of Avila and the Politics of Sanctity* (Cornell University Press, 1996), pp. 50-66.

I would engage conversation with one or two of the other sisters, who, little by little, illuminated me about convent life. From what I could tell, the sisters wore habits that were at least two layers thick, and the fabric was a coarse wool, not a light cotton. I couldn't imagine it, nor could I understand how serene and unruffled they always were. I never once saw them with a drop of sweat, whereas I, on the other hand, always had a handkerchief out, petrified that a drop from my forehead would fall onto one of their manuscripts. We were always asking one another questions, curious about each other's worlds and with a profound and healthy mutual respect. There was a steady, precious rhythm to those days that quietly fed my soul. I went back to Chicago full of stories and with a clearer sense of purpose and meaning.

Two and a half years and five doctoral exams later, I was back in Spain, now in Madrid, allowing the focus of my dissertation to take shape in questions like: What was it like for Teresa, lacking a theological education and writing in a climate of suspicion about mental prayer and open hostility to women's teaching authority? How did she successfully navigate such difficult waters? How might understanding this climate illuminate our reading of her? And were there any strategies that Teresa could teach us today?

As I learned more about the Inquisitional context of Teresa's *Interior Castle*, it became clearer to me just how extraordinary the book really is. Ironically, the *Interior Castle* owes its very existence to the harsh climate of inquisitional scrutiny[2] that had moved inquisitional officials to sequester Teresa's first book on prayer, *The Book of Her Life*, in 1575. But Teresa wanted God, not the Inquisition, to have the last word. If that isn't the instinct of an authentic theologian, I'm not sure what is. As she wrote her way through the *Interior Castle*, Teresa shared with her contemporaries a concrete and quite extraordinary vision of God—a God whose tender longing for us "undoes" us, gradually teaching us what love truly is. The world would not have had exposure to this God without Teresa's courage

---

2   "Harsh" is a good approximation, in English, of what Teresa herself called her times: "tiempos recios." Describing this climate in *The Book of Her Life* in 1562, she writes: "They approached me with great fear to tell me that these were very harsh times, and that perhaps someone would mount a complaint against me before the inquisitors…" See Teresa of Avila, *Life*, 33:5.

and "*muy determinada determinación*" to take up pen repeatedly and search prayerfully for the words to communicate the love of God that gives life. I think it is also very safe to say that Teresa would not have been made a doctor of the Roman Catholic church—the Doctor of Prayer, no less—in 1970 without the *Interior Castle*, which provides a depth and sophistication far beyond what she was capable of when she wrote *The Book of Her Life*. The *Interior Castle* is an attempt to show how, through prayer, God thoroughly reforms and reshapes us, inviting us into a collaborative partnership capable of changing the world. ("We always hear about what a good thing prayer is… yet only what we ourselves can do in prayer is explained to us; little is explained about what the Lord works in a soul; I mean about the supernatural."[3]) But Teresa does more than just chronicle the soul's journey to God; she introduces us to a God who is keenly interested in us. She shows us that we are soulful people, capable of more than we know, and made of and for relationship with others. As we grow into relationship with God, she claims that we, too, will learn, through that relationship, how to engage the work of renewing the world, working for dignity, renouncing and denouncing injustice, growing in truth and love and fidelity, and drawing others into this life-giving, creative activity.

Teresa is a good lifelong companion. Her emphasis on the constant reformability and transformability of the human person is an insight that bears multiple explorations. Twenty-six years into my career as a university professor, I still teach Teresa, inside and outside of the classroom, most recently now to women recovering after domestic violence and relational trauma. What gets incredibly interesting, in these situations, is how much these women teach *me* about Teresa and what she has to offer to us today. As a brilliant friend once said to me as I was first getting to know him: "I went to the University of Chicago, but the poor have been my real teachers." Latina women rebuilding their lives after domestic violence have proven to be the ones who best teach me what Teresa's theological synthesis really means. She teaches that we must recognize and protect the high dignity of the soul, and that our journey toward meaningful relationship, with God, self and others, is one that involves constant change and challenge. "The things of the soul must always be considered as plentiful, spacious and

---

3   Teresa of Avila, *Interior Castle*, I:2:7.

large; to do so is not an exaggeration. The soul is capable of much more than we can imagine, and the sun that is in this royal chamber shines in all parts," she writes. And then she gives us her simple and basic life principle: "Whoever does not grow, shrinks."[4]

Teresa helps us to recognize the movements, habits, and forces in our lives that support authentic relationship with God, self, and others, and those that do not. She encourages us to create communities of solidarity, support and mutual care, capable of bearing witness to the energy of God's love wanting to come alive in the human community today. Teresa's own life gives us evidence of the malleability and strength of the human spirit, and her words continue to invite us to explore and model the reality of human resilience.

---

[4] Teresa, *Interior Castle*, I:2:8 and *Interior Castle* VII:4:9.

Interpretation Theory: Discourse and the Surplus of Meaning (Texas Christian Press, 1976) by Paul Ricœur

The Hermeneutical Challenge of Life

Sandra M. SCHNEIDERS,
Jesuit School of Theology of Santa Clara University

How does one who has been avidly reading books of every variety for more than half a century, even if limiting the choice to books read as an adult in an academic and/or ministerial context, select *one* as the "most important book I ever read"? Obviously, one has to add some further qualifiers, so I refined the question by asking myself what book (besides the Bible) is related most significantly to the most—quantitatively and qualitatively—significant aspects of my life? Surprisingly, one book immediately "leaped out" of the stack, namely, Paul Ricœur's *Interpretation Theory: Discourse and the Surplus of Meaning*, a collection of lectures which Ricœur delivered at Texas Christian University in Fort Worth, TX in 1973 and published in 1976. Coincidentally, that was the very year I began my professional life as a theologian at the Jesuit School of Theology and the Graduate Theological Union in Berkeley, California, having received my doctorate from the Gregorian University in Rome just a month before, in December 1975.

That coincidence is one of many that I discovered as I thought about Paul Ricœur, his work, and my experience. For example, I began my graduate studies not in theology but in the field of philosophy, defending my master's thesis on the metaphysics of free will in the work of the neo-Thomistic philosopher Jacques Maritain in 1967, the same year that

Ricœur published his stellar phenomenological study on that very topic, *The Symbolism of Evil*, which was a part of his two volume *Philosophy of the Will*. In 1975 I was finishing my doctorate in theology and biblical studies with a dissertation grappling with the issue of New Testament interpretation while, between 1974 and 1979, Ricœur published a number of essays later collected as *Essays in Biblical Interpretation*. The year 1976 saw the publication of the series of lectures by Ricœur that now constitute *Interpretation Theory*. And in 1977 Ricœur published his treatise, entitled *La Révélation*.

I was not, of course, consciously shadowing the great French philosopher whose work I was only beginning to study seriously as I worked, during the 1980's, on my own book on biblical hermeneutics, *The Revelatory Text*, which appeared in 1991. But, in retrospect, I realize that the questions which were burning issues for me even during my first years as a professional scholar, and which I grappled with in that book, were not the questions which my Catholic neo-Thomistic philosophical and historical-critical biblical education had prepared me to raise, much less answer. Those questions, which circled around the relationship between revelation and the biblical text, and between biblical revelation and Christian spirituality, were being discussed in other circles—philosophical, linguistic, literary, psychological, psychoanalytical, inter-religious, and aesthetic—and probably the most significant, original, and fertile mind at work on these questions was Paul Ricœur. During the first fifteen years of my professional theological work Ricœur produced major studies in every one of these areas, including work on symbolism, metaphor and language, the nature of texts, narrative and identity, aesthetics, imagination, memory, and, of course, the nature, process, and results of interpretation. It has been said that he nearly single-handedly redefined and revitalized the hermeneutic tradition. And, in a publishing environment in which the shelf life of most books is a few years at best, very few if any of Ricœur's major writings on these topics have actually fallen into desuetude.

During the first fifteen or so years of my professional career I struggled, by my participation in what seemed to some colleagues to be two unrelated fields, New Testament interpretation and Christian spirituality as an academic discipline, to formulate my concerns, to limn the contours of my "project" which was more a glimmer in my mind's eye than an articulated question. I was reading the continental "new hermeneuts" and their American exponents, the philosophers of language, theological aesthetics, philosophical hermeneutics, developments in literary criticism of the bible, new approaches to foundational theology and new methodology in biblical studies, and studies of revelation in the theology of religions. When I finally delved into the hermeneutical work of Hans-Georg Gadamer and Paul Ricœur I felt like I might be getting "warm." At a professional conference, a colleague, Dr. Loretta Dornisch, who had done her own dissertation on Ricœur, suggested that the best way to understand his hermeneutical project was to read his *Interpretation Theory*. I bought the book immediately and read it avidly, more than once, struggling with Ricœur's luminous but dense prose and amazed by his enormous erudition and the supple architectonics of his reasoning.

Reading the slim book, whose size massively belies its depth and scope, was a kind of intellectual homecoming for me. Someone actually understood my questions! And, indeed, had some answers. The subtitle of the book itself encapsulated the hint of a way forward: "Discourse and the Surplus of Meaning." The four sections of the book were each directed to one of the spheres of my concern, which I had not been able to get into fruitful conversation with each other, but which Ricœur masterfully sequenced in the trajectory from revelatory discourse to transformative understanding: "language and discourse"; "speaking and writing"; "metaphor and symbol"; "explanation and understanding." In other words, the areas I had been trying to understand in relation to each other, and as operative in the mediation of revelation through the biblical text, were not only addressed but interrelated: language as meaningful, textuality as mediation, linguistic creativity, the relation between the objectivity of texts and their subjective appropriation, and the participative and transformative character of the interaction between subjects through inscribed discourse were all discussed in remarkable depth and clarity in less than a hundred pages!

In subsequent years I have taught courses, lectured, and published on biblical hermeneutics, spirituality as a hermeneutical discipline, New Testament spirituality, and related topics—always using *Interpretation Theory* as background or even as a basic text, and finding more depth in it each time I re-read it in a different context. My personal copy is so annotated, underlined, outlined, highlighted and bookmarked that it constitutes a kind of private intellectual autobiography. This probably explains why, when I asked myself what book has been most significant for the most significant aspects of my thought, *Interpretation Theory* emerged from the pile as the singular candidate.

I never had the honor of meeting Paul Ricœur, even though he held a visiting professorship in the Divinity School of the University of Chicago from 1971-1991 and I am fairly certain we were in various academic venues at the same time. But in preparing this essay I came to realize that he has functioned, during most of my mature intellectual life, as both mentor and model. His mentoring of my intellectual development should be clear from the foregoing. But his modeling of what a true Christian intellectual should be has been a challenge and encouragement throughout my professional/ministerial life. I will mention only a few of the traits everyone recognizes in Ricœur which have been personally important for me.

First was his un-polemical but completely non-apologetic personal synthesis of his vibrant Christian faith with his "secular" academic identity and vocation as a philosopher. From his early absorption in the mystery of evil through his work in biblical hermeneutics Ricœur never pretended to be a religiously neutral bystander. As André LaCocque wrote in his obituary for the Society of Biblical Literature when Ricœur died in 2005, "In a thoroughly dechristianized country as is modern France, such an intellectual position [Ricœur's openly Christian stance in the academy] demanded great courage." As LaCocque put it, the maintenance of an appropriate distance between his faith and his philosophical inquiry "cannot be understood as an intellectual dichotomy." Ricœur was anything but a biblical fundamentalist, but he never lost his sense of wonder and gratitude before the divine condescension manifest in revelation.

Second, Ricœur was renowned among his peers for his capacity to take his intellectual critics and rivals absolutely seriously, without a hint of condescension or arrogance. He strenuously argued with many of the currents of thought and their proponents in the philosophical and even theological world in which he worked, but he dismissed no one and never resorted to ridicule. He was able to find in every seriously argued position, no matter how contrary to his own, the kernel or even the small grain of truth that should be listened to and could be learned from. For example, while much of mainstream biblical scholarship was dismissing structuralism as a "mountain laboring to produce a mouse" Ricœur folded it into his philosophical hermeneutics as an important testimony to the necessity for, and project of achieving, a certain controllable objectivity in the process of interpretation in which subjectivity could too easily become subjectivism.

Third, even though, as one of the intellectual giants of his day, he could easily have left the late twentieth century's struggles with massive moral evil to others with more time for such than he, Ricœur was no ivory tower intellectual but a committed and vocal proponent of social justice, and foe of war, racism, and sexism.

Finally, Ricœur's example has validated for me an approach to productivity in the intellectual life that came naturally to me but that, early in my career, I feared represented a lack of discipline or capacity for conceptualization. Probably half of Ricœur's major works consist of collections of essays on related topics or on a central theme on which his thought had developed and matured over the years. Although *Interpretation Theory* is composed of four lectures delivered at one event, many of his major works, for example, *Conflict of Interpretations*, and his volumes on political issues and on biblical interpretation, bring together lectures and/or essays written over a span of years in a variety of contexts and for various audiences. This process of "thinking through writing" rather than writing only what has been completely thought out and can be presented as one's definitive position on a subject is, I think, very congenial both for some writers and many readers. It represents, in Ricœur at least, an embrace of the tentative, cumulative, and self-corrective character of sustained reflection on profound subjects. Such reflection is indeed the "never-ending story" of engagement with reality through written discourse, and the literary genre of collected essays exposes not only the conclusions, but the processes of such engagement.

In a way it is appropriate that I selected a work of Paul Ricœur as the most important book I have read. Given his ground-breaking work on the autonomy of texts and their ability to generate worlds their authors could not have imagined, it is fitting, and a privilege, to express my appreciation for a scholar I never met but who has influenced me more than most I have, precisely and exclusively through his texts.

Jesus: An Experiment in Christology (New York: Seabury Press, 1979) by Edward Schillebeeckx

Jesus and Hermeneutics Brought Alive

Ormond RUSH, *Australian Catholic University*

Scripture was my favourite subject at the seminary. And in the late-60s and 70s, our lecturers were all into the historical-critical method. I had a particular interest in what was then the flavour of the month, the so-called "search for the historical Jesus." No doubt I was hermeneutically naïve about the limits of the historical-critical method and clearly too optimistic about being able to successfully get back into that "world behind the text." But the prospect was then exciting. Jesus fascinated me. *What was he like?* It was a spiritual quest as much as an intellectual one. Also during those seminary days, a few of us did extra studies at the local University of Queensland. One was a biblical studies course I took in 1971. I well remember as very provocative for me at the time a question posed as an essay topic: "What is the significance for contemporary theology of the quest for the historical Jesus?"

In my early years of pastoral ministry, after ordination in 1975, I continued to read anything scripture-related, especially in Jesus studies. My young priest friends and I were idealistically determined to always "keep up our reading." Soon I was thirstily imbibing Hans Küng's *On Being Christian*. Fairly soon after, a translation of Schillebeekx's *Jesus* was published in 1979, originally written in the same year as Küng's, 1974. I was then living in a rural parish called Charters Towers, a dry and dusty former gold mining town inland from the coast of northeastern Australia. In the evenings, I would plough through Schillebeeckx's *Jesus*, not an easy read. They must have been long evenings; it took me two months to read the 750-page tome. Perhaps triumphantly, on the inside cover of my copy I wrote in pencil: "finished 7 July 1980."

The book enthralled me with its portrait of Jesus and its proposals for reconstructing how his first disciples might have come to interpret him, a trajectory that begins before his death and then continues after his resurrection. Addressing a Europe in a crisis of belief, Schillebeeckx wanted to present a Jesus that gave due respect to historical enquiry but with a view to the context of contemporary European believers and non-believers. As I look back 35 years later, it is probably the most influential book of my life, both spiritually and intellectually.

I soon became aware of the book's weaknesses. Not all scholarly reviews at the time were positive (many were glowing). Soon after I had finished reading it, the scripture scholar Raymond Brown came to our diocese for a series of talks. I happened to be the diocesan media director. I thought it would be good to interview him for a local radio station, where I had a regular spot. As I got to the end of the interview, I thought I'd squeeze in a question about the book (selfishly, for my own sake, not for the sake of an audience that really didn't need to hear about a Belgian-born Dutchman called Schillebeeckx). Brown surprised me by being critical. There were particular points of exegesis he disagreed with; parts of the book were overly speculative; and he believed that the book would have been better if he had widened both the scope of the scholars he cited and those he asked to read the manuscript before publication. Nevertheless, despite all the criticisms it received (along with the accolades), the book remains symbolic for me along, as Schillebeeckx would say, "the narrative" of my life.

I cannot here summarize all the fine details of his densely argued thesis. But two things remain important for me: the book brought Jesus alive for me; and it brought hermeneutics alive for me. First, despite its thick scholarship, it stirred me with its fresh perspective on Jesus. In this regard, two chapters in particular still remain for me special jewels in the crown. In Part Two on "the Gospel of Jesus Christ," the first chapter treats "Jesus' Message of Salvation" (pp.115–178) and the second chapter "Jesus' Manner of Life" (pp. 179–271). They examine Jesus' fundamental focus, the reign of God, his parables, his practice of table fellowship, and his vision of God and God's vision for humanity: "Laughter, not crying is the deepest purpose that God wills for [humanity]" (p. 178). And most importantly of all, Jesus' own intimate experience of the God he prayed to as *Abba*: "The source of this message and praxis, demolishing an oppressive notion of God, was his *Abba* experience, without which the picture of the historical Jesus is drastically marred, his message emasculated and his concrete praxis (though still meaningful and inspiring) is robbed of the meaning he himself gave to it" (p. 269). Jesus is our window into God, our entry into God. Lapidary phrases from the book still ring out in my classes: Jesus' human story is "the story of God" (p. 650), "the parable of God himself" (p. 650), "'God translated' for us" (p. 670); he is the "mystic and exegete of God" (p. 673).

Second, the book brought hermeneutics alive for me. The sheer boldness of his project excited me. In a deliberate "Christology from below," he was attempting to trace the genesis of Christian belief in Jesus Christ by reconstructing the hermeneutical process that gave rise to the gospels. Beginning with the pre-Easter disciples and how they might have interpreted Jesus, he goes on to show how this remained, post-resurrection, the basis of a fuller yet continuous interpretation of him. Working back from the final New Testament formulations, he proposes interpretive frameworks that might well have been operating for those who first witnessed Jesus, his way of life, his actions and teachings. That he was the final prophet, sent by God, was a key initial interpretation.

The hermeneutical principles that guide the *Jesus* volume would all be summed up in the introductory section of Schillebeeckx's sequel: *Christ: The Experience of Jesus as Lord*. This serves, as Schillebeeckx once said, as a conclusion to the first volume. Here he talks more explicitly and more expansively about hermeneutics. He proposes two major theses that capture what the *Jesus* volume had set out to demonstrate. There is no divine revelation without human experience; and, all human experience is already interpretation. While divine revelation cannot be reduced to human experience of it, revelation can only ever be mediated through such interpretive experience. What we have in the four Gospels are the results of a long interpretive process, grounded in the reality of Jesus of Nazareth. No one portrait says it all, because he was interpreted differently. But each captures the same Jesus faithfully.

I followed Schillebeeckx as his thought developed in later years, with his hermeneutics, for example, embracing critical theory. But the *Jesus* book remained symbolic for me. When I was asked by the bishops of my state in 1987 to study at the Gregorian University in Rome for a licentiate in Fundamental Theology, my hermeneutical turn kept spinning. For my minor dissertation, I chose to write on the theological methodology of Francis Schüssler Fiorenza. There a name kept cropping up, Hans Robert Jauss, with his notion of reception hermeneutics. It was Jauss' hermeneutics that later became the focus of my doctoral studies, also at the Gregorian.

Basically, for Jauss, there are three elements that make for effective communication of meaning: the one wishing to communicate; the actual articulation of the communication in words or action; and, the ones who are receiving that communication. All three are important. But this third in the triad was particularly significant for Jauss: the receiver. Much of this I had come to know through Schillebeeckx, but already the need to tweak his hermeneutic was a little clearer to me. However, I continued to learn from him through his ever-developing thought, which always would challenge my own limited horizons.

Recently reading over Schillebeeckx's *Jesus* again, I realized that, in that first reading back in 1980, the seeds of a book, were being sown, a book I would come to write three decades later: *The Eyes of Faith: The Sense of the Faithful and the Church's Reception of Revelation*. In its central section, it attempts to show how the New Testament faith interpretation process in the early church that Schillebeeckx had explored is for us *the* paradigmatic example of what came to be called the *sensus fidei* ("sense of the faith") of Christian individuals (like Luke) and the *sensus fidelium* of a whole community (like Luke's community and the wider circle of Christian communities) at work in the early church.

For the cover of the book, I deliberately chose a Giotto fresco from the Scrovegni Chapel in Padua, with Jesus in the middle washing Peter's feet, surrounded by disciples with those piercing Giottoesque almond eyes looking down at him enquiringly: who is this Jesus who makes God's salvation so tangible? The image well captures Schillebeeckx's own piercing enquiry in his book. But *Jesus* is not just about Jesus. It is as much about those who first interpreted him. And the divine authority the church acknowledges for their witness to Jesus authorizes us to imitate them in an ongoing enquiry of faith, with our own *sensus fidei*. But that is another issue, for an emerging synodal church.

I've been thinking, as I look now at my heavily annotated and underlined copy of *Jesus*: when you take up a book and read, you never know where it could lead you, long after you've finished it the first time.

Just Jesus, 3 Volumes (Crossroad, 2000) edited by Jose Ignacio, Jose Ignacio Lopez Vigil, Maria Lopez Vigil

A Certain Jesus

William REISER, S.J., *College of the Holy Cross*

During my second year of college, one of our religion assignments was to read a life of Christ and then write a review. I looked through the shelves and found a number that looked interesting. On the shelves were Giuseppe Ricciotti's *The Life of Christ* (1947), Fulton Sheen's *Life of Christ* (1958), the three volumes of L. C. Fillion's *The Life of Christ: A Historical, Critical, and Apologetic Exposition* (1940), and Ferdinand Prat's two volumes, *Jesus Christ: His Life, His Teaching and His Work* (1950). To be honest, I cannot recall whether I chose Fillion or Prat to read and review. I may have done both.

But I also discovered Romano Guardini's *The Lord* (1954), with its stunning Rouault painting on the dust jacket. I read it, slowly, over the course of a year. The butcher at our local grocery store had already read it several times and urged me to give it a try (a memory I cherish). Fillion and Prat struck me as more academic and scholarly, while Guardini was more reflective and existential.

The book that eventually caught my imagination, however, was Alban Goodier's two volumes *The Public Life of Our Lord Jesus Christ: An Interpretation* (1936). I was a first-year novice and had just finished making the Spiritual Exercises. Each evening we had a half-hour devoted to reading the life of a saint or a life of Christ. That's when I discovered Goodier.

I loved it. I must have read it three or four times before moving on to his volume on the Passion.

Over the years I've taught courses on Jesus. I have a number of favorite writers, especially James Dunn, John Meier, Jon Sobrino, and N. T. Wright. For the past several years in my introductory class, as well as in courses for the Permanent Diaconate program, I have used José Pagola's *Jesus: An Historical Approximation*. It is superb.

Yet the book that made the deepest and most lasting impression on me originated as a series of radio broadcasts south of our border—one hundred and forty-four, to be exact. The scripts plus commentary appeared in 1982 as *Un tal Jesús: La Buena Noticia Contada al Pueblo de América Latina*. The two volumes of *Un tal Jesús* were eventually translated and published, first, in the Philippines under the title of *A Certain Jesus* and then, thanks to Crossroad, in three volumes as *Just Jesus*. Each volume opens with three forewords: one from an editor of Claretian Publications for the Philippines edition, one from Ignacio Ellacuría, and one from me. I was stunned to see that my remarks followed Ellacuría—an association that I treasure, even though our paths were very different.

Un tal Jesús was not written as a life of Christ but as a re-telling of familiar gospel scenes in a way that was fresh and imaginative. The humanness of Jesus is foregrounded thoroughly and consistently. He is humorous, compassionate, outgoing, prophetic. He possesses a relationship with God that is remarkably (yet not unbelievably) intimate, profound—and that seems to be growing as his mission unfolds.

I have re-read and re-played the story of the healing of the leper (Mark 1:40-45) countless times, and each time, by the end, my eyes are moist. Jesus and John (the disciple narrating each of the episodes) go to visit the leper's cave (the man has a name, a family, and before the onset of his disease, worked as a fisherman in Simon's village) in order to bring some food that Simon's wife had prepared. While John is urging caution, the leper appears. Desperate and lonely, Caleb cries at one point that the place is so forsaken that not even God would ever pass this way. Drawing close, Jesus asks him to show them his sores. As Caleb unwinds the cloths, he discovers that the sores have gone. John exclaims, "What have you done to him, Jesus?" To which Jesus answers, hesitantly, "But, John, I ..." No sense of magic there, but a subtle move toward mystery. The Jesus unafraid of desolate places lures the imagination.

The context of this retelling of the gospel is thoroughly Latin American. The idiom, the culture, the food, the ordinariness of village life, with its gossip and petty rivalries, the hard work in fields or fishing the lake, the voices of children and of the ancients—all of that seems so much like the village life that is woven into the narrative world of the gospels themselves. But what drives the story forward is Jesus' vision of the reign of God. And that reign is first and foremost a reign of justice. And why does justice figure into the story so prominently?

Because another feature of the Latin reality is the five hundred years of oppression it endured, from the arrival of the *conquistadores* to the emergence of the dictatorships. More than anything else, that reality draws the tightest connection between the two worlds: Israel under the foot of the Roman empire, and the historical experience of the peoples of Central and South America under the feet of powerful international political and economic interests—the enduring empire of capitalism.

For me, it's all about imagination. The gospel lives within us through image and story, scenes to which we become present over and over again. I cannot go back to Goodier because biblical scholarship has advanced so much, and in time *Un tal Jesús* will feel dated as well. Yet what has tied me to it is twenty years of traveling to the Andean region of Bolivia and the same number of years of speaking with and listening to people close by from Guatemala, Mexico, and Ecuador.

Essentially, I guess, I am a storyteller, less obviously in the classroom than in church; but a storyteller nonetheless. Images become the vehicle for opening minds and hearts, and for communicating the deepest truths about the human world. Teaching theology is, essentially, the cultivation of imagination. All that we believe ultimately derives from narratives, both the many narratives that make up the biblical tradition and, increasingly, the countless local narratives that provide form and identity to peoples throughout history.

In the past few years, I have been teaching a course called Defense Against the Dark Arts; the class is about theology and imagination. The idea arose because several of our majors (knowing my affection for the series) asked if I would offer a course on J. K. Rowling. Before too long

I realized that practically no student I've taught in recent memory had read the whole of the New Testament, whereas some have read the Harry Potter series eight or more times! One student confided to the class that she read the books so many times because it was a world she could retreat to; others chimed in. How, I wondered, could imaginations become just as much at home in the gospel story as in the world of Hogwarts? And I continue to wonder. But what has become clear is that the ultimate defense against the Dark Arts—the many "spells" and unseen forces that paralyze and destroy us through fear—is imagination, because imagination is the place where hope resides and fears are tamed.

Just Jesus, then, opens a space for imagination. But unlike a work of fantasy, *Just Jesus* connected to the world of my pastoral experience and the way I had come to read the gospels. Three times, over the course of nine months, I read the books and listened to the episodes with people from the Hispanic community. Each time, the response was enthusiastic and (for me) gratifying. It seemed sometimes that we were making an annotated retreat together as gospel scenes came alive; or, perhaps more precisely, as the humanity of Jesus became increasingly real. *Just Jesus* sensitizes the imagination to discover mystery in the ordinary: an imagination that feels more at home with the church as a field hospital (to draw on an image that Pope Francis likes), with a Jesus who was comfortable living with Simon and his family, who worked, who wept and who laughed, and who brought the divine presence even into the most desolate places.

In his Foreword, Ignacio Ellacuría notes that those who are accustomed to viewing Jesus "from this side of his resurrection and ascension into heaven" may find the Risen Jesus less scandalous than the Crucified One. It is the humanity of the crucified one—the Palestinian Jesus—that *Just Jesus* foregrounds. I think, though, that we are now safely beyond the theological quarrels about the historical versus the divine Jesus that we witnessed in the years following Vatican II and the debates about liberation theology. This has happened not just because we have retrieved the connection between Easter and the cross (after all, it was the *crucified* one who was raised), but especially because we have reconnected the cross with the prophetic ministry that led up to it. And that prophetic ministry was squarely centered on the poor, for whom the Church has made a fundamental option. "*Just Jesus* does not try to replace the gospels," Ignacio wrote, "but shows how these should be read, deepened and lived." I would add that it also helps to create the imaginative landscape for truly evangelical prayer and practice. For when we really listen to them, the gospel narratives infuse our imagination with hope. Without that, the Church would be without prophets; and we would be a people who have forgotten how to dream.

"Justice in the World" by 1971 Synod of Bishops, Second General Assembly
(in *The Gospel of Peace and Justice: Catholic Social Teaching Since Pope John*, edited by Joseph Gremillion, Maryknoll: Orbis, 1976)

A World and Church Committed to Justice for the Poor

Michael CROSBY, O.F.M.Cap.

To answer the question of why the Synod of Bishops' document, "Justice in the World," comes first to my mind as the most formative text in my experience and work, let me paraphrase a previous contributor, Sandra Schneiders: "I refined the question by asking myself what book (besides the Bible) is related most significantly to the most—quantitatively and qualitatively— significant aspects of my life?"

Most of my professional ministry has involved two main areas: one quarter has been devoted to socially responsible investing and the other three fourths have been my work in writing and speaking on contemporary biblical discipleship. It is perhaps not surprising that, not a book but, in fact, a Catholic Church document has been most influential for me. The coordinators of this NCR project have thought it could also be included, even if it is not a book.

My first assignment as a Capuchin Franciscan priest was to a "changing parish" in Milwaukee. Having experienced the upheaval that took place after Milwaukee's civil disturbances in 1967, I volunteered to work in the "inner city." My Province has parishes from Milwaukee to Detroit.

St. Elizabeth's in Milwaukee was in the midst of transition from white to black. I was sent there "to reconcile" the parish. I arrived in 1968 and left, considering myself a failure, in 1973. I had not been prepared by my seminary training to deal with economic injustice, classism and racism as they impacted Catholic parochial life.

Three years into my time there I remained befuddled by the question: "How can [white] Catholics have so much hatred toward others [blacks]?" It had become clear to me that the "bottom line" for most of our parishioners was not the gospel of Matthew, Mark, Luke or John but the "bottom line" of economics; more concretely, their rapidly declining property values. The consequence: we lost three thousand families those first three years. As African Americans moved in, many, if not most of the large population of ethnic Germans and Poles left.

At the same time some real enlightenment came with the 1971 Synod of Bishops. In my studies I had read all the various encyclicals and other documents in the area of what was called "Catholic Social Teaching." Of them all, only "Justice in the World" summarized so clearly and succinctly what we were facing in our parish. These insights, written for the first time (I believe) with strong input from the perspective of those bishops victimized by globalized injustice, echoed my own experience. The "world" they described was the "world" I had experienced but couldn't name. They declared: "Even though it is not for us to elaborate a very profound analysis of the situation of the world, we have nevertheless been able to perceive the serious injustices which are building around the world of men a network of domination, oppression and abuses which stifle freedom and which keep the greater part of humanity from sharing in the building up of a more just and more fraternal world" (#3).

I don't think, in all the books I have written since that document, that I have not quoted from the above statement or from an equally compelling challenge that began the section on "The Gospel Message and the Mission of the Church" which offered a new understanding of sin not just as *individual* but as *social* as well: "In the face of the present day situation of the world, marked as it is by the grave sin of injustice, we recognize both our responsibility and our inability to overcome it by our own strength. Such a situation urges us to listen with a humble and open heart to the word of God, as he shows us new paths toward action in the cause of justice in the world" (#29; see also #51).

True to the humility it invoked, a subsequent passage of the text acknowledged that the "sin of the world" also could be found in the Church itself. This emerged in one of the few admissions I have ever seen in an official "church teaching" of two things: sin in the church and the need for conversion (especially among its leaders). The Bishops stated: "While the Church is bound to give witness to justice, she recognizes that anyone who ventures to speak to people about justice must first be just in their eyes. Hence we must undertake an examination of the modes of acting and of the possessions and the life style found within the Church itself" (#40). Whether or not this examination has yet been done, I'll leave to the Bishops. But to someone like me, who is concerned about justice in our political economy as well as in the Church, it gives great consolation to know that the Bishops themselves have admitted, at least in this document, their own need for conversion. This is even clearer early in the Document when they stated that, as they analyzed the world and listened to the Gospel, they recognized their own need to "be converted to the fulfilling of the divine plan for the salvation of the world" (#2).

Another thing I learned during my time at St. Elizabeth's, from Dr. Martin Luther King, Jr., was the connection between racism and militarism. I saw this again at the local level, when young black men were coming home in caskets while so many young white men were able to have access to deferments. That led me to protests, including one in 1969 when I got arrested *in the Pentagon* for praying for an end to the war. Why would a priest working in a parish be concerned about the Vietnam War? I just had to look at the grave sin of racism and militarism in our neighborhood to know the answer.

Since 1971 members of my Province have realized the need to address issues of social injustice within our Province (especially vis-à-vis our non-clerical, non-white, and non-heterosexual brothers) as well as in our far-flung ministries (from the inner city areas in the Midwest, to native American reservations in Montana, to our "mission" in Nicaragua under the regime of Anastasio Somoza). Some of the friars who spent time in Washington, DC, became convinced that they needed to be based within the Province's territory to help us in what a writer like Paul Freire (highlighted in this book by Thomas Groome) called *conscientization*: the need to do social analysis of our own situation, to recognize the injustice involved and, for us as Franciscans, to bring the mission of Jesus to bear upon this reality in a way that would bring "good news to the poor." The result was the creation of our Province's "World Justice and Peace Office." Although I was still in the parish, I was on its Board of Directors.

In 1973, as part of an ongoing effort of the Catholic bishops of "the North" and "the South" of the Americas, an organization called CICOP (Catholic Interamerican Cooperation Program) had a meeting in Dallas. As a member of the Board of the Office I attended that meeting. The keynote speaker was Radomiro Tomic, the Chilean Ambassador to the United States (under Salvatore Allende, who later that year was killed in a U.S. supported coup [09.11.73]). The more Tomic analyzed what the Synod of Bishops called the "situation of the world marked by the grave sin of injustice" as it directly impacted countries like his Chile, the more I saw the parallels within our own parish boundaries. He spoke of outside ownership, deficit balance of payments and control of the economy by elites with resulting social consequences (poor housing, poor healthcare, less healthy foods). The reality of Chile, I realized, was a macro version of what was going on economically and politically in the St. Elizabeth parish.

That realization was bad enough. It brought home very clearly what the Bishops had said in their Document about listening "with a humble and open heart to the word of God." After doing his social analysis, Tomic turned to the word of God to see how it applied to the situation of the people of his country. The gist was: "When we now go to the Gospel to see what the Scriptures say about this, the only passage that seems to be honest is the one that says: 'To those who have, more will be given in abundance, but from those who do not have, even that will be taken away.'" (see Mt. 13:12; Mk. 4:25; Lk 8:18). Sitting there at that CICOP meeting, hearing that Scripture passage used in that way, I was led to make a commitment: "From now on you have to spend your life to change that abuse of the scriptures. You have to bring good news to those who are poor. This means solidarity with those who are poor because they struggle for justice."

My life since then has been an effort to realize that promise I made to myself. After giving myself five years to "reconcile" whites and blacks at St. Elizabeth's in Milwaukee and going into depression at my sense of failure, I asked to be relieved of this ministry. Still I knew what I felt called to do: work in the area of social (in)justice.

What first began as an effort to bring good news to those people who are poor as the result of economic and political policies and/or practices in my local community became a new challenge. Businesspeople in corporate meetings and shareholders at annual meetings urged me to "go back" and try to make my own church more just. So, if I was to deal with racial apartheid in South Africa, I had to overcome sexual apartheid in my church. If I was to talk about human rights and greater equality in the workplace and the boardrooms, I had to work to bring about equal access in the sanctuary among those called to priesthood.

Why? Because the bishops themselves have said so: "While the Church is bound to give witness to justice, she recognizes that anyone who ventures to speak to people about justice must first be just in their eyes." The call to conversion is an equal opportunity challenger. And, I have discovered, this call for justice in my own church is usually much harder to proclaim (and even harder to see accepted by its leaders) than any work I have done to bring about greater justice in the corporate and political worlds.

Toward the end of their document on Justice, the Bishops refer to their reflections as an "examination of conscience which we have made together." This examination has a contemporary echo in another examination that Pope Francis says must be memorized and memorialized (i.e. "do this") by every Catholic: the examination of the entire world as announced by the Matthean Jesus in the Beatitudes ("Blessed are….") and in Chapter 25 ("Lord, when did we see you…?").

The Law of Christ: Moral Theology for Priests and Laity (The Mercier Press, 1963) by Bernard Haring

A New Orientation for Moral Theology: From a Manualist and Legalist Approach to a Christic and Personalist Model

Charles E. CURRAN, *Southern Methodist University*

For me, Bernard Häring's *The Law of Christ* was the most important book I have ever read. We all recognize, however, that the most important book we have ever read depends heavily on what we were looking for at the time we read it.

Here was my situation and mindset at the time I first read *The Law of Christ*. I was finishing my theological studies at the North American College in Rome in the spring of 1959. I had been ordained a priest in Rome in 1958 for the diocese of Rochester, New York. In early spring, I received a letter from my bishop saying that I was to come back to Rome in the fall of 1959 to pursue a doctorate in moral theology at the Gregorian University to prepare me to teach moral theology at St. Bernard's Seminary in Rochester.

As a seminarian, I had studied moral theology at the Gregorian University with well-known and distinguished moralists such as the German Jesuit Franz Hurth and the American Jesuit Edwin Healy. I enjoyed their classes, in which they basically followed the purpose of the manuals of moral theology in preparing seminarians for their role as confessors by knowing what acts are sinful and the degree of sinfulness. The ethical model was a legal one—law was the objective norm of morality. In addition, Josef Fuchs also taught me in two courses, and he pointed out that the approach of the manuals was not the only possible approach to moral theology. (In those days I did not know Fuchs very well, but later we became quite close.) With this background in the spring of 1959, I started thinking about my future studies and how I wanted to teach moral theology. At this time a friend pointed out to me the three-volume Italian translation (*La Legge di Cristo*) of Häring's work, which was originally published in German in 1954. The Italian translation had just been published in the period of 1957-1959. The English translation of *The Law of Christ* was published only in 1963.

The Law of Christ opened my eyes and my mind to see a new approach to moral theology. The very subtitle of the work—*Moral Theology for Priests and Laity* indicates that the focus was on the moral life as a whole and not just on what acts were sinful and the degree of sinfulness. The very first chapter of *The Law of Christ* insists that responsibility, not law or commandment, is the focal center of Catholic moral teaching. The basis for the importance of responsibility is found in the very understanding of religion itself. Häring had written his own doctoral dissertation on the understanding of the Holy and the Good. Religion has the essential character of response to the loving coming of the Holy One. The essential religious form of response and responsibility to the Holy brings about a truly religious ethic. For Christians the I-Thou relationship of intimacy with God flows from the Word of God who is God made flesh. God comes to us in Christ, and we respond in Christ to God's gift. However, this Christian personalism is not narrow individualism. Yes, God calls us personally by name (Häring frequently insisted in his classes on this fact), but in God's presence we also find our neighbor and the way to fellowship and community in the Church and the broader human society.

In this first chapter, Häring goes on to examine the most significant moral concepts in light of this criterion of responsibility. Commandment and law must be understood as religious concepts. The commandments of God are words of divine love addressed to us in the great commandment of love; the fulfillment of the command is the response of obedient love. Such an approach differs from the manualistic concept of law, which is based on the sovereign will of God and not on the all-holy essence or nature of a loving God.

The three theological virtues of faith, hope, and love must be seen in light of a response-relationship with God. The virtue of religion is our response to the majesty of God, our creator and father. The other moral virtues do not directly and immediately respond to God, since they are directly concerned with the created order. The believer, however, detects in the order of creation the loving work of the Lord and creator, and thus this relationship with all that God made is grounded in the personal relationship with God in Christ Jesus. The manuals of theology had paid very little attention to virtues. In fact, in treating virtues they treated the sinful acts that go against the virtues!

Reading further in the book, I recognized that Häring also appealed to value theory and value experience as proposed by Max Scheler and Dietrich von Hildebrand to ground the theory of responsibility. A profound difference exists between mere theoretical knowledge of the law that something must be done or avoided and insight into value as the basis of response and obligation. The deepest knowledge of value arises from an intimate connaturality with the good. All values are rooted in the basic value, which for the believer is the loving God. The specific types of value include the various virtues.

The manuals almost completely neglected scripture except for an occasional proof text—the scriptures were used to support a position that had already been arrived at primarily by human reason. But Häring sees scripture as the basis for developing moral theology. The title of the whole work is taken from Romans 8:2, which is quoted on the title page of the first volume—"For the law of the Spirit of the life in Christ Jesus has delivered me from the law of sin and death." Unlike the manuals, Häring insisted on the theological character of moral theology. The first page in the foreword to volume I begins with a sentence: "The principle, the norm, the center, and the goal of Christian moral theology is Christ." I later came to realize that Häring's approach to Christology was what was called a Christology from above. Christ is the Word of God who comes to us as the God-Man with the Father's love. We, then, are also joined with Christ in responding to the gift of the Father. Other Christologies begin with the human and historical Jesus, but Häring sees Jesus the Christ as the mediator bringing God to human beings and bringing us to God.

The manuals of moral theology usually devoted a separate volume to the sacraments, but the treatment was almost totally canonical—what is necessary for the valid and licit administration and reception of the sacraments. *The Law of Christ* does not have a separate volume covering all the sacraments. Volume 2 discusses life in fellowship with God, and here Häring treats the sacraments in general under the development of the virtue of religion. For Häring, religion is a living dialogue between God and the human person. The sacraments are the most intimate and personal encounter with God. The sacraments, however, do not involve just the narrow I-Thou relationship to God. They are essentially a social reality uniting us with all the members of the mystical body of Christ.

After reading the Italian translation of *The Law of Christ* in spring 1959, I learned that Häring was then teaching at the Academia Alphonsiana in Rome. At that time the Alphonsiana could not give doctoral degrees, but in 1960 they were given the right to confer the ecclesiastical doctorate in moral theology. My bishop insisted that I get my degree in moral theology from the Gregorian University, but in the fall of 1959 I also enrolled for classes at the Alphonsiana. In the next two years, I took four classes with Häring. His Latin lectures were stunning and stimulating. I invited a good number of my fellow students from the graduate house of the North American College to come and listen to him. To a person, they were greatly impressed. From Häring and other professors at the Alphonsiana I learned a new approach to moral theology, which I tried to develop when I started teaching at St. Bernard's Seminary in the 1961-62 school year.

My relationship with and respect for Häring grew with the years. I was the person who first brought him to the United States to give lectures. Later he lectured and gave retreats all over the United States, to say nothing of doing the same thing in practically all parts of the world, especially Africa and Asia. I came to the conclusion in the late 1960s that Häring's tremendous involvement in spirituality and working for reform in the Church meant that he would probably never again publish as important a theology book as *The Law of Christ*. Looking back, I do not think that *The Law of Christ* is a classic. It is a transitional work that probably will not be read very much in the future. Most Catholic moral theologians, however, would agree that it was the most important book in moral theology in the twentieth century, because of its influence in changing the approach to moral theology even before the Second Vatican Council.

The Long Loneliness
(Harper & Row, 1952) by Dorothy Day

Fascinated and Challenged

Julie Hanlon RUBIO, *St. Louis University*

When I first read Dorothy Day in 1987, seven years after the famous writer, activist, and founder of the Catholic Worker movement had died, I was immediately pulled in. I had moved to Washington, D.C. and was living and working at Mary House, a shelter for pregnant women and their families. As I read about Day's life and work, I was drawn into a long argument with her that has marked my work, my family life, and my struggle to be a Christian.

Mary House was founded in 1981 by Bill and Sharon Murphy, who had met while serving at a 1400-bed shelter, the Community for Creative Non-Violence, in Washington, D.C. They had a vision of a smaller-scale way of ministering to the homeless. They started with their own home, which already held their four children. In the late 1980s, most women who lived there were fleeing violence and poverty in El Salvador, Nicaragua, or Guatemala.

At Mary House I learned a balanced approach to serving the marginalized. Because Bill and Sharon knew that they wanted to be doing this work for a long time, they took time to care for their children and themselves. Their version of living simply included some luxuries. They took time off from hospitality after guests left in order to allow their family some space. They sent their children to private schools, occasionally ate at local restaurants and took vacations. Some days Bill declared that the Spirit was calling for some time off, so he took it and encouraged me to do the same.

In contrast, I recall an especially long morning I had spent volunteering at the local Catholic Worker shelter cleaning turkey carcasses on the day after Thanksgiving. Side by side with people who thought nothing of spending hours getting meat for soup from others' trash and seemed to never take a day off, I began learning about the Catholic Worker Movement that Day founded.

The first thing I remember about the movement is how I disliked it. I found their lack of rules disturbing. How could they let people stay as long as they wanted? Why such a concern with not drawing firm lines between guests and staff? Why wouldn't they apply for non-profit status so they could receive government money and tax-deductible donations? Why was such extreme voluntary poverty necessary to good service? Why were they so obsessed with religion?

But little by little, I was being drawn in.

I started reading a book of Day's essays. Here I encountered her unique vision of hospitality, community, and spirituality. I argued with Day, but I kept thinking about her ideas, too. Through accompanying the women at Mary House to their appointments with doctors and social workers, I came in contact with some of the government bureaucracy that Day criticized. I saw the personalism she spoke of not only at the Catholic Worker, but at Mary House, where "service" included having long dinners and great parties with guests.

Later (I can't recall precisely when) I found an old copy of Day's autobiography, *The Long Loneliness*. Day as a person fascinated me. She had been a journalist, a radical, a bohemian. An intellectual and a college-drop out. A single mother who left the man she loved to start the Catholic Worker Movement and raise her daughter Tamar in its quirky, loving embrace.

She was a loyal convert to a church she relentlessly challenged. She called the church "the cross on which Christ was crucified" and mourned its distance from the teachings of Jesus in the Sermon on the Mount. She always acknowledged her own sin, which made it easier for her to see the need for a church, for other people of faith (living and dead) to inspire, support, and challenge her.

Though I knew plenty of traditional and progressive Catholics, I had never met anyone like Dorothy Day.

I was fascinated and challenged by her piety. She went to daily Mass, prayed with a breviary and a rosary, and could not live without frequent retreats and confession. She spoke casually about the mystical body of Christ and loved the traditional practices that I had never considered relevant to the life of a progressive Catholic.

I was fascinated and challenged by her voracious reading. I began to make a list of the books she had read. Because of her I returned to Dickens, relished the long novels of Tolstoy and Dostoyevsky, delved into the writings of Merton and the Berrigan brothers.

I was fascinated and challenged by her insistence that it was not enough to support good causes. To be Christian, one had to adopt the precarity of voluntary poverty and "live with [the poor], share with them their suffering too. Giving up one's privacy, and mental and spiritual comforts as well."

I found in her a compelling vision of how to live as a radical, intellectual Catholic, a way to unite the life of the mind with faith in God in the community of saints and sinners that is the church.

From Day's essays and autobiography, I moved on to other books of hers (*Loaves and Fishes*, *On Pilgrimage*, her letters, and her diaries) and books about her (biographies by William Miller, Jim Forest, Robert Coles, and Paul Elie). I started using excerpts of her books for morning or evening prayer. Though I would put my Dorothy Day books away for a time I always returned to her when I needed to reground myself.

At St. Louis University, I started teaching Day in nearly every course I taught (Marriage and Family, Social Justice, Faith and Politics, and Christian Ethics). Some students argued with her just as I had. Others were way ahead of where I had been in college and found in her a kindred spirit. Some who joined the movement came to speak in my classes. They always impressed my students and quietly challenged the compromises of my life as a professor.

I spent some time volunteering at the local Catholic Worker, tutoring, cooking meals, and taking kids on excursions in St. Louis. I brought my students to the house so they could see what it looks like to build "a new society in the shell of the old," to practice love as "a harsh and dreadful thing." Every time I taught Day I would be convinced again to question everything about my life. Every time, I would argue back, "There are other ways to authentically practice Christian faith."

When I became a mother, I turned to Day's writing on pregnancy and thought about how she raised her daughter Tamar. I took my children to Karen House, wanting them to love the Catholic Worker vision as I did, though they, like my younger self, were mostly unimpressed. Because of her, I constantly struggled with myself about how much upper middle class parenting I could embrace (A game system? A neighborhood with excellent schools?) while still calling myself a Christian.

While one of my sons was a college student in New York, I visited Christie Street and Mott Street, in Little Italy, where some of the earliest Catholic Workers opened their doors. I could almost see Day walking the streets, buying vegetables from the market, greeting the men in the soup line, listening to opera with her window open in summertime. A part of me still wished I could follow her.

On a trip to Washington, D.C., I visited the crypt of the National Shrine, the site of Day's famous prayer (recounted in *The Long Loneliness*) "that some way would open up for me to use what talents I possessed for my fellow workers, for the poor." Day attests that when she arrived home, Peter Maurin was on her doorstep, and that night the Catholic Worker Movement began to be born.

Like Augustine's *Confessions*, Day's *Long Loneliness* is a conversion story. Yet I find hers much more compelling. Like Augustine, Day took up celibacy, and her diaries and letters tell us that this was no easy choice, because she never stopped caring for Forrester, her first love.

But her struggle was not only to leave behind a life she could no longer call good, but to live in community as if the Gospel were true and possible. In Robert Coles' biography, he tells of taking his students to see Day. They asked how she wanted to be remembered. She spoke first of her life with the poor, of how she tried to serve good coffee and good soup to those who came to the Catholic Worker, but also of learning from those she served. Second, she said she wanted people to say, "She really did love those books!" She found the meaning of her life in trying "to live up to the moral vision of the Church, and of some of my favorite writers."

Even though I have found a certain peace in my much less radical life choices, I confess to being perpetually unsettled by the beauty and hardship of Day's life.

This is what I love about Dorothy Day: her relentless quest for a moral life shaped by a vision of radical discipleship and by novelists whose stories captured what is true and beautiful, and what it costs to be a Christian. Because I started reading her nearly thirty years ago, and keep reading her even now, my quest to live a Christian life is much more difficult, and for that I remain ever in her debt.

Memento Mori (Macmillan, 1959) by Muriel Spark

A Reminder of What's to Come

Valerie SAYERS, *University of Notre Dame*

I first read Muriel Spark's hilarious, disturbing, consoling *Memento Mori* in my year of discernment—1973: the year I graduated from college and decided that if I meant to stop resisting the vocation of writer, then I had better devote some time to actually writing. I left New York City and returned to South Carolina, where I moved in with my widowed mother and the two siblings still at home. I meant to grieve my father's recent death and to write, though it is still unclear to me whether those two plans were separate and distinct. To support myself, I took a job teaching subjects I didn't know anything about (business English, economics, human relations) in a two-year technical college. The plan was: teach through the day, prepare my classes in a few efficient afternoon hours, and write at night, every night.

At that point I was as ambivalent about writing as I could possibly be. Pleasurable as it was on rare occasion, writing was also painful. Every page I composed was embarrassing, by virtue of both its quality and its self-revelations—though frequently I was writing so cryptically that I wasn't even revealing any sense, much less any self. I wrote compulsively (and obscurely) about the Southern landscape and social terrain; neurosis, psychosis, guilt, and death (I was reading far too much Dostoyevsky); and my complicated relationship to Catholicism. I'd started college in what was still a kind of golden age for Catholic novelists: I'd been introduced to Waugh, Mauriac, Greene and O'Connor (to whom, as a Southerner,

I didn't need an introduction). Happily, as I tore through their work, it only suggested to me how different their sensibilities were from mine.

Muriel Spark was one of those writers I'd been meaning to track down and now intended, in my year of trying the life of a writer, to read systematically. I was keenly aware that I needed to be reading more contemporary females, since I had only been introduced to a sum total of three (dead) women novelists in all my college years. I chose Spark's *The Prime of Miss Jean Brodie* to crack first, because I had seen the movie and found it charming, sexy, and more than a little alarming. The novel was something else again, layered with crystalline political perspective and clear moral authority, both delivered with skewering wit. I was a Faulkner fan and in my college days had thought of myself as an experimentalist (experimental prose is always well-suited to the obscure and embarrassed writer). Now Spark's crisp, direct style appealed to me enormously and began to change the way I conceived of my own voice. I picked up *Memento Mori* next, at random I supposed (Dr. Freud would have had a different opinion). It was a slender volume, a length well-suited to the tired business-English instructor with classes to prepare and fledgling stories to produce.

Originally published in 1959, *Memento Mori* is light, airy, deft. The plot is simple: a circle of upper-crust London old folks receive, in turn, puzzling phone calls reminding them that they will die. Meanwhile, they visit each other's hospital beds and funerals, still competing for power, money, and prestige. They have led mostly charmed lives, and one of the central characters, Charmian, has the very concept built into her name. Likewise, her husband, Godfrey Colston, is conveniently God-free and frequently cold as a stone. Charmian's former maid, Jean Taylor, is more plainly named and, as it happens, the lone central character who does not come attached to money or fame. Sharply intelligent, a devoted Catholic since her conversion to please Charmian, she is a resident of a public old folks' ward whose residents provide Spark with frequent opportunity for low comedy.

Memento Mori is an allegorical satire of the privileged and the vapid, its mocking purposes as baldly apparent as the symbolism inherent in its characters' names. Godfrey likes to lecture Catholics on their beliefs and berate them for their loose adherence to rules. When his cook answers his interrogation by saying she "doesn't really fancy the idea" of cremation, he pounces: "*'Fancy the idea'*....It is not a question of what you fancy. You have no choice in the matter, do you see?" All free will, Godfrey pays five pounds to both his wife's aging maid and a friend's young granddaughter in exchange for their baring the tops of their stockings while he silently regards their garters. Before a reader can ponder the innocence of 1959, however, Spark provides a wealth of sex and violence to challenge that perception. By novel's end, Godfrey's sister, Dame Lettie, who has been plagued with the most regular calls reminding her of impending death, meets that death at the hands of a burglar who "wrenched the stick from the old woman's hand, and with the blunt end of it, battered her to death. It was her eighty-first year." The swift, unsentimental dispatch of Dame Lettie is in narrative keeping with the way she has lived her life, brusquely judging and ordering everyone around—but that doesn't make it any less shocking.

Spark's disturbance of my readerly sense of equilibrium was certainly in opposition to any ideas my young aspiring-writer self had about what pieties constituted a "Catholic novel." She appeared to be, in her gusto for come-to-Jesus moments of the violent variety, a relative to O'Connor—but perhaps because I feared identifying with a writer born forty-five miles down the road from me, and certainly because she scared the wits out of me, I'd always kept Flannery O'Connor at a grudgingly respectful distance. I turned to Spark with more visceral appreciation. As I read through the dozen novels she'd written to date, I was dazzled by her use of a genre I came to think of as Surrealism Lite: characters in *Memento Mori* name the real humans they suspect of harassing them by telephone, but a detective concludes that it is no human but Death on the line. The following year Spark would publish *The Abbess of Crewe,* a wild fusion of theological vision and political satire confronting, of all absurdities, Watergate, thus confirming my sense that her appetite for experimental genre was as lusty as her predilection for the simple, straightforward sentence.

If I was stylistically in her thrall, however, it was Spark's attitude toward theology that instructed my own progress as a Catholic novelist most directly and permanently. Nowhere is that attitude more apparent than in *Memento Mori.* The maid Jean Taylor is the Catholic conscience of the novel, a clear exemplar of a generous ideal Spark contrasts to the materialism of the Colstons. But Spark is delightfully aware that the neat opposition of saintly Catholics would be very dull stuff if the Catholics, like the other characters, did not come in every moral flavor. Charmian's Catholicism was, it turned out, a fleeting diversion; and Taylor herself, heroic in her suffering, often succumbs to jealousy. Neither does Spark limit her theological idealism to Catholic characters: the promiscuous Lisa Brooke, aged seventy-three, "reminding herself how attractive she still was, offered up the new idea, her celibacy, to the Lord to whom no gift whatsoever is unacceptable."

That early line in the novel elated me: biting, absurd, sexually frank, fully devoted to the ironic pleasures of the satirist's voice, it nonetheless embraces a piece of Catholic identity equally familiar and comforting to the cradle Catholic (me) and the convert (Spark). The novel's epigraphs come from Yeats, Traherne, and The Penny Catechism ("What are four last things to be ever remembered?"); at novel's end, Jean Taylor "lingered for a time, employing her pain to magnify the Lord, and meditating sometimes confidingly upon Death, the first of the Four Last Things to be ever remembered." *Memento mori* ("Remember you must die"), indeed.

My reading of Spark was not simply giving me a sense of new aesthetic possibility, but giving me permission to use Catholicism if and when it needed to appear in my fiction, and to use it explicitly, in a way that did not require obscurity, embarrassment, sexual abstinence, or misplaced deference. I realized that it was their romanticizing of Catholicism that had made me uncomfortable with Waugh and Greene's portrayals of Catholic characters. Spark, like O'Connor, is having none of the soft stuff—but neither does she ban Catholicism from nearly all her work, as O'Connor does. Spark's fiction strikes a balance between the intellectual, the psychological, the theological, the comic, and the absurd; and that was precisely what I wanted to do too.

Of course I did not end up a writer like Muriel Spark—I am neither of her time nor her place nor her gifts—but I still aspire to her sublime wit and forthright embrace of faith, even as she retains her right to criticize the institutional Church and the faithful. I still re-read *Memento Mori* every few years and laugh recklessly. What's more important, though: I remember the first of the Last Four Things. Muriel Spark is on the line, reminding me what's to come.

Method in Theology (Seabury, 1972) by Bernard Lonergan

The Centrality of Conversion

Dennis M. DOYLE, *University of Dayton*

Method in Theology is the work of a genius, Bernard Lonergan, a Jesuit philosopher and theologian who lived from 1904 until 1984. I first read it as part of my dissertation research in the early 1980's. It turned out to be the book that has had the most influence not only upon what I think but also upon how I think. *Method* builds upon Lonergan's earlier work, *Insight: An Inquiry into Human Understanding* (1957).

In *Insight,* Lonergan explores how the human mind can understand and know things, as well as how a basic continuity in the process of knowing stretches across math, science, social science, metaphysics, ethics, and religious belief. If you start reading *Insight* with naïve credulity, Lonergan will lead you in the direction of critical thinking. If critical thinking runs you into the ditch of a dead-end skepticism or an anything-goes relativism, Lonergan will pull you out of that ditch by teaching you how to affirm yourself as a knower. He will prompt you to demonstrate to yourself that human understanding and knowledge, though limited, are real. He will help you to recognize and to overcome various forms of bias. He will convince you that values are anything but purely subjective. He will make you aware of various forms of differentiations in your own consciousness, and of how different types of human operations lead to different forms of expression of knowledge. He will argue persuasively that your ability to know anything requires the existence of a universe that can be understood and known, and that if anything at all is really intelligible, then there must be an ultimate context of intelligibility. Upon the basis of this ultimate context of intelligibility, you can reason that there must be God. Not only is there God, but you can also reasonably affirm special revelation through Christ carried forth in history in the Catholic Church.

Method, though building upon *Insight,* offers a more ecumenical approach intended for use by theologians in various traditions. Moreover, Lonergan adds to his earlier focus on intellectual reasoning some balancing emphases on willing and loving. If *Insight,* in retrospect, can be said to be mainly concerned with what Lonergan would later come to call intellectual conversion, *Method* expands the range of concerns to include also moral and religious conversion.

Intellectual conversion entails understanding what you are doing when you are knowing. You realize that knowing something requires more than just taking a look at what is there outside of yourself. It also requires using your mind to understand and to make judgments. And so you come to grasp how reality is much more than just what meets the eye. But it is also more than just your subjective ideas. Lonergan explains how objectivity is the result of authentic subjectivity. Moral conversion involves a shift in your criteria of decision-making from selfishness to higher values. Religious conversion is a falling-in-love with God.

Lonergan wrote *Method* at a time when theology was still completing a transition from being mainly done only in seminaries to being done also in universities. On the one hand, does theology really belong in universities? Can it be legitimate to bring faith perspectives into academic classrooms? Should universities confine themselves only to academic religious studies? On the other hand, do scholars who study the bible and tradition only with historical methods belong in a theology department?

Method shows how theology can be a fully reasonable and critical discipline while at the same time retaining its traditional role as "faith seeking understanding." Lonergan lays out a basic organizational plan for the academic discipline of Theology as divided into eight functional specialties (or sub-disciplines). The first four functional specialties—Research, Interpretation, History, and Dialectic—operate in a way that is logically prior to "conversion." The final four functional specialties—Foundations, Doctrines, Systematics, and Communications—require "conversion" as a prerequisite. For Lonergan, you will recall, conversion is threefold: religious, moral, and intellectual.

Scholars working within these functional specialties should be in dialogue with each other. Those who are operating in specialties that call for "conversion," for example, are not exempt from the canons of reason that bind those working in the pre-conversion specialties. They are, however, specializing in intellectual regions that presuppose choices and decisions in favor of a particular religious tradition.

Theology so understood combines reason and faith in such a way that it benefits greatly from the context of a university that supports many academic disciplines. It builds upon studies that are scientific, hermeneutical, historical, and analytic. It requires many dimensions of its own discipline to be performed in a way that is logically prior to any faith stance. At the same time, it does not banish all particular, intellectual faith commitments from the academic court. A Catholic university, for example, can house theologians and sponsor research performed not only by Catholics, but by scholars from a wide range of religious traditions in a way that can combine both insider and outsider perspectives.

Method presents theology as a discipline that mediates between a religion and a culture. On the one hand, there is something very traditional about theology, because the theologian is drawing upon and interpreting a tradition that exists prior to oneself. On the other hand, there is something very progressive and even creative about theology, because the theologian needs to appropriate the tradition into the present context. As the world of today is characterized by cultural pluralism, so there are many particular contexts into which Christian tradition needs to be appropriated.

Also, in addition to honoring the standard academic criteria associated with science, social science, history, and philosophy, a theologian needs to appropriate Christian tradition in harmony with religious, moral, and intellectual conversion. To speak theologically in an authentic manner requires not only reasonable intellectual judgments. It includes also the desire to be truly good as well as being in touch with the gift of love with which God floods our hearts. It helps tremendously if the theologian participates in a faith community that strives to live out its vision in an authentic manner.

What Lonergan's eight functional specialties offer us is something of a map of theology as an academic discipline. A map, however, is not the territory. There is always something abstract about a map. In real life theology does not always fit neatly into exactly eight categories that follow one another in a particular order. Lonergan's *Method* does not offer a recipe that is to be followed with precise measurements in ordered steps.

Recently, however, I spent some time at a German university as a guest professor. At an initial lecture in which I explained Lonergan's eight functional specialties, some members of the Catholic theological faculty made the point that such an abstract approach, though helpful in some ways, did not really describe what they do. At a second lecture, however, I named many members of the faculty and explained where their sub-disciplines fit on Lonergan's map. The professor of Bible Studies who emphasizes textual criticism is connected with Research and Interpretation. The professor of Church History is connected with History. The professor of Philosophical Theology is connected with Dialectic. The professor of Fundamental Theology is connected with Foundations. The professor of Dogmatics is connected with Doctrines and Systematics. The professor of Religious Pedagogy as well as the Professor of Moral Theology are connected with Communications. Unfortunately, not many of the same people attended both lectures. Those present at the second lecture, however, were no longer suggesting that the map did not apply to them. Such an exercise would probably not work as well at a U.S. university where theology faculties are not so traditionally structured.

Method performs a valuable service in explaining how theology can fit within a university setting. In an age where few people conceive of theology as one unified discipline with many interacting parts, it may be about time for a *Method in Theology* revival. It sometimes seems as though the theology departments of today are mainly inhabited by people so focused on their sub-disciplines that they have no idea that they should be collaborating with their colleagues in a larger unified project called Theology.

Beyond its map of theology, however, *Method* lays out in a coherent framework an encapsulated overview of Lonergan's mature thought regarding human consciousness, meaning, society, religion, philosophy, history, faith, revelation, doctrine, and community.

If you are a person who does not like to think, you should definitely stay away from this book. Otherwise, please do not feel intimidated. The book is quite readable and yields much fruit even from a first pass. It is also the kind of book, however, that you will not exhaust in one reading. You will get more out of it every time you read it. After all, it is a work of genius.

Middlemarch: A Study of Provincial Life (Harmondsworth, Penguin, 1965) by George Eliot

Encountering George Eliot

Anne E. PATRICK, *S.N.J.M., Carleton College*

The sexist remarks of a famous literary critic led me to start reading George Eliot in June 1976, just after receiving my master's in Divinity from the University of Chicago. At the time I was casting about for a case to include in my doctoral dissertation, which would demonstrate the usefulness of H. Richard Niebuhr's "ethics of responsibility" for literary criticism of fiction. In 1976 I had not read much Niebuhr; what preoccupied me then were things that F.R. Leavis, a Cambridge University professor, had written about Eliot, whose original name was Mary Anne Evans (1819-80). In *The Great Tradition* (1948), Leavis had pronounced her one of a handful of truly excellent novelists, despite some unevenness in her writing.[1] Leavis believed that Eliot's strengths were due to her "maturity," and her weaknesses to "immaturity," evident (to him) in an alleged emotional involvement with certain of her fictional characters, which he assumed was due to her being female!

Leavis acknowledged *Middlemarch* (1871-72) as Eliot's masterpiece, but felt she had over-identified with its heroine, Dorothea Brooke, idealizing this young woman and her friend Will Ladislaw and largely exempting

---

[1] F. R. Leavis, *The Great Tradition* (1948; reprinted New York University Press, 1973). In this very influential book Leavis maintains that novelists comprising "the great tradition" of English fiction are Jane Austen, George Eliot, Henry James, Joseph Conrad, and D. H. Lawrence (p. 27).

them from the irony she displayed toward other characters. And when Leavis turned to Eliot's final novel, *Daniel Deronda* (1876), which dealt with themes of Jewish identity, he found her guilty of even greater lapses: "The Victorian intellectual certainly has a large part in her Zionist inspirations, but that doesn't make these the less fervidly emotional; . . . for the relation between the Victorian intellectual and the very feminine woman . . . comes very naturally and insidiously.... Deronda...decidedly, is a woman's creation."[2] What on earth does that mean? Leavis tells us yet more baldly in "George Eliot's Zionist Novel" (1960): "The provincial girl of lower middle-class origin, who by sheer ability established herself as a figure of the English intellectual world while still in young womanhood, *was* a woman. She was fully a woman, with a woman's needs."[3]

By 1976 I tended to think it more likely that Leavis himself was guilty of emotional indulgence, and to suspect that misogyny had kept him from appreciating a good deal of what was going on in Eliot's fiction. To test that hypothesis I set out to study her works on my own. That summer I read *Middlemarch* and *Daniel Deronda*, and then turned to Evans' essays, which were brilliant and surprisingly amusing. I also read a biography by Gordon Haight, and finally approached her early fiction, having been spared a premature exposure to *Silas Marner* in high school.

From this reading there developed a deep and enduring friendship with Mary Anne Evans, who like me had read Thomas à Kempis' *Imitation of Christ* appreciatively as a teenager, but unlike me had left off the pious Christianity of her childhood when she encountered critical biblical scholarship in her twenties. I, on the other hand, had spent (most of) my twenties in a starched white coif and long black serge habit, reading what was available on convent bookshelves and syllabi for courses taken at Catholic institutions during an 11-year quest for a B.A. in English the old-fashioned, pre-sister-formation way. After two years in my community's novitiate in Rome, NY, I was sent out to teach at age 19. I spent nine more years collecting credits mainly through courses taken after school, on Saturdays, and during the summers. I followed a similar plan for acquiring a master's degree in English, taking courses at the University of Maryland on the

---

2 Ibid., p. 82.
3 F. R. Leavis, "George Eliot's Zionist Novel," *Commentary* 30 (1960), p. 319.

basis of what was offered from 4-6 or 7-9 p.m. or in summer sessions. I had a reduced teaching load during my final semester there, and was able to write the interdisciplinary thesis "Eschatological Perspective in the Major Novels of Graham Greene" that helped me gain admission to the University of Chicago Divinity School's program in Religion and Literature in 1973, despite having only eight undergraduate credits in religion, two of them in Gregorian Chant.

I had felt the calling to become a theologian ever since studying the documents of Vatican II in 1967 and hearing talks by Monika Hellwig and Bernard Cooke around the same time. In the summer of 1969 I studied German toward that goal, and later asked my community to be freed for full-time theological studies in 1973. My strategy was to enter divinity school through the program that built on my literary training, and then take theology and ethics courses so as to emerge a theologian. In choosing Chicago over other options I wanted to avoid something I feared, perhaps unjustly, from Catholic institutions, namely being condescended to as a woman religious. Yet I also wanted a place where I could learn from outstanding Catholic scholars, and Bernard McGinn and David Tracy were on the Chicago faculty.

By the time I met the great critics of religion—Nietzsche, Freud, Marx—and contemporary atheists and agnostics, thinkers such as Paul Ricœur had come up with ways of understanding the issues that made it possible for me to develop a "second naïveté" sort of faith. In Mary Anne Evans' day, however, the only honest option she could see was to renounce the consolations of Christianity in favor of scientific humanism. I admired the courage and intellectual honesty she showed in making this decision as a young woman, and the open-mindedness she later displayed in coming to see value in religious traditions she did not personally espouse. I knew, of course, that her contemporaries John Henry Newman and Matthew Arnold had found different ways of dealing with the Victorian crisis of faith, and I think part of Eliot's appeal to me was sensing the analogy between the issues church membership raised for her in the 1840s and those surfacing in the 1970s over sexism in Christianity.

By 1976 I understood the options for Catholics who believed in the equal dignity of both sexes to have been framed by Mary Daly, who renounced all patriarchal religions, and Rosemary Radford Ruether, who believed the Christian gospel was at its core egalitarian, and our task was to reinterpret and reform the tradition. Four years earlier I had published my first essays in feminist ethics: a piece in *Sister Formation Bulletin* calling for the inclusion of women in all Catholic ministries, and a critical investigation of "Sex-Role Stereotyping and Catholic Education."[4] Imagine my delight when I discovered that George Eliot had anticipated me by more than a century, portraying Dinah Morris as a highly effective preacher in *Adam Bede* (1859), and demonstrating the problematic effects of sexist attitudes and social arrangements in many works, including *Middlemarch* and *Daniel Deronda*!

I was captivated from the beginning of *Middlemarch*, when Eliot introduced her main character, Dorothea Brooke, as bereft of the "coherent social faith and order" that had obtained when St. Teresa of Avila accomplished great deeds in sixteenth-century Spain.[5] Eliot regarded all her novels as "experiments in life," and in this work she sets up an experiment featuring two young persons, Tertius Lydgate, a doctor who aimed to do significant research while caring for patients, and Dorothea, an equally idealistic woman from the landed class, who felt in her late teens that the only way to accomplish important things was to marry a middle-aged pedant, Edmond Casaubon, and help him publish his "Key to All Mythologies." In the end Lydgate leaves Middlemarch thoroughly discouraged by difficulties experienced there, and blames his misfortunes on his self-centered wife, Rosamond Vincy. Dorothea's first husband dies before she has to deal with his outdated project, and she ends up content to do good in the world as the wife of Will Ladislaw, "an ardent public man" who worked on reforms through Parliament. Although Dorothea's influence was not "historic," she is judged a moral success, whereas Lydgate, who showed such promise in his youth, dies embittered and unhappy. Dorothea also suffered, but she came to recognize the unity of all life and her part in it, and she was able to surmount experiences that led to feelings of grief and despair. Lydgate, however, never stopped seeing himself

---

4   Anne E. Patrick, "Creative Ministry: Apostolic Women Today," *Sister Formation Bulletin* 19 (Fall 1972): 8-15; "Sex-Role Stereotyping and Catholic Education," *Momentum* 3 (December 1972): 7-13.

5   George Eliot, *Middlemarch* (1871-82; reprint, Harmondsworth: Penguin Books, 1965), p. 25.

as the alienated victim of the otherness around him, especially the female otherness he chose to marry.

By the time I finished reading *Middlemarch* I had no doubt that the esteemed critic F.R. Leavis had missed one of the most important ethical insights George Eliot derived from this "experiment in life," namely the harm done to women *and* men by the sexist attitudes and social arrangements that characterized Middlemarch.[6] The novel also demonstrated other concepts that became important to me, including the social dimensions of conscience, but it was Eliot's critique of gender stereotyping that made the greatest impact on me initially. Finding so much evidence against the sexism of a very influential literary critic in 1976 gave me confidence in my own judgment and increased my sense of the importance of bringing a feminist perspective to Catholic theology and ethics.

---

6 A thorough report on my findings is published as "Rosamond Rescued: George Eliot's Critique of Sexism in *Middlemarch*," *The Journal of Religion* 67 (1987): 220-38.

Mujerista Theology:
A Theology for the Twenty-First Century
(Orbis Books, 1996) by Ada Maria Isasi Diaz

Bringing the Struggle of Latinas to the Table

Michelle Gonzalez MALDONADO, *University of Miami*

In 1989 a brief autobiographical essay by Ada María Isasi-Díaz changed my life. I was a senior at Georgetown University taking a class on feminist theology. I loved the subject. However, as a twenty-year-old Latina, I had never read a theological word written by a Hispanic or been taught by a Hispanic professor in any subject. Before discovering this essay, I did not even know that a thing called Latino/a theology existed. I knew I wanted to write theology, but I thought to accomplish this meant sacrificing my culture, my identity, and my feminism. Something I was not very willing to do. And then I read Ada María's brilliant reflection on her Cuban heritage, the women's ordination movement, and the ambiguity and tensions of their intersection within her life.

"A Hispanic Garden in a Foreign Land," reappeared in my life when it was reprinted in Ada María's collection of essays, *Mujerista Theology: A Theology for the Twenty-First Century*. At the time of its publication I was completing my Masters at Union Theological Seminary. This text not only initiated a theological movement that would bear the book's title, it explores themes that continue to be central in theological discourse even today. It has set the stage for many of the questions that Latino/a and feminist theologians continue to explore in their scholarship. My reflection on this book will highlight some of the major essays within it that have had a lasting impact on my theological worldview.

Ada María's text offered an introduction to Latina feminist theology that explored key themes within theology. The book is deeply informed by her Cuban roots and weaves autobiographical anecdotes with theological reflection. The deep particularity of her experience opens up a world where the reader connects with her, and consequently her insights, in ways that traditional academic theology is incapable of doing. The book not only argues that action is fundamental to academic theology, but also that without it theology is ultimately not authentic. Ada María defines herself as an "activist-theologian" who understands the theological task as ultimately liberative.

A clear intent of this book was to make the experiences and struggles of Latinas conversation partners within the larger discourse of liberation and feminist theologies. Latino/a experience is often rendered invisible within the black/white paradigm of racial discourse in the United States or sidelined as the inferior stepchild of Latin American scholarship. The book was published at a time when womanist (African-American feminist) theology was becoming more widely read. The term *mujerista* was a way to bring the struggles of Latinas to the table. In her introduction Ada María is very clear about the intent of her *mujerista* theology: to provide a venue for the voices of grassroots Latinas, take seriously their experiences as a theological resource, and challenge those theological teachings that oppress Latinas. This last point is significant for it becomes a theological norm in her work, one that embraces a preferential option for the oppressed as normative.

Her opening essay emerges from the pain of leaving her homeland and her struggles to find a home first in a convent, then later in the women's ordination movement. There she is shocked to discover racism and ethnic prejudice. She then turns to her mother's legacy, acknowledging both its positive and negative aspects. From Ada María I learned that I was able to be critical of my Cuban heritage while at the same time embracing it, and that this was not a betrayal.

The next essay is the writing by Ada María that I have assigned most often in my classes, "To Struggle for Justice is to Pray." Autobiography also opens this chapter, and here we encounter her time as a missionary in Lima, Peru. Two profound insights are found in this brief essay. The first is the lived experience of the poor as the foundation for her theology. This insight, which resonates with the writings of Latin American liberation theologians, reads more powerfully within her own personal narrative than it does in the jargon of traditional academic theology. The second is her realization that spirituality is not reserved for the elite and does not have to be nourished by disembodied prayer. Instead, it is in the midst of concrete, embodied social justice that she becomes closer to the sacred. One does not have to take refuge from this world to be spiritual; one can encounter God in the messiness of life.

In her essay defining *mujerista* theology she focuses on the preferential option for Latinas, the significance of liberative praxis, and the importance of daily life. In Ada María's work, daily life (*lo cotidiano*) is not only material, but also cultural. It is something that is conscious, not merely repeated mechanically. It does not refer exclusively to the private or domestic sphere. Epistemologically, it is linked to what is known as "common sense." Due to its material and epistemological value, for Ada María *lo cotidiano* exemplifies the unity of action and reflection. She partially blames the failures of liberationist movements to transform structures of oppression on the neglect of *lo cotidiano*.

Lo cotidiano is a central characteristic of *mujerista* theology. Since its inception, *mujerista* theology has emphasized the concrete lived experiences of Latinas as the starting point for theology. For Ada María this is the site of struggle, resistance and transformation. It is the space of popular religion, inhabited by the saints and *virgenes* of Latino/a devotions. The category of *lo cotidiano* is not only descriptive, but also hermeneutic and epistemological.

As she states in the chapter entitled "*Mujerista* Theology Challenge to Traditional Theology": "*Lo cotidiano* also includes the way we Latinas consider actions, discourses, norms, established social roles, and our own selves. ... *Lo cotidiano* is a way of referring to Latinas' efforts to understand and express how and why their lives are the way they are, how and why they function as they do" (pp. 67-68).

This emphasis on *lo cotidiano* protects *mujerista* theology from essentialist claims. The centrality of daily life is not, however, uncritical, only that which contributes to the liberation of Latinas is salvific. It also does not reduce theology to pure relativism. The liberative principle remains the norm within her theology. However, daily life reminds us of the partial and fragmentary nature of all our knowledge.

"Elements of a *Mujerista* Anthropology," is the essay I have cited most frequently in my own scholarship. In *mujerista* theology three phrases are critical to anthropology: *la lucha, permítame hablar*, and *la comunidad/la familia*. These are not the only sources, nor are they necessarily exclusive to Latinas. However, they are starting points for reflections on theological anthropology that takes as its starting point Latinas lives. To speak of these three phrases is to offer an arena for Latinas' theological contributions: Latinas' daily lives, their contributive voices, and their relational conception of selfhood. Family and community are fundamental dimensions of human nature. This essay captures the maturity of Ada María's scholarship, where she is beginning to make theological claims based on the insights gathered from the Latinas that inform her work.

I remember years ago sitting at a conference watching Ada María being criticized for her use of ethnography and her refusal to make essentialist claims about all Latinas. I think back at this moment with a smile on my face because her critics could not have been more wrong. Today we see more and more the ethnographic turn within the study of religion and the insider/outsider voice of the academic who does not remain radically distanced from their subjects of study. Today we see discourses such as Latino/a, Black, and Latin American theologies being criticized for their essentialist claims about the populations they claim to represent. We cannot make those critiques of Ada's work. She seemed to have known long before many of us how to say something about a particular population, yet have it impact a much broader readership.

The autobiographical voice Ada María embraces within many of her writings is an example of the significance of daily life in her work. I must confess that these are my favorite moments in her writings. For Ada María has a way of telling a story while educating us about sophisticated theological concepts all at the same time. While today we exist in an academy that constantly reminds us of the importance of context and culture, there is still hesitancy amongst academics to reveal themselves entirely. Thus, a certain detachment remains the norm in theological discourse. This is not the case in Ada María's voice. She is not afraid to show us that she is passionate about a topic and why.

I must conclude with a note on Ada María. As I have written in reflections on her after her death, Ada María was a mentor, an inspiration, and a friend. She was just as warm, brilliant, and passionate in person as she is in her writing. She was an inspiration for many young Latino/a theologians. And she always went out of her way to read and comment on our work. Her commitment to the everyday Latinas whose insights informed her work was unmatched. These "organic theologians," as she described them, both supported and informed her scholarship. They are part of this broader legacy Ada María has left us. She concludes *Mujerista Theology* with the words "*la vida es la lucha,*" (to struggle is to live). We continue the struggle in her memory and she lives on in that struggle.

New Seeds of Contemplation
(New York: New Directions, 1961)
by Thomas Merton

Discovering the True Self in God

Ilia DELIO, O.S.F., *Villanova University*

I discovered Thomas Merton in the midst of a laboratory. I was a doctoral student in Pharmacology at New Jersey Medical School working on a model of motoneuron disease known as ALS (Lou Gehrig's disease). I remember standing in the middle of the lab one day, procrastinating by thumbing through *Time* magazine. I enjoyed reading the book review section and was struck by a new biography of a monk named Thomas Merton. I had never heard of Merton but the summary of the book was intriguing. I went home that evening and reread the book review. The highlights of his life were fascinating: an intellectual from Columbia University whose cultural and literary life were relinquished for a life of solitude and silence in a Trappist monastery. I was drawn to Merton like a magnet. I bought Monica Furlong's biography and read it in a single evening. I then went and purchased Merton's *Seven Storey Mountain*, and after finishing this book, I knew that I wanted to follow Merton's path. The rest, as they say, is history.

What drew me to Merton (and still does) was his deep inner search for truth and light; his inner yearning for God. I encountered his *New Seeds of Contemplation* while teaching a graduate spirituality course at Washington Theological Union. This book, in particular, encapsulated his spirituality for me—not in a biographical sense—but by his profound soulful depth, which at times seem to touch infinity. In fact, it is the opening chapters of this book that I return to again and again because they are, to me, like the opening chapters of Genesis, revealing the truth of creation and our capacity for God.

Two particular ideas stand out in the beginning, which I think govern the flow of ideas throughout the book: prayer and self-identity. Merton explores the integral link between prayer and identity in his opening chapters, "Pray for Your Own Discovery" and "Things in Their Identity." He plumbs these ideas with the mind of a philosopher and the pen of a poet: "The seeds that are planted in my liberty at every moment, by God's will, are the seeds of my own identity, my own reality, my own happiness, my own sanctity. To refuse them is to refuse everything; it is the refusal of my own existence and being: of my identity, my very self."

Often we think of ourselves as finished products, as if God created us and then disappeared. But Merton, like the spiritual writer Beatrice Bruteau, realized how short-sighted this thinking can be. The "I" is not a finished product, something left over from God's creative activity; rather, it is the very process of God's creative action. Merton too had something of this idea when he said "Our vocation is not simply to be, but to work together with God in the creation of our own life, our own identity, our own destiny." To know this truth, Merton wrote, we are to "pray for our own discovery."

To pray, in the monastic sense, is to enter into dialogue with God, heart to heart. Prayer is that deep silent encounter in which the innermost center of our being continuously stretches toward that which is not yet seen or fully known; yet, it is a type of deep knowing that we belong to God. Merton drew on the integral relationship between God and the human person, as if defining the double helix of divinity and humanity: our lives are intertwined with God's life. "God utters me like a partial thought of himself," he wrote. Hence the only path to true happiness is prayer, and prayer begins with self-discovery.

Merton's chapter on self-identity is a classic on par with Saint Augustine's opening page of the Confessions: "You have made us for yourself, O Lord, and our hearts are restless until they rest in You." Merton wrote: *"The secret of our identity is hidden in the love and mercy of God."* In fact, one could hear the voice of Augustine echoing throughout Merton's prose. For the New Seeds of Contemplation aims to do what Augustine himself did, to discover the ground of our happiness, our true vocation as human persons. Merton's work, like Augustine's *Confessions*, is not a "how to" book, but a foundations book: the ground of contemplation, the realization that there is no *cogito* or *ego* only *SUM*. Contemplation is the transcendence of all divisions into the higher reality of oneness-in-love: "It is our emptiness in the presence of His reality, our silence in the presence of His infinitely rich silence, our joy in the bosom of the serene darkness in which His light holds us absorbed, it is all this that praises Him."

It is apparent that the Gospel Parable of the Seeds (Lk 8:4-15) influenced Merton's thought. A farmer knows that seeds must be planted on rich fertile soil, free of rocks and debris, if good seeds are to bring forth good life. Similarly, to say that God utters me like a partial thought of himself is to say there is a seed of God planted in my life, but the inner soil of my heart must be fertile and free of hardened rocks if this seed is to grow into the fullness of my life. Merton becomes eloquent at times, his artistic prose drawing the lines between Creator and creature, like a painter scanning the canvas of the soul. Nowhere is he more expressive than in his chapter on the true and false self:

> Every one of us is shadowed by an illusory person: a false self. This is the man that I want myself to be but who cannot exist, because God does not know anything about him.... My false and private self is the one who wants to exist outside the reach of God's will and God's love—outside of reality and outside of life. And such a life cannot help but be an illusion.... The secret of my identity is hidden in the love and mercy of God.... Therefore I cannot hope to find myself anywhere except in him.... Therefore there is only one problem on which all my existence, my peace and my happiness depend: to discover myself in discovering God. If I find Him I will find myself and if I find my true self I will find him" (pp. 34-36).

The search for true identity requires an honest self-love. Love of self is not selfishness but a humble recognition of our lives as true, good and beautiful. Without real love of self, all other loves are distorted. Lack of self-knowledge, Saint Bonaventure once wrote, makes for faulty knowledge in all other matters. Merton realized that so many people are weighed down by deep hurts, anger, resentment, lost loves, broken relationships, desperately seeking to fill their lives with happiness and peace. As he himself was searching for truth and identity, he came to a deep insight—that each human person already has what they are looking for: "Within myself is a metaphorical apex of existence at which I am held in being by my Creator."

Merton thought that to live the truth of our own existence is to be a saint. "A tree is holy," he wrote, "simply by being a tree"; flowers are saints gazing up into the face of God. We humans are no less called to be ourselves, and in being ourselves, to radiate the glory of God. However, very few people grasp the holiness of their lives. Rather, there is an implicit belief that God is watching from above and that we have to make our way to heaven to see God. Merton said, "We cannot go to heaven because we do not know where heaven is or what it is," so God comes to us. God comes down from heaven and finds us, just as God sought Adam in the Garden of Eden (cf. Gen 3:9). There is nothing we can do or say that can alienate God from our lives. We can disown God but God cannot disown us because God cannot disown God's own self; the self that is the very source of our lives (2 Tim 2:13).

Merton understood this inscrutable mystery by saying, "Our discovery of God is, in a way, God's discovery of us." Our praying to God is God praying in us. Our lives and God's life are so intertwined that loving God is God loving God's own self in us. Prayer is waking up to this reality, coming to a new consciousness of God's in-dwelling presence. "We become contemplatives," Merton wrote, "when God discovers himself in us." So God does not desire that we become anything other than the true self, which God has loved from all eternity.

The chapters unfolding in *New Seeds* flow from this foundational truth of self-discovery in God. For if our life's journey is knowing the truth of ourselves in God, then all wars would cease, violence would be banished, the world would be a sacred sphere, broken bones would be healed and hearts mended. If we could discover this great mystery of God in us, we would be truly free and out of this freedom the seeds of our lives would sprout into a new world of justice and peace.

Night (Hill and Wang, 1960) by Elie Wiesel

Memoir, Expose, and Testimony

Dianne BERGANT, C.S.A., *Catholic Theological Union*

Shortly before the opening of the Second Vatican Council, a remarkable new religious publication was born. It was called *Jubilee*, from the Latin *Jubilate, Deo* (Sing joyfully to God). Founded by Ed Rice and co-edited by Robert Lax and Thomas Merton, the magazine was relatively short-lived (1953-1967). However, in that brief period of time, it fulfilled its goal to "produce a Catholic literary magazine that would act as a forum for addressing issues confronting the contemporary church." One of the issues of this magazine included a chapter from *Night*, a recently published (1958 in French; 1960 English translation) book by Elie Wiesel. This chapter made a significant impression on me, an intellectually searching, recently professed, young woman religious. It prompted me to seek out the book which, after all these years, continues to touch my heart and sear my conscience.

It is difficult to identify the genre of this book. It is a memoir written by a man who has committed his entire life to 'remember' what happened to him and to millions of other Jews whose horror has come to be known as the Shoah (Hebrew for "catastrophe") or Holocaust (Greek for "burnt"). But this is more than a memoir. It is also an exposé of the depths of depravity to which individuals and society can descend. While this slim volume is certainly both memoir and exposé, perhaps it is best regarded as a testimony to the indomitability of the human spirit. This book has left its mark on me in all three ways.

Wiesel tells of his first night in Birkenau, the first death camp to which he was sent. He had been a pious boy whose life was dedicated to the study of the Talmud. However, his very first encounter with the atrocities he would witness stripped him of his innocence. He became aware of the mystery of iniquity as he watched babies being thrown into a burning pit. This was the night of the death of God in the soul of this innocent boy:

> Never shall I forget that night, the first night in camp,
> that turned my life into one long night seven times sealed.
> Never shall I forget that smoke.
> Never shall I forget the small faces of the children whose
> bodies I saw transformed into smoke under a silent sky.
> Never shall I forget those flames that consumed my faith forever.
> Never shall I forget the nocturnal silence that deprived me
> for all eternity of the desire to live.
> Never shall I forget those moments that murdered my God
> and my soul and turned my dreams to ashes.
> Never shall I forget those things, even were I condemned
> to live as long as god himself.
> Never.

What is one to make of such sentiments? How can one measure the power of evil that can, in one glance, totally destroy one's concept of God?

What did I know of suffering? There had been illness and death in my family, but never brutality. I was not aware of human inhumanity against another. I too grew up with the concept of God as caring, generous, and, when necessary, forgiving. I had not yet meet Job, nor been startled by his bold question: Why have you allowed this to happen? But even as I was horrified by this scene, I realized that I was reading the account in the comfort of my room; I was not, like Wiesel, standing before the pit, unsure of my own fate. My image of a loving God was not threatened, as was his. However, this was perhaps the first time that I wondered about my understanding of divine providence.

It was not the actual physical suffering as reported by Wiesel that struck me most. It was the inhumanity that these prisoners were forced to endure that took my breath away and left a knot in my stomach. Wiesel was an only son, a position of no mean status in a devout Jewish family.

And yet the merciless deprivation of food and water and sleep he was forced to bear and the excruciating labor that stifled every ounce of his energy reduced him to the level of brute self-survival. He confesses this as he recounts his father's last agony:

> I remember that night, the most horrendous of my life:
>
> "The SS had flown into a rage and was striking my father on the head: "Be quiet, old man! Be quiet!"
> "Eliezer! Eliezer! Come, don't leave me alone…"
> His voice had reached me so far away, from so close.
> But I did not move.
> I shall never forgive myself.
> Nor shall I ever forgive the world for having pushed me against the wall, for having turned me into a stranger, for having awakened in me the basest, most primitive instincts. His last word had been my name. A summons. And I had not responded.

Having drained this sixteen-year-old boy of all physical, emotional, and spiritual resources, his tormentors forced him to decide between responding to his dying father and protecting the possibility of his own survival. Terror forced him to make a decision that tore at his heart and would tear open that wound for the rest of his life. To compound his torment, he blamed himself for his cowardice and would continually blame himself for his craven weakness.

What did I know about sin? I certainly was guilty of the typical childhood misbehavior: disobedience, fighting, cheating, lying, etc. However, I had never before envisioned the blatant evil depicted in this short passage. I had never before conceived of the scope and character of torture that could so strip a vulnerable boy of the fundamental bond of love and devotion between himself and his father. I couldn't image treating my own father that way. Yet, I realized that such weakness is in all of us, and all an enemy had to do was discover it and exploit it. It made me realize that in the right circumstances, every human being is probably capable of almost anything. For the first time, the expression, 'There but for the grace of God' took on meaning for me.

Having been liberated from the death camp and having almost died from illness after his liberation, Wiesel felt compelled to bear witness to the atrocities perpetrated against the Jewish people. He was and continues to be convinced that if we forget, we are guilty; we are accomplices to those atrocities. However, he was stunned, as was I, that no one seemed to care. When he first came to the camp, he believed that some country in the world, some group of people, some individuals would do what they could to end such crimes. But it did not happen, and he soon lost hope in any form of human indignation. In fact, when the captives, within whose number he was included, were being transported in cattle cars or forced to run through the countryside, civilians considered them curiosities, gawked at them, or even made sport of their condition. No one appeared concerned or willing to alleviate their suffering, much less step forward in the name of simple decency.

This apparent indifference persisted even after the war ended and attempts toward recovery were under way. Wiesel wrote the first draft of this book in Yiddish. It was then translated it into both French and English. However, it was rejected by every major French and American publisher. This happened despite the endorsement and efforts of the great French Catholic writer and Nobel laureate François Mauriac. Only after months of personal visits, letters, and phone calls did Mauriac finally succeed in getting Wiesel's manuscript into print. For some reason, the urgency of the message was not realized.

Despite the horrors that robbed him of his innocence, shattered the structure of his Jewish piety, and stripped him of his inherent concern for others, Wiesel clung to life. Even when life appeared to be nothing more than a struggle for survival, he clung to life. Even when the God to whom he had committed his life seemed to have abandoned him, he clung to life. Even when he experienced to the core of his being the world's disdain for the Jewish people, he clung to life. His spirit may have been compromised, but it was not destroyed.

The message of *Night* has never ceased to challenge me. Its account of human depravity reminds me of the enemy that stalks our streets seeking a place in the human heart. Its portrayal of self-sacrifice in the face of personal tragedy inspires me to courage and valor. Its unmasking of individual and societal disinterest in the suffering of others accuses me of my own complacency. It reminds me of the teaching of another Jew, also a victim of the cruelty of others:

> "…as you did it to one of the least of these who are members of my family, you did it to me." (Mt 25:40)

Pedagogy of the Oppressed (Herder & Herder, 1970) by Paolo Freire

A Pedagogy for Oppressors

Thomas GROOME, *Boston College*

Liberation: In the Beginning . . .

I grew up in a traditional Irish home, yet one where I often heard the rhetoric of *liberation* and *freedom* associated with living our Catholic faith. By today's categories, my father could be described as a socialist, though he would eschew the label. For his politics, he was simply following the logic of his Christian faith. A local politician elected many times to public office, his invariable platform was care for the poor and downtrodden, decent housing, medical care, good education for all, and the rights of workers to a fair wage. He constantly critiqued the colonizing influence that England had had on Ireland. He took an active part in the Irish War of Independence from British rule that began in 1916 (he was 18 at the time)—and drags on to this day in Northern Ireland. So his life work was a struggle for Irish freedom—to be enjoyed by all its people.

In the broader Irish society, too, the language of *liberation* was fairly commonplace. The great Daniel O'Connell (1775-1847), whose philosophy of peaceful resistance influenced Gandhi and Martin Luther King, was hailed in Ireland as "The Liberator." O'Connell's work, which culminated in religious freedom for Catholics in 1829, was termed "Catholic emancipation." If one of us nine kids balked at going to Sunday Mass, my mother would remind us that this was what the Liberator had won for us with "emancipation." So instead of a duty, Sunday Mass was an act of freedom.

It was to my great amazement—and delight—then, that upon beginning my doctoral studies at Union Theological Seminary and Columbia University in 1973, I discovered an emerging world of "liberation theology." My first encounter was with Gustavo Gutierrez's *A Theology of Liberation*; upon finishing it, I wrote home to say, "Dad, you've been right all along." I was also introduced to the emerging feminist theology literature; Bev Harrison was my major advisor at Union. However, the most significant "homecoming" was when I discovered a *liberating pedagogy*. I first read Paulo Freire's *Pedagogy of the Oppressed* in 1973 (published in English in 1970) with heart-throbbing excitement. My life has never been the same since. Given when I read it, no book has influenced me more than *Pedagogy of the Oppressed*.

My Friend Paulo

I presume a first-name familiarity here because I had the blessing of becoming a friend of Paulo's. I met him when he visited Union Theological during my time there and at other places along the way. However, it was when I had the privilege to host and co-teach with him in a course at Boston College's Summer Institute that our friendship was cemented. I was honored when he had my book *Christian Religious Education* (Harper and Row, 1980) translated into Portuguese and wrote the Preface for the Brazilian edition.

I also became friends with his dear spouse, Elza, during their two summers at Boston College. People should know that Elza was the trained educator of the two; Paulo's degree was in law. It was Elza who often gave him the pedagogical language to say what he wanted to say. She was also a catalyst to his feminist consciousness—which emerged after his writing of *Pedagogy of the Oppressed*. The day after Elza went home to God, I felt honored when Paulo called me to share his grief, and just to reminisce for a while about her, knowing that she was also my friend.

What I Learned from Paulo

Meanwhile, what did I learn from Paulo Freire that has shaped my own work at the interface of theology and education ever since? Without being exhaustive, I can think of the following cumulative points.

1) First, education is always a "political activity," deeply influencing the quality of people's lives in the world and likewise their socio-cultural-political context. Education's politics must be for humanization and the liberation of all; nothing less is worthy of our human vocation. Teachers inevitably have political power within every teaching/learning event; they can choose to use this power to control and limit or to empower and enable people toward humanization

2) To be humanizing and liberating, the pedagogy employed must be one that conscientizes its participants. Conscientization is a process of becoming aware of one's place in the world and its forms of oppression and then of committing to act as a historical agent of social liberation. Reaching beyond "awareness," conscientization is only achieved when it acts with imagination and commitment to change oppressive social structures.

3) A pedagogy of conscientization/liberation must begin by enabling people to *name* their own *realidad:* to express in their own words what they perceive as their socio-cultural-political context. They must speak their own word and name their own reality rather than having the educator name it for them. Thus, emancipatory pedagogy is one of dialogue—what he calls a "dialogic action"—rather than a monologue by the educator. "Dialogue is the encounter between people, mediated by the world, in order to name the world" (*Pedagogy*, 76). He was convinced that enabling oppressed people to speak their own word was already an act of social transformation: "To speak a true word is to transform the world" (ibid, 75).

4) I once heard him refer to himself as a "vagabond of the obvious." What he meant was that much of what people think they "see" is what they have been told to see through the codification of their socio-political context. The challenge then is to pose the kinds of questioning and reflective activities that encourage people to "decodify" their reality, to see and name for themselves what is obvious about it. This amounts to seeing beyond what "they say" to what is truly there—often "staring them in the face"

and yet ignored. As people come to see for themselves, they can imagine what ought to be done so as to act toward freedom.

5) A key to implementing Paulo's pedagogy was to engage people with "generative themes," by which he meant real life issues that pertain to their quest to live humanly and with dignity. To begin with such generative themes and have people name and reflect critically upon them through dialogue is the opposite of what he famously named "banking education"—the process of depositing information in passive receptacles. It is through dialogical education around their own generative themes that people can move from dependency to agency for their liberation, to act as "subjects" (not "objects") to change their *realidad*.

6) Within dialogic education, Paulo saw all participants as co-teachers and co-learners together; all are to learn from each other. Yet, such egalitarian and dialogical education does not rob educators of their word or exclude them as resources to their co-learners. Indeed, he recognized that sometimes the educator needs to "occupy the vertex of the triangle in contradiction to the oppressors and to the oppressed" (*Pedagogy*, p. 164). Also, "Not all lecturing is banking education; it depends on the content and the dynamism of the presentation, whether I tell people what to think or invite them to think for themselves" (Freire at Boston College, Summer 1983).

7) For Paulo, education should always be a "utopian activity," full of trust in people and confidence in their potential to be agents of their own liberation. This perhaps was his conviction that amazed me most, given that much of his work was with poor illiterate peasants. A phrase he repeated often in our teaching together, especially when people seemed overwhelmed by what he was proposing, was, "The best way to accomplish those things that are impossible today is to do whatever *is* possible." As in the parable of God's reign being like a mustard seed or pinch of leaven (Luke 13), so in the struggle for liberation and justice, he was confident that even small efforts can bring results beyond proportion.

All of these features I've tried to adopt in my work of educating-in-faith across the years, often adjusting to another time and cultural reality (as Paulo would encourage). However, it is likely his turn to a praxis epistemology that has been most influential on my own pedagogy and that which I recommend to religious educators. As he advised, "Liberation is a praxis: the action and reflection of people upon their world in order to transform it" (*Pedagogy*, p. 66). By giving priority to historical praxis, Paulo was rejecting the one-way "theory to practice" assumption that marks so much of education. Instead, he wanted the knowing process to begin with people's critical reflection upon their own lives in the world. However, while he favored beginning with people's own historical praxis (as Dewey might say, their own "experience"), his intent was to honor the three ways of knowing outlined by Aristotle as *theoria, praxis,* and *poiesis.*

In other words, though beginning with people's historical praxis, for Paulo this is to lead them into the "theory" of whatever discipline is being taught and to engage participants' imaginations to craft (poiesis) what should be done. Echo here my own favored approach to educating-in-faith that I named "shared Christian praxis." It engages people's reflection on life, in the light of Christian faith, within a community of conversation, toward lived faith that is liberating for all.

For this essay I returned and re-read *Pedagogy of the Oppressed* for the umpteenth time. Now I have some more critiques than I had at first blush in 1973. For example, his notion that the oppressed have responsibility to liberate their oppressors is true to an extent, but could be unfair or even destructive in some contexts, for example, in situations of domestic violence. Then I favor *conversation* as a more engaging term than *dialogue*. Also, I wonder if his political analysis, even of his Brazilian context, is now well-dated. And the gender exclusivity of the text reads as more irritating than ever. With the years, too, I've come to realize that for our first world context, Paulo's pedagogy is as much for oppressors as it is for the oppressed.

And yet, anyone familiar with my own work in religious education and practical theology across the years will readily recognize why I say *Pedagogy of the Oppressed* was the most influential book I ever read and especially for when I read it—at the beginning of my scholarly vocation.

Personal Writings
(translated and edited by Joseph A. Munitiz and Philip Endean, New York: Penguin Classics, 1996) by Saint Ignatius of Loyola

Pilgrimage of Life

Lisa FULLAM, *Jesuit School of Theology of Santa Clara University*

Ignatius of Loyola begins his *Autobiography* with a major life change when he was about 30 years old. Recuperating from reconstructive surgery following a battle wound, he read the lives of the saints and began to wonder what would happen if he did the kinds of things that saints did. Noting how his emotions and imagination were caught up in these reveries, he redirected his life from that of a bawdy and scrappy courtier to that of a pilgrim, a companion of Jesus, the founder of a spirituality that has shaped the lives of innumerable pilgrims since, myself among them.

I was in my thirties, in the process of my own major shift of direction in life, when I first read the *Autobiography*. Mine was less drastic than Ignatius'—I was neither as boisterous as the pre-conversion Ignatius, and am nowhere near as saintly as he became—though we both found ourselves tossed back into school when we'd anticipated being fully fledged. Emily Saliers of the Indigo Girls sings about reading the diary of Virginia Woolf and finding herself on "a kind of a telephone line through time. And the voice at the other end comes like a long-lost friend." So it was for me, too, when I found an unlikely friend in a 16th century courtier-turned-pilgrim.

At the urging of some of his close associates, Ignatius agreed to meet with the Portuguese Jesuit Luis Gonçalves da Camara, to tell his life story. The process was unusual: in intermittent meetings from 1553-1555, Ignatius would converse with Gonçalves da Camera, who then would go write down what he recalled of Ignatius' words—sometimes immediately, sometimes weeks later. The *Autobiography* covers the years from 1521-1538, from Pamplona, where Ignatius was wounded, to his first year working full-time in Rome as leader of the nascent Society of Jesus. The original plan had been to continue the story, but Ignatius died in 1556 before the project could be resumed.

It is just as well that the *Autobiography* ends where it does. Here we have the pilgrim Ignatius discovering how God was working in him, and we see his fits and starts as he discovers what his new direction in life will entail. It is in this phase of his life that the bulk of Ignatius' *Spiritual Exercises* was composed, shaped by Ignatius' own spiritual journey, by those he led in the Exercises, and by adjustments made to mollify the Inquisitors who show up repeatedly in the text to evaluate, threaten, and often to imprison Ignatius. It is in this period that the contours of Ignatian spirituality take shape. Here we meet Ignatius in all his early full-speed-ahead enthusiasm. In the *Autobiography*, the mature Ignatius introduces us to himself as he was starting out and, more importantly, to God who called him from courtier to pilgrim.

What drew me was not merely the coincidence of a redirection of life in our mid-adult years, but the intensely imaginative, even playful spirituality Ignatius forged. Ignatius framed spiritual life as adventure and he headed out to discover who God was calling him to be, with whom and for whom. Ignatius' God is deeply kind, even—perhaps especially—when we might be slow on the uptake, but willing to strive. This is a cataphatic spirituality—all creation reveals its creator, an insight that this veterinarian can wholeheartedly endorse. Ignatius was formed academically in the Renaissance humanism of his time, reflecting a wide-open attitude to learning and intellectual endeavor that is a criterion in my own faith and work. Ignatius' fearlessness is both encouragement and challenge to me, as is the commitment to social justice that flows naturally from all the traits of this path.

But how did *Ignatius* come to know this particular way God works with some souls? That's his topic in the *Autobiography*: the shaping of a pilgrim. Ultimately, all spirituality is biography; here I will point to three key aspects of Ignatian spirituality as we see them in the *Autobiography*: availability, discernment, and companionship.

Availability

Every worthwhile spirituality has a radical edge that, if lived out, shapes its adherents in a distinctive way. The edge of Ignatian spirituality is availability to respond to the call of God. Ignatius describes this over and over in his writings as standing "as with one foot raised," ready to go wherever the greater glory of God might be served. People who speak of Ignatian "indifference" have it exactly backward: the goal is not indifference but rather passionate connection to the most important person—Jesus—and the most important thing—availability for wherever God sends us for the help of souls, in light of which central commitments all other attachments are held.

We see this throughout the *Autobiography*, first in Ignatius' willingness to set aside both the courtier's life against the desires of his family and his own delights. Ignatius made this shift on the basis of a glimmer of insight: when he let his imagination roam into what he might do if he were to do "this which St. Francis did, and this which St. Dominic did," he found himself at peace and happy, while fantasies of what his return to court life might hold left him dry and discontented. Still recovering from surgery, he would ponder his plan, "wishing he was already completely well so as to begin on his way" (p. 11). Ignatian availability is the profound and joyful freedom of a companion of Jesus.

Ignatius' first desire was to spend his life in Jerusalem, visiting holy sites and being of help to pilgrims. Refused by the Franciscan community there and forced to return to Spain, he discerned that further study would help him be of greater service, (and, not incidentally, would help him defend himself from the Inquisitors). Availability for that mission led Ignatius in his early 30's to sit in a Latin class with boys half his age, then on to further studies in Alcala and Paris. His priestly ordination in 1537 is mentioned in passing in the context of the narrative of the work of

Ignatius and his companions in Venice; in Ignatian spirituality everything is to be understood in the context of discerned availability for the work of God on earth. In our own time, Ignatian educators speak of forming "men and women for others," people available for the service of God and the help of souls.

Discernment

Discernment is the ability, in Ignatius' language, to distinguish between the kinds of spirits that can stir the human heart. Is what I hear the Good spirit of God, or, what one spiritual director of mine used to call "the not-the-Good spirit"? Availability without discernment leaves one tossed whichever way whichever spirit may be blowing, as aimless as a dry leaf in the wind. Discernment without availability is abstract and narcissistic, a theoretical pondering that remains fruitless from lack of the courage or willingness to respond.

Ignatius introduces us to his own process of learning discernment with a joke at his own expense. After his decision to reorient his life to the service of God and the help of souls, Ignatius had no clear idea what to do next. He set out for the Benedictine monastery at Montserrat. Along the way he met a Moor, who expressed doubt at Mary's perpetual virginity. Ignatius was stumped—in his new state as a servant of God, should he avenge Mary's honor by killing the Moor, or let him go because servants of God shouldn't go around killing people? He decided to let his mule decide. At the fork in the road ahead, if his mule followed the Moor's, Ignatius would kill him. If not, he would let the man go in peace. It ended happily for all concerned when Ignatius' mule took the other road. Ignatius tells this story not to celebrate his cluelessness, but "so that people can understand how Our Lord used to deal with this soul: a soul that was still blind, though with great desires to serve him as far as its knowledge went" (p. 14).

Discernment in the Ignatian sense is an ongoing communication of the soul with God, adjusting to the needs of the situation. Sometimes even good discernments don't work out, like Ignatius' decision to remain permanently in Jerusalem, an intention he returned to late in the *Autobiography*, and again this proved impossible. When one's discernment is thwarted, the available soul remains ready to change direction, to respond anew to God who continues to work in us. It is a truism in Ignatian circles that God is always already ahead of us, at work in the world and in our own souls even before we are aware of God's presence and action. To be Ignatian, then, is to become a mystic, seeking God in all things. Discernment is the subtle process by which the soul attends to its creator, serving God and the world in companionship with Jesus, growing in sensitivity to the voice of the Spirit.

Companionship

Pilgrims know that it is those who walk with them and those who support them in other ways that make their pilgrimages possible, whether that support comes as alms, advice, or a roof for the night. Throughout the *Autobiography*, Ignatius introduces us to his companions, usually by name. We meet his confessors, his teachers, his supporters, everyone who had a hand in keeping this pilgrim on track. Early in his narrative, we meet the scrupulous Ignatius, drawn to conventional acts of asceticism like refusing to trim his hair or nails, fasting and abstinence from meat, repeated confessions driven by obsession about the status of his soul, and long hours of prayer. Patient spiritual guides helped him, but in the end, "once he began to be consoled by God and saw the fruit he was bringing forth in souls as he dealt with them, he left aside those eccentricities." Note: it was not mystical experience solely, but mystical experience affirmed in and by his community that showed him a better, more moderate way of life.

In Ignatian spirituality, Jesus is the companion par excellence. Ignatius' *Spiritual Exercises* consists of imaginative explorations into the life of Jesus, along with related meditations that, taken together, compose an emotionally powerful invitation not just to *love* Jesus, but to *fall in love* with him. In the gospel stories we encounter Jesus who companions, heals, forgives, and teaches those who will throw in their lot with his; in the *Spiritual Exercises*, we are invited to join in that company ourselves. Intimacy with Jesus draws us into companionship with those he loves, by our companionship building the beginnings of the kingdom of God.

Throughout the *Autobiography*, we see Ignatius gathering around himself men and women who shared his intense religious devotion. He described this as driven by anxiety at first, a need for affirmation from other spiritually astute people, but when his anxiety lessened, his natural openness to companionship continued. Late in the *Autobiography*, we meet some of the men who will be the first Jesuits. Sharing a common commitment to the help of souls, they united around the emerging spirituality of those trying to discern and step confidently wherever and for whatever mission the greater glory of God sent them.

This institutionalization of Ignatius' charism was not without cost. Early on, Ignatius welcomed insights and companionship from all, but as the Society began to take shape, Ignatius went on the defensive, saying "we need to be very much on our guard and not take on conversation with women unless they be illustrious" (p. 97). The Society remains resolutely opposed to the discerned availability of women called to its ranks, despite the admission into the society during Ignatius' lifetime of Juana of Spain, who joined the Society as a scholastic and remained a Jesuit until her death. Ignatius himself would spend the rest of his life leading the Society from an office in Rome, a pilgrim rendered immobile so that the Society as a whole could be available for mission. His availability kept him off the road, though his correspondence spanned the globe.

But I'm getting ahead of the story in the *Autobiography*. There we met the pilgrim Ignatius as God was schooling him into a companion of Jesus and a helper of souls, even my stumbling and imperfect pilgrim's soul, across that "kind of a telephone line through time." Perhaps there might be something in that pilgrim's path for you, too.

The Seven Storey Mountain
(Harcourt, Brace and Company, 1948)
By Thomas Merton

First Fervor

Donald COZZENS, *John Carroll University*

I was seventeen and knew two things for certain. In fact, these two certitudes were crystal clear to me as a first-grader at Holy Name Elementary School. I wanted to be a priest and I was in love with JoAnn Mahoney. While there was never a serious doubt about seminary studies, I nevertheless felt the ripples of tension and unease rooted in mandatory celibacy. JoAnn Mahoney and celibacy! Still, in the spring of my senior year of high school I sat at my parents' dining room table and wrote the rector of Cleveland's Saint Mary Seminary seeking admission.

Now you should understand that my desire to be a priest was a pontifical secret. None of my classmates, not one, knew of my intention. The reason for the secrecy remains somewhat of a mystery to me to this day. I suspect my fear was that my high school friends would think me pious. And I definitely did not want anyone, especially JoAnn, to think of me as pious.

But one of my teachers, a Sister of Charity with the eye of a Father Brown detective, was on to me. Sublimely discreet, she said one day after class when my senior friends were out of earshot, "You might like this book." She handed me, as if it were D. H. Lawrence's *Lady Chatterley's Lover*, a first edition copy of Thomas Merton's *The Seven Storey Mountain*. I thanked her politely enough and stuck the book behind my fourth year Latin grammar text, fearing someone noticed her offering and might ask me about it.

Months later, I plunged into *The Seven Storey Mountain* with a first-year-seminarian's thirst for spiritual adventure and with the idealism typical of a religious novice. Merton's repudiation of his dissolute living, especially his early sexual indulgence at Cambridge and later at Columbia, was comforting. See, I told myself, women and beer and smoky jazz clubs left Tom Merton with a stale taste in his mouth, an emptiness in his soul, and rumblings of regret in his gut. He was, he wrote, "sick of being sick." By the mysterious workings of grace, Merton began to understand it was union with God and the saints that really mattered. To his surprise, he wanted nothing less than holiness. And I wanted what Merton wanted. His spiritual autobiography was the perfect book for me at the perfect time.

At the same time I was reading *The Seven Storey Mountain*, I was corresponding with a young nun in Baltimore, Maryland, whom I had met just before she entered the Carmelite monastery there. Teresa of Avila had encouraged her sisters to befriend a seminarian or priest and to pray for him daily. Sister Colette of the Trinity became my prayer friend and soul mate.

Letters from Sister Colette and reading *The Seven Storey Mountain* confirmed my budding passion for contemplative spirituality. I would be a diocesan priest, but a diocesan priest with a monastic, contemplative spirituality. So, the monk and the nun, more than the seminary's formation program, shaped my interior life. The three of us, Merton, Sister Colette, and I, were all guilty of the spiritual elitism that Merton came to regret after *The Seven Storey Mountain* shocked the publishing world with its unprecedented commercial and critical success. Only later did we see our Church's triumphalism, the smugness that Flannery O'Connor called "the great Catholic sin." Merton's own critique of his autobiography went further. He recognized and regretted his excessive moralizing and the dualistic thinking that shaped his early understanding of holiness. Along with Merton, Sister Colette and I moved beyond our early naïveté as we recognized the possibility of contemplative living for all of God's pilgrim people.

I missed all this in my first reading of *The Seven Storey Mountain*. The book was a light unto my feet. Like a pin to a magnet, I was drawn to the author's personal, engaging, heroic writing that fired my first fervor (so be the mixed metaphors). I agreed with the *Chicago Sun* reviewer who wrote that the book was "a hymn of positive faith sung in the midst of a purposeless world searching for purpose, a book that can be read by men [sic] of any faith or none at all."[1] But, as a seminarian, I had plenty of purpose in my own life—the priesthood and the ministry that I would exercise as a "doctor of souls." So, let me tell you why Thomas Merton's *The Seven Storey Mountain* has so influenced my spiritual journey.

**

Merton's spiritual autobiography is a vivid, compelling adventure story of a lost soul searching for healing and wholeness—for salvation. In telling his story, Merton becomes a kind of a modern Odysseus[2]. And so Merton emerged as a hero to me in my early years as a seminarian. In writing of his bouts with spiritual confusion and conflicting desires, Merton was writing about my own confusion and discordant desires. In struggling to surrender his willfulness to a willingness that forced nothing, he helped me to temper my own Pelagian efforts to grow spiritually.

It's pretty clear now that *The Seven Storey Mountain* served as my "spiritual director" during my first years of seminary formation. Merton's vivid writing, his spiritual honesty, and his heavenly quest fired my soul far more than any of the preached retreats we seminarians endured. Reading Merton I came to understand what the spiritual masters meant when they spoke of "living in the presence of God." He gave me a glimpse of the quality of his own soul, a soul now being molded by the rhythm of monastic life and contemplation born of solitude and silence. His was to be a lyrical spirituality inspired by the Fathers of the Church, neo-Thomistic theology, and traditional monastic devotion. Later, it would become an earthy spirituality, truly prophetic and nourished by Kentucky's rolling hills and Gethsemani's forest trails, by clouds and rain and the changing seasons.

In the final section of *The Seven Storey Mountain,* Merton writes of being on retreat at Gethsemani just months before entering and being moved by the monks' final chant of the day, the *Salve Regina.* "…[T]hat long antiphon, the most stately and most beautiful and most stirring thing that was ever written, that was ever sung" (p. 335). Yes, I said to myself as I underlined these words in my text. I knew precisely what he meant.

---

1   James O. Supple, December 28, 1948.
2   Anthony T. Padovano, *The Spiritual Genius of Thomas Merton,* Franciscan Media, 2014, p. 47.

Diocesan seminarians traditionally end their day with the singing of the *Salve Regina* in their darkened chapel lit by a single candle next to a statue or icon of Mary. Here Merton was speaking for seminarians everywhere. I like to think that the most treasured seminary memory we priests hold is this chanting of the *Salve*.

Not too many years ago, Cleveland priests were gathered at our seminary to mark its 150th anniversary. Invited to the celebration were all the priest alums, including those men who left the priesthood to marry. A few of those who had left active ministry came with their wives. The celebration ended with Vespers and the chanting of the *Salve*. From my position near the back of the chapel, I was moved when I saw that these married men, holding the hands of their wives, had tears running down their cheeks as the *Salve* awakened in them still sacred memories—their wives surprised by the wave of emotion rising up in their husbands.

**

I seldom preach a retreat without quoting Thomas Merton. Not so much from *The Seven Storey Mountain,* as from the books that flowed from Merton's pen after the publication of his autobiography. Books like *Seeds of Contemplation, The Sign of Jonas, No Man Is an Island, Thoughts in Solitude, New Seeds of Contemplation,* and *Conjectures of a Guilty Bystander,* along with Merton's poems, journals and collected letters. But it was *The Seven Storey Mountain* that first shaped my spirituality and led me to these later works that define Merton as a spiritual master.[3] Here are two of my favorite Merton maxims: "A retreat is a time to do nothing for as long as you can." And, "In humility is perfect freedom." This latter quote is Merton at his laconic best. Here we have a true seed of liberation. When we put our ego-self aside, something rather strange occurs—we don't care too much what others think of us. We're free to be who we are meant to be—our true self. Surely a key foundation stone of spiritual freedom.

**

From time to time, I've been asked if I ever considered joining a religious order. The thought of being a Dominican or a Jesuit priest never crossed my

---

3   See the Introduction in Lawrence Cunningham's *Thomas Merton: Spiritual Master,* Paulist Press, 1992.

mind. No, my vocation was to the diocesan priesthood. But the thought of being a Trappist priest, a contemplative priest, that idea did break into my consciousness, but rarely. And those occasional imaginings were due to *The Seven Storey Mountain*. No, my truth was the diocesan priesthood. But as my seminary years passed by and ordination drew near, I came to see more and more clearly that my ministry as a priest needed to be grounded in a contemplative spirituality.

Moreover, Merton and others, but especially Merton, have convinced me that the path to ecumenical and inter-religious communion—and to peace and justice—is found in the contemplative centers of our world and in the hearts of those of us trying to lead contemplative lives. Thomas Merton, I believe, like the great Karl Rahner, understood that the Christian of the twenty-first century will be a contemplative or not at all.

Tattoos on the Heart: The Power of Boundless Compassion (Free Press, 2011) by Greg Boyle

The Slow Work of God

Thomas P. RAUSCH, S.J., *Loyola Marymount University*

A couple of years ago I was rushing through Los Angeles International Airport, hoping to grab a quick coffee and a scone before my flight at Starbucks. But as I entered the American Airlines concourse, what I saw was not the famous Seattle coffee concession but a Homegirl Café, busy with several Mexican-American girls waiting on the early morning commuters. Gosh, I thought to myself, Greg has created a whole industry. My favorite book is Greg's *Tattoos on the Heart: The Power of Boundless Compassion,* a *New York Times* best-selling book and named one of the Best Books of 2010 by *Publishers Weekly.*

Greg is Father Greg Boyle, a Jesuit brother and friend, a few years behind me in the Society, known to all of Los Angeles and far beyond for his work with the "homies," the homeboys and homegirls whose lives and bodies have been so marked by the culture of violence that is the gang life of East L.A. Greg grew up in Los Angeles, the gang capital of the world, but in a very different, decidedly middle class neighborhood. He entered the Society of Jesus in 1972 and was ordained in 1984. Originally scheduled for ministry at one of our universities, after Spanish language studies in Bolivia and daily contact with the country's poor, he asked to be assigned to Dolores Mission, the poorest parish in the Archdiocese of Los Angeles in the midst of two large housing projects and some eight gangs. He was the youngest pastor in the archdiocese.

Realizing how many young lives were blunted by the gangs, he began by riding his bike through the neighborhood in the evening, trying to get to know the young people who at first ignored him. But gradually, as he visited them in jail or the hospital, they realized he was there for them. They started calling him "G," for Greg, or "G-Dog." In 1988 he buried his first victim of gang violence. Twenty years later he had presided at over 165 such funerals for young men from the neighborhood. *Tattoos on the Heart* is the story of his efforts to provide jobs as a way out of gang life for these young men and women through Homeboy Industries. His favorite saying is "Nothing stops a bullet like a job."

Homeboy Industries began when a Hollywood agent came to see Greg after the death of his wife, wanting to do something to address the growing gang problem. After shooting down a number of his suggestions, none of them practical, Boyle suggested that he buy an old bakery for sale in the neighborhood; he would try to bring rival gang members together, to work with each other in what he would call The Homeboy Bakery. Soon he had gang members arriving, looking for a job. One of them, just released from prison, arrived with FUCK THE WORLD tattooed on his forehead. Imagining him trying to get a job at McDonalds and scaring away the customers, one of Greg's first services was a tattoo removal program.

The stories he tells would break your heart. There was Jason, a young crack dealer, the son of two addicts, who, after rejecting a number of invitations, finally showed up at Greg's office and with his help found a job. Having left his anger behind him, he eventually had a home and family, and was looking forward to his daughter's baptism. He had bought her a new dress. A week before the baptism he was gunned down in the streets by someone from his past. Or Luis, also a drug dealer, but one of the biggest and smartest in the community, who for years had avoided the law. After his daughter Tiffany was born, he too came to Greg, was hired to work at the bakery and with his natural leadership ability was soon appointed foreman. He took being a father seriously, got a small apartment, the first home he had ever had, and with it a whole new life. One evening while loading his car, he too was shot and killed by some gang members who found themselves in his neighborhood. As Greg said at his funeral, Luis "had come to know the truth about himself and liked what he found there."

There are too many stories like those of Jason and Luis, kids who Greg befriended, young men who, through unconditional love and care, discovered the truth about themselves, turned their lives around, rejoiced in their children, and looked to a future with hope. They came from broken homes, abusive, addicted or absent parents, dysfunctional families. Lacking love and self-respect, they were burdened with shame that was situational as well as personal. You find yourself identifying with them, marveling at their humor, their resiliency, only to have them end up one more victim of the violence of the streets. Like the sixteen-year-old girl, pregnant, who says to Greg, "I just want to have a kid before I die." Or Benito, a funny, energetic twelve-year-old killed in a drive-by. Many do turn their lives around. Those stories are there too.

My favorite is about Bandit, well-named for "being at home in all things illegal." He came to see Greg after a lot of time locked up for selling crack. Greg took him to a job developer, who got him an unskilled, entry-level job at a warehouse. Fifteen years later, he calls Greg; he now runs the warehouse, has his own home, a wife and three kids. He wants Greg to bless his oldest daughter; she's not in trouble, but is going to college at Humboldt, the first in her family to do so, wants to study forensic psychology. Greg tells Bandit how proud he is of him, who answers with tears in his eyes, "I'm proud of myself. All my life, people called me a lowlife, a *bueno para nada*. I guess I showed them." Greg calls this the slow work of God, helping the soul to feel its worth. It is the strategy of Jesus, not centered on taking the right stand, but rather on standing in the right place—with the outcasts and those relegated to the margins.

Father Boyle is an acute observer; he writes with a poetic sense, an ear for dialogue and an eye for detail. The book's title comes from a moment when he complemented a homie, trying to get him to see the goodness within; the kid responded, "Damn, G . . . I'm going to tattoo that on my heart." The book's subtitle is *The Power of Boundless Compassion*, and that's what he offers. Bringing enemies together in the bakery, they work side by side with each other and become friends, breaking down the illusion of separateness to replace it with kinship. Boyle finds the holy in the comic and the ordinary. He meets people who are living heroic lives, like the mother of Rigo, who every Sunday takes seven buses to visit him in prison while he serves his time. Rigo's father used to beat him, once with a pipe.

G brings a depth of spiritual wisdom to the book, citing saints and mystics of the Christian tradition and his own rich insight. He writes about a God who loves us passionately, about the shame and "dis-grace" that cripples so many young people growing up in poverty and violence, and the toxic effects of neglect. In a course he taught at Folsom Prison none of the inmates could define compassion, until one old-timer said, "That's what Jesus did. I mean, Compassion . . . IS . . . God." He writes about giving young people time to do the slow work of finding themselves. His topics include gladness and joy, kinship, and success, which so often we turn into an idol. For those of us driven by the need to be successful, he quotes Mother Teresa, who once said "We are not called to be successful, but faithful." To this Greg adds, with genuine humility, "If you surrender your need for results and outcomes, success becomes God's business. I find it hard enough to just be faithful."

From its original location in the old bakery building, Homeboy Industries has grown into a $8.5-million glass and concrete headquarters in a gang neutral location on the edge of Chinatown. It houses Homeboy Bakery, a beautiful Homegirl Café, along with a catering service, various craft industries, and a Homeboy Diner at City Hall. It currently employs 250-300 former gang members, while some 1,000 from the community take advantage of its services each month, including 500 monthly treatments at its clinic for tattoo removal.

The stories in his book, told originally in Father Boyle's homilies at Mass in some twenty-five detention centers, probation camps, and juvenile facilities, brought tears to my eyes numerous times, as they will to yours. This is a holy book about the power of unconditional love and compassion.

A Theology of Liberation: History, Politics, Salvation (Orbis, 1973) by Gustavo Gutiérrez

Liberation: Professional and Personal

James B. NICKOLOFF, *Barry University*

On April 9, 1972, as a 24-year-old Peace Corps Volunteer living and working in the town of Andong, South Korea, I received the sacraments of initiation as well as reconciliation and thus officially became a member of the Catholic Church. In retrospect, it does not seem strange to me that I took this step in a traditionally Buddhist-Confucianist country, for I come from a largely non-religious family and likely needed to consider the Christian story in an exotic (to me) setting before committing myself to a spiritual path.

But Korean Catholicism is unusual. Perhaps because it was founded by Korean laypeople and not by foreign clerics, it is both deeply Catholic *and* strikingly Korean. The "Koreanness" of the Church goes beyond liturgical music and church decoration, and even a Western neophyte like me could not fail to sense a genuine inculturation of the story of Jesus. I now know the correct theological term: incarnation.

Eight short years later I found myself working as a Jesuit seminarian at St. George's College in Kingston, Jamaica. In Jamaica, as in Korea, I was radically "other"—a good experience for a middle-class Euro-American male. But in Jamaica I found a Catholic Christianity dramatically *dis*-connected from the island nation's real culture. I am referring to the world of the poor, often called "roots" Jamaicans, who flock to evangelical and fundamentalist churches and mostly shun the Catholic Church.

The gap between *ecclesia* and culture in Jamaica became the subject of my master's thesis. (It was not well received by my Jesuit superiors). And when I later began doctoral studies, a single question guided my reading: what does "authentic inculturation" of the Christian message require, especially ecclesiologically?

With this question floating in my consciousness, I came upon the works of Latin America's liberation theologians for the first time, thanks to Jesuit teachers like Don Gelpi, Hal Sanks, and John Coleman. The works of Gustavo Gutiérrez quickly seized my attention since they were rooted in the Peruvian Church's own extraordinary efforts at incarnation. Overcoming five hundred years of Euro-centrism meant eliminating the ecclesial distance from the poor majority of the country. But to take on the flesh of oppressed indigenous, mestizo, and black Peruvians required one thing above all—and of all: *liberation*, and several kinds of liberation simultaneously. Gustavo's formulation (I call him "Gustavo" here not to assert any personal privilege but because he is almost universally called "Gustavo") of liberation as a three-fold process involving social structures, personal self-regard, and relationship with God is classic and has been the subject of intense debate for nearly fifty years. Nevertheless, I still find that few people, including professional theologians, actually "get" his proposal.

While the strength of his model, indeed its whole point, lies in the unity Gustavo claims for the three-fold process of liberation, he is careful to distinguish the three levels (of the single process) as well. In particular, his rejection of both a causal and a chronological relationship among them impressed me since in the U.S. a powerful therapeutic culture tells people that they must first "get their own acts together" before they should take part in the struggle for social-political-economic liberation. Gustavo knew from experience (and from his formal study of psychology) that psychological transformation can and does take place *in* the (usually communal) fight for structural liberation. And one's relationship with God may undergo transformation at the same time, in the same process.

For Gustavo, psychological transformation, the middle term of the three-fold process of liberation, is not more important than (and is not prior to) the other two levels, but it does mediate a sound relationship between

A Theology of Liberation: History, Politics, Salvation

political action and Christian faith. What he has in mind by psychological conversion is the movement from fear, resignation, and isolation to trust, initiative, and solidarity—that is, liberation. In my experience, it is this second level of liberation and its mediating role that most critics of his theology have failed to understand. Those who see his theology as mainly a justification of political revolution (Cardinal Ratzinger for a long time) and those who see his work, especially in later years, as merely a "spirituality" narrowly conceived are mistaken. Human liberation ("salvation" for Gustavo) occurs in three ways—simultaneously.

It was clear to me after reading *A Theology of Liberation* that I needed to know—feel, taste, smell—the milieu that had shaped such a notion of liberation. It took some doing, but I managed to persuade both my reluctant Jesuit superiors ("You'll get caught up in the revolution and never finish writing your dissertation.") and my exacting doctoral committee in Berkeley ("Will you have the academic resources to produce a rigorous piece of work?") to let me travel to Lima in May, 1986. Within three weeks of my arrival, a miracle occurred. I don't know what else to call it. One day a phone call came for me at the main Jesuit residence, and on the other end was the inimitable voice of Gustavo. He had a proposal: if I would agree to cover Saturday confessions and one Sunday mass, I could live with him in the rectory and converse with him about my dissertation (when he wasn't in Rome, New York, or São Paulo).

I am still embarrassed to admit that I hesitated before accepting Gustavo's invitation. The problem was this: I could see that in no time he would recognize (a) how little theology I actually knew and (b) how shallow my commitment to the poor really was. He was taking a risk with the invitation, but there was also a risk in my saying "yes" to the "father of liberation theology"! Friends and my own better sense prevailed, and I moved in and worked with Gustavo for nearly two years.

Further surprises were in store as I took up my work in the parish of Cristo Redentor. Among the Saturday penitents were young people who told me, with anguish but also with audacity, of struggles with their sexuality. I had long known about my own homosexuality but had not seen it as relevant in my present circumstances. I soon learned, however, that because these *jóvenes* came from very poor families and had no opportunity to visit gay clubs or gay political meetings located in the wealthy section of the city, they were deprived of the chance to meet openly gay people. And talking things over with a counselor or therapist would never have occurred to them. It gradually dawned on me that they faced a lifetime of struggle for mere survival—alone—in the harsh world of Lima. Unlike their heterosexual counterparts in the barrio, who at least had the right to marry and face the challenges of life with a partner approved by family, church, and society, the young gay or lesbian person faced a perpetual and involuntary solitude, either by remaining single (and being stigmatized for doing so) or by entering into what could never be a wholly fulfilling heterosexual marriage. Condemned to loneliness of one kind or another, these persons had to be among the most marginalized of Peru's poor. Besides touching my heart, their stories made me ask for the first time about the relationship between sexual orientation and poverty, and these two in connection with Christian faith.

Their anguish also made me go to Gustavo to disclose to him what I was hearing (without breaking the seal of confession). I suspected that his fame and status in the Latin American Church, of which parishioners were quite aware and very proud, might prevent some from being completely transparent with him in the way that they could be with an obscure and impermanent pastoral associate. But as I pondered a conversation with Gustavo, I knew I could not talk about "them" as if I were a complete outsider to their experience. With this in mind, I asked Gustavo if I could have a talk with him, and in his typical manner he replied, "*¿Se trata de algo importante o algo muy importante?*" ("Is it something important or something very important?") When I replied *"bastante importante"* ("rather important"), he said, "Fine. Let's have lunch together next Saturday." Lunch, for Gustavo, meant spending several hours over a meal in a quiet restaurant. I knew the die was cast.

I began the momentous meal by telling him about the suffering of his young homosexual parishioners. As all who know him will testify, Gustavo cannot help but respond to others' pain with compassion—in the true etymological sense of the word. But then I told him the second piece of the story, that I myself am gay and could not act as if I know nothing about the experience of homosexual attraction. At this point, Gustavo fixed his eyes on me and in a gentle voice said, *"Jaime, yo no sé nada de esa experiencia. Tú tienes que ser mi profesor."* ("Jaime, I know nothing about that experience. You have to be my teacher.") Humility, we all know, lies at the heart of good theology.

But then it was Gustavo's turn to surprise me as he proceeded to tell me about a friend of his, a former student, who came from a wealthy family in Lima, discovered his own homosexuality, found a partner, and moved to the U.S. so they could live more freely. After some years abroad, however, he missed his family so much that he returned to Peru, leaving his partner behind. But in Lima he found the same lack of understanding, even rejection, as before, and in his misery took a gun and shot himself in the head on Christmas Eve. Our lunch conversation had turned deeply personal—and serious. Gustavo's eyes were filled with tears.

Decades after leaving Peru (and the Jesuits), I am still unable to uncouple sexual, socioeconomic, personal, and structural liberation. Nor can I separate these from Christian faith and the Church. The same humble people who drove Gustavo to elaborate a revolutionary theology fifty years ago taught me that a genuinely incarnate faith and an inculturated Church must be rooted in human liberation. There is no other way, *gracias a Dios*.

The Varieties of Religious Experience: A Study in Human Nature (Longmans, Green & Co., 1902) by William James

The Individual Subject as Primary

Sidney CALLAHAN, Mercy College/The Hastings Center

Whenever I take up and reread *The Varieties of Religious Experience: A Study in Human Nature* by William James, my spirits soar. My mind takes off and my faith becomes more deeply grounded. No wonder that after a hundred and some years these twenty Gifford Lectures published in 1902 are required reading for anyone interested in the psychology of religion.

Here the brilliance of William James dazzles and delights readers with displays of originality built on wide knowledge. And why not? His wealthy and eccentric father, Henry James Senior, had supported William's prolonged studies, here, abroad, and back again. Along the way James mastered languages, philosophy, literature, science, medicine, psychology and the art of drawing. Only after much intellectual and psychological turmoil was James at last able to settle into an academic berth at Harvard teaching philosophy and psychology. During the turbulent years William struggled to gain direction, overcome health problems and fight through serious suicidal depressions. His passionate temperament, amazing energy and formidable will finally triumphed. Over the decades, he taught his academic classes, lectured widely, and produced a huge amount of writing for both academic and general audiences.

James always speaks directly to the reader. He invites you to join him in whatever urgent inquiry he is pursuing. In *Varieties* he takes on the most basic religious questions that individuals face in their lives. Why and how does a person come to believe—or doubt? And why does it matter to the universe? James's focus is always on the individual subject as primary; he is not interested in the external study of religious institutions or abstract theological doctrines.

As an empirical, scientific psychologist James seeks to understand the inner story—the subjective, emotional, and intuitive dimensions of personality. Feelings count most in determining faith and behavior. You may not always agree with James, but you cannot help being impressed by the energy and acuteness of his arguments. It helps that William has mastered an informal streamlined prose (quite different from that of his brother, Henry James, Jr. the literary star.) Yet his dramatic firsthand accounts of individual conversion or despairing depression are gripping reading. James punctuates these narratives with nuanced analysis and ironic sparks of wit.

My own debts of gratitude for this book by James start with his initial arguments dealing with "the neurology question." Skeptics and materialists in his day, as in ours, confidently took the line that religious beliefs merely manifested the superstitions of a brain's disorder. But James argues that religious experiences cannot be dismissed as neurotic brain products. Why? Because in the natural scientific order *every* human mental thought—skeptical, materialist or believing—originates in the brain. We fail to notice this because only the ideas we *already* disagree with are deemed neurotic.

In science and philosophy we must rationally judge the value and worth of beliefs and feelings by other criteria and standards. *On the whole,* we ask, do religious ideas and experiences meet three criteria: Are they morally helpful? Do they make cognitive sense with everything else that is known? And are they immediately luminous, i.e. generating emotional feelings of light, trueness, goodness, joy and love? In other words, good or bad, general effects should be the standards of evaluation; by their fruits shall you know them.

James then proceeds in the rest of the lectures to give multitudes of examples demonstrating the mainly positive effects of religious experiences. He writes chapters on the reality of the unseen, conversion, saintliness, mysticism, philosophy and happiness. These treatments remain classics, along with his discussions of individual differences in religious temperaments, such as the healthy-minded and sick souls.

These arguments in defense of religion by James were liberating for me as a convert to Roman Catholicism. My religious mother had been afflicted by schizophrenia and in my aggressively secular family there lurked the suspicion that my ardent religious enthusiasms were signs of pathological tendencies. Yet my faith could meet James's three-fold criteria of validity. I was morally helped, intellectually strengthened and joyfully blessed—for all the long productive life to come. James served as a sophisticated defender of the faith in atheistic academic milieus encountered. There too religious fervor and commitments also carried the odor of craziness.

Indeed, James was quite ready to propose that a more sensitive and even neurotic temperament might be more receptive to valid religious truths than a more stolid unimaginative nature. Here James himself was a case in point, although he never claimed any truly mystic experiences and remained outside of any committed Christian denomination. He was always an in-between thinker, too religious for the secular materialists and not avowedly religious enough for the orthodox.

For many the scientific empirical investigatory approach James employs is quite convincing and effective in defending religion's value. He gathers religious testimonies from past history and across cultures. In *Varieties* James gives many, many accounts of enthusiastic ecstatic religious experiences as well as descriptions of the tortures of despair over the meaninglessness of human life. Counter-conversions and indifference also make appearances. Believers can be grateful for the preponderance of so many testimonies of the joy and ecstatic happiness provided by the wonder of God's love. (Irish Catholics can be quite reticent on such matters!) Despairing doubt is more generally acceptable in postmodern times. Yet a whole range of voices appears in *Varieties*.

Readers hear from Christian saints, mystics, literary geniuses, mediums and mind cure practitioners, scientists, missionaries, ancient sages, Eastern mystics, and ordinary people of all classes. Over a hundred accounts are presented. Augustine, John of the Cross, Teresa of Avila and George Fox rub shoulders with Tolstoy, Emerson, Walt Whitman and less familiar scientific authorities of James's era. In the end, this cloud of witnesses brought forth to testify to the positive fruits of religious belief give support to one's own faith.

James was interested in everything to do with religion. He honed in on how individual temperament interacted with belief and religious experience, or lack of it. Some personalities were incapable of faith, he believed, because their deeper intuitive sources were "frozen," or blocked by the social circles of disbelief they inhabit. Others were religiously "tone deaf." Still others could never reach a level of self-consciousness to question or doubt. But in conversions or counter-conversions inner fields of energy could shift, hot spots of burning interest could cool, or vice versa. James did not think that science or psychology yet understood these dynamics of the inner life of human beings. He did not presume to say whether supernatural influences could be at work. Science was still in its infancy and the mysteries of a pluralistic universe should be acknowledged.

Certainly James was prescient and well ahead of his time in giving serious weight to innate individual differences, to scientific evolution's processes, to the power of emotion, intuition, mind, and fluctuating levels of consciousness. For him, reality is dynamic, flowing, integrated and full of probabilities. All of these ideas make James sound fresh and up to date. Academic psychology has only belatedly returned to James's concerns with the power of the mind, the centrality of emotion, and the quicksilver stream of consciousness. Religious experience is now a respectable field in academic psychology.

So in sum, I owe James for being a guide to my intellectual vocation. Trying to understand the relationship of religion and psychology is the life for me. In *Varieties* James is necessarily ecumenical because of his broad basic definition of religion. Religion is the realization that there exists in reality an invisible order and it is humanity's happiness to integrate itself with it. The vast unknown realms in the pluralistic universe exist as MORE. Since things are not well with us humans, high religions of deliverance like Christianity and Buddhism can provide ways to holiness and happiness.

William James was criticized in his day (and ours) for his radical empiricism and pragmatic lack of interest in abstract philosophy, metaphysics and theology. Well yes, true enough. And as a second generation Scots-Irish, Protestant Yankee he doesn't really get the communal embodied corporate spirituality of Roman Catholicism. But no one is perfect. James was amazingly humble in his search for the MORE. The mystery of reality and religion never stops calling forth his passionate efforts to understand. I am not the first to join his unique and exhilarating campaign through the fields of religion and human nature. But others may not have had him confirm their sanity, appreciate their ardent joys and endorse their intellectual and vocational path. Yes, I am in love with William James, but even more I wish I could *be* William James.

What Happened at Vatican II
(The Belknap Press of Harvard University Press, 2008) by John W. O'Malley

Understanding Vatican II: Finding the Way Forward

Katarina SCHUTH, O.S.F., *Saint Paul Seminary School of Divinity, University of St. Thomas*

Change is recognized as a constant in human life. Yet some people resist understanding and responding positively to it while others welcome it. Those who find change difficult may be fearful of the new situation, challenged by what it will demand, or wed to the present state of affairs. Those who are more likely to accept change may be more adventurous, or accommodating, or comfortable with what is being proposed. In determining the response, an important factor is often the level of understanding the person brings to the situation. Scripture readings, particularly in the Easter season, document reactions to the tremendous events that brought about great change in the lives of the early disciples. As they begin to understand the Scriptures, they are led to peace. This is most dramatically recorded in the story on the road to Emmaus (Luke 24:13-35). Beginning with Moses and the prophets, Jesus interpreted the Scriptures and opened the eyes of the disciples. Through his explanation, the Risen Lord was made known to them.

This passage brings to light how essential it is to be familiar with and comprehend new circumstances in order to respond positively to them. Centuries after the Emmaus journey, the decrees of the Second Vatican Council generated many changes that elicited a wide variety of reactions.

To this day the Church is grappling with this disparity, a task made more challenging as Catholics who were alive during the council decrease in number. The loss of so many people who experienced its impact firsthand and possessed a depth of knowledge about and a favorable reception of its teachings leaves a lacuna that must be filled. For this reason, *What Happened at Vatican II* by John O'Malley is not only a timely and influential book. It is an indispensable resource for ensuring continuing implementation of the directives of this great event.

When the Second Vatican Council commenced on October 11, 1962, few people could have imagined the impact this exceptional occurrence would have on the Church and on the whole world. The unexpected announcement of the council was made on January 25, 1959, just three months after Pope John XXIII's election. Until its conclusion on December 8, 1965, Catholics everywhere were attuned to the developments that would change their participation in and perspective of the faith they had experienced as virtually unchangeable before the council. Some fifty years later it is evident that the event affected not only the spiritual lives of Roman Catholics, but also many other aspects of life for them and the rest of the world. The Church was dealing with many concerns of the day, among them the secularization of society, the separation of Church and State in Catholic countries, the spread of Communism, and the proliferation of nuclear weapons. As a result of the council, people of other faiths, political leaders, and interested observers gained a fresh perspective on the significance of the role of Catholicism. Changes in relationships among people were vital. Leaders also were compelled to accommodate to a new vision of the Church in the modern world as it affected governing structures, church-state matters, and the social order.

The magnitude of these effects is vividly described by John O'Malley in *What Happened at Vatican II*. Throughout the book, he highlights the intent of the council and communicates details about how decisions were made, who was involved, and what was at stake. The council fathers soon recognized that the process they were engaging would set in motion sweeping changes. O'Malley examines their attitudes toward and readiness for change, which differed as enormously as their expectations and hopes for certain outcomes. He outlines three fundamental principles of the council:

aggiornamento, development, and *ressourcement;* these three he calls the "issues under-the-issues," all of which imply change.

For Pope John XXIII, the word *aggiornamento* meant "bringing up to date," that is, developing the Church to meet the needs of the modern world. The broad scope of updating led to some of the most heated discussions. As O'Malley notes, "development" seemed less contentious as long as it was taken to mean "an unfolding of something already present implicitly or in germ" (p. 300). Problems arose when decisions seemed not to further but to contradict the direction of a particular matter so that it was changed and not simply extended. The word *ressourcement,* likened to renaissance, "advocated skipping over what was currently in place to retrieve from the past something more appropriate or more authentic" (pp. 300-301). The sources of the Christian tradition were to be re-examined by methods of modern scholarship, often with the hope of returning to the purposes and practices of the early Church.

Concern about where these changes would lead resulted in some of the most contested and difficult decisions of the council. It is easy to imagine how the content of important decrees was applauded by some participants and feared by others. Whatever the issues, the minority held onto their views, while the majority was eager to move forward. To this day, disagreements are being played out between those who favor the decisions of the council and are committed to putting them more fully into effect and those who disagree with the implementation of council decrees, if not the decrees themselves. With the hope of "reforming the reform," as it is often labeled, the stance of the latter group is expressed with growing harshness in a spate of recent literature. Their goal is to roll back the changes, based on the opinion that it is necessary to undo the damage to the Church that originated with the council. At the same time, the fiftieth anniversary of the council has resulted in many other works, the purpose of which is to convey what the authors believe was the intent of the council and its many positive outcomes. Thus, these writings seek to promote understanding and ongoing implementation of the council's decrees.

What Happened at Vatican II contributes convincingly to the discussion. O'Malley's indispensable historical context is enhanced by deep analysis based on a thorough understanding of the interchanges during the council. This is made even more vivid by his presence in Rome during that time. His chronological account of the four sessions reveals the progression of ideas and the growing recognition of how exceptional this council was to be. As his powerful narrative shows, already present as the council began were efforts to minimize change, to remain with the 'status quo.' This stance was largely rejected by the bishops who had come from all corners of the world, critical of the Eurocentric emphasis of the Church. In a fair way, the text presents these divergent positions and uncovers the nature of what actually happened in the discussions and the reasons for the outcomes. This method weakens the present efforts of those who propose the so-called "reform of the reform." O'Malley explains the positive role the council plays in the Church today, and discusses not only its successes, but also the hope of seeing the advancement of additional intended outcomes.

Among the most profound new understandings that resulted from the council—and one that can certainly be considered a "success"—was a grasp of the universality of the Church. This new vision came about by the mere presence of bishops gathered from all over the world. Potential changes in the church were already in the forefront, but changes brought about by the situation in the world had an equally profound effect. The end of colonialism and the growth of the new churches in Asia and Africa, for example, introduced unfamiliar questions. The depth of the impact on norms and ideals are described in this compact and powerful paragraph from O'Malley:

> For the new churches it recommended adaptation to local cultures, including philosophical and theological adaptation. It also recommended that Catholic missionaries seek ways of cooperating with missionaries of other faiths and of fostering harmonious relations with them. It asserted that art from every race and country be given scope in the liturgy of the church. More generally, it made clear that the church was sympathetic to the way of life of different peoples and races and was ready to appropriate aspects of different cultural traditions. Though obvious-sounding, these provisions were portentous. Where would they lead? (p. 298).

Embedded in this description are a multitude of adjustments that resulted from incorporating the practices of cultures beyond those of Western

Europe. Language, music, art, governance, the role of missionaries, ecumenism and interfaith relationships, the exercise of authority, and organization of the new churches were all in play. Obviously, change was inevitable, but the emerging question was how the leaders would handle it. A variety of concerns surfaced: the manner and style of authority, the role of papal authority in relation to bishops in the local church, the meaning and exercise of collegiality, and the relationship between the center and periphery of the Church. Some of these concerns are still in the process of being understood, accepted, and implemented, while others have shifted in importance and focus. The future will depend greatly on the direction provided by the pope and other church leaders. When Pope Francis was chosen to lead the Church, the power of papal influence was evident in his positive approach to the teachings of the Second Vatican Council and his insistence on their enactment.

As a result of Pope Francis' leadership, O'Malley's list of the realization of council decrees successfully put into practice will surely grow deeper and longer: the reform of the liturgy and wide appreciation of the vernacular, development in the understanding and use of Scripture, the increased role of laity in church affairs, updating of religious life, closer ecumenical and interfaith relationships, and freedom of religion. But much remains to be accomplished, a task articulated by Massimo Faggioli in *A Council for the Global Church: Receiving Vatican II in History*: "To choose to celebrate the council fifty years after its opening implies the possibility of becoming more conscious of the theological praxis of the Catholic Church, and also of the questions that were left unresolved by the council and await response" (p. 35).

In *What Happened at Vatican II,* readers learn to go beneath the surface to understand the significance and repercussions of this momentous event. With greater appreciation and understanding, the response of faithful Catholics, like that of the disciples on the road to Emmaus, will be similar: "Were not our hearts burning within us while he spoke to us on the way and opened the Scriptures to us?" As the disciples grew in faith when the Scriptures were opened to them to reveal the true meaning of the life, death, and resurrection of Christ, so careful readers of *What Happened at Vatican II* will acquire insights that show the way forward and change forever their perception of the council.

www.ingramcontent.com/pod-product-compliance
Lightning Source LLC
Chambersburg PA
CBHW020050170426
43199CB00009B/229